TERRORISM IN INDIA

TERRORISM IN INDIA
1917–1936

MANOHAR
2025

First published 1937
Reprinted 1974, 2020, 2023, 2024, 2025

ISBN 978-93-90035-17-5

Published by
Ajay Kumar Jain *for*
Manohar Publishers & Distributors
4753/23 Ansari Road, Daryaganj
New Delhi 110 002

Printed at
Replika Press Pvt. Ltd.

ORIGINAL TITLE PAGE

TERRORISM IN INDIA

1917—1936

Compiled in the Intelligence Bureau, Home Department, Government of India

PRINTED BY THE MANAGER, GOVERNMENT OF INDIA PRESS, SIMLA
1937

CONTENTS

PREFACE.

In 1917 there was published, under the authority of the Home Department of the Government of India, a confidential publication entitled *Political Trouble in India, 1907—1917*, written by Mr. J. C. Ker of the Indian Civil Service, who had been Personal Assistant to the Director of Criminal Intelligence from 1907 to 1913. This book set out to give a connected account of seditious and revolutionary activity in India between the years 1907 and 1917. The significance of the two dates deserves notice. The fact that the year 1907 was the fiftieth anniversary of the Indian Mutiny of 1857 was an important factor in developing discontent, which was prevalent at the time on account of political and economic circumstances, in several parts of India, along channels of criminal and revolutionary activity. The year 1917 marked the close of a phase when a period of widespread politico-criminal conspiracies had culminated in the combination of those activities with enemy intrigue during the early years of the Great war and in the crushing of those activities for the time being through the machinery of special war-time legal enactments. Effective repression was supplemented by the famous pronouncement of 20th August, 1917, by the Secretary of State for India as to the intentions of His Majesty's Government in respect of Indian constitutional progress. The result was that, in 1917, crimino-political agitation was more or less dormant, while constitutional political activity was at a high pitch. The opportunity which then occurred for a review of political trouble in the past ten years was, therefore, in the wider sense, opportune.

Twenty years have passed, during which political agitation in India, both constitutional and criminal, has continued and developed to an extent and in a manner which could hardly have been visualized even by the writer of the review of events down to 1917. The compilation to which I am now writing a preface has no such comprehensive aim as the book to which it is, in part, a sequel. It would not be possible to cover the whole field of what would come within the definition of political trouble in India in the years 1917 to 1937, in one volume. The growth and development of Communism and cognate revolutionary movements in and affecting India has been dealt with in a series of publications compiled and issued from the Government of India, Intelligence Bureau. Reports and surveys of particular aspects of illegal political agitation have been compiled from time to time and these include two monographs dealing with the subject of terrorism. No attempt, however, has been made to review the course of the terrorist movement over the whole period. The need of such a review has been felt increasingly as, in the process of time, individual officers of Government who had been prominently engaged in the fight against this form of revolutionary conspiracy have passed out of the service, and the mass of official and judicial record dealing with the subject has grown beyond the capacity of assimilation by their successors. The opportunity arose towards the end of 1936 to make an officer available to undertake the task of bringing the history of Terrorism up to date. Though mainly accidental, it is of interest and significance that the result of this officer's labours should appear in the form of the present book just at the time when the introduction of the new Constitution embodied in the Government of India Act, 1935, and the assumption of the reins of government in six Indian Provinces by the Congress Party has caused a fundamental reorientation of political agitation and gives ground for hope that political progress may be directed and controlled by popularly elected governments under which the incentive to opposition by means of the revolver and the bomb will be largely, if not entirely, eliminated.

The present book consists of a narrative, which I anticipate will be of considerable value to a fairly wide circle of readers interested in the administration of India, and of appendices which are intended to assist those, mainly police officers, whose duties require them to make a detailed study of the whole or portions of the past history of Terrorism. The production has been entirely in the hands of Mr. H. W. Hale, Indian Police, who has been temporarily posted to the Intelligence Bureau.

For a few months, part of Mr. Hale's time was definitely allotted to work on this production, but for the past four months he has had to carry out the full duties of one of the posts of Assistant Director and his work on this book has been overtime. The book in its final form represents an immense amount of research among scattered and diffuse contemporary records. I will conclude with a most sincere tribute to the industry and ability with which Mr. Hale has produced a concise and readable, but reasonably complete, picture of a most important aspect of Indian politics and administration.

J. M. EWART,

Director, Intelligence Bureau.

The 1st September 1937,

TERRORISM IN INDIA.

CHAPTER I.

INTRODUCTION.

Terrorism—its Objects. The various aspects of Revolutionary activity in India have been dealt with by Mr. J. C. Ker, I.C.S., in his book, "Political troubles in India, 1907—1917". Since that date aspirants for violent reform have adopted several methods, and the present book is an attempt to describe the course of that particular phase of revolutionary activity occurring between 1917 and the end of 1936. Terrorism, as distinct from other revolutionary methods such as Communism or the Ghadr Movement, may be said to denote the commission of outrages of a comparatively "individual" nature. That is to say, the terrorist holds the belief that Indian independence can best be brought about by a series of revolutionary outrages calculated to instil fear into the British official classes and to drive them out of India. He commits other outrages for the purpose of collecting funds for the purchase of arms, for the making of bombs and for the maintenance of his party, hoping that the masses will be drawn to his support either by fear or admiration. In "The Revolutionary" pamphlet* which was very widely distributed by hand and through the post in Bengal, the United Provinces and the Punjab in 1925, the writer puts forward the argument that as India is held by a handful of men under arms, so an armed revolution is the only way to establish his ideal of a "Federal Republic of the United States of India" and, although he states that terrorism is not the object of the Revolutionary Party, he says that terrorism is the only course to be pursued and in support of his argument quotes the example of Ireland and the guerilla warfare

*See Appendix 9.

which was carried on there. Again, in the pamphlet setting forth the objects and rules of the Hindustan Republican Association* it is freely stated that terrorism is an important item of the party's programme. To quote from another pamphlet, a manifesto entitled, "The Philosophy of the Bomb"* which was distributed in January 1930, and written probably by Bhagwati Charan, a notorious terrorist of the Punjab, "The revolutionaries already see the advent of the revolution in the restlessness of youth, in its desire to break free from the mental bondage and religious superstitions that hold them. As the youth will get more and more saturated with the psychology of revolution, it will come to a clearer realization of national bondage and a growing, intense and unquenchable thirst for freedom. It will grow, this feeling of bondage, this insatiable desire for freedom, till, in their righteous anger, the infuriated youth will begin to kill the oppressors. Thus has terrorism been born in the country. It is a phase, a necessary and inevitable phase of the revolution. Terrorism is not complete without revolution, and revolution is not complete without terrorism...... terrorism instils fear in the hearts of the oppressors, it brings hopes of revenge and redemption to the oppressed masses, it gives courage and self-confidence to the wavering, it shatters the spell of superiority of the ruling class and raises the status of the subject races in the eyes of the world, because it is the most convincing proof of a nation's hunger for freedom." Another manifesto *, issued by the Hindustan Socialist Republican Army and distributed at the Lahore Congress in December 1929, begins, "The food on which the tender plant of liberty thrives is the blood of the Martyrs". It goes on to say, "...........terrorism is never the object of revolutionaries, nor do they believe that terrorism alone can bring independence...........the British Government exists, because the Britishers have been successful in terrorising the whole of India. How are we to meet this official terrorism? Only counter-terrorism on the part of revolutionaries can cheek effectively this bureaucratic bullying..

---

*See Appendix 3.

....terrorism has its international aspects also. England's enemies which are many are drawn towards us by an effective demonstration of our strength. That, in itself, is a great advantage."

In 1929, when a house in Mechuabazar Street, Calcutta, was searched, a leaflet* was found which, in urging the young men of Bengal to resort to violence, mentions several youths who had been "martyred" for terrorist crimes, and tells its readers to read and learn the history of "Pearse....a gem of young Ireland..........(who) stimulated new animation in the nation and........roused an indomitable desire for armed revolution". Again, after the spectacular raids in Chittagong in April 1930, leaflets were posted in Chittagong and other parts of Bengal containing the words, "it (the Indian Republican Army, Chittagong Branch) also entreats all the members of the INDIAN REPUBLICAN ARMY and the people of Chittagong to begin a vigorous campaign of murdering these people, wherever found, to avenge the murders of their forefathers and thus to relieve the country of the pernicious exploitation which they are doing in this land of OURS......The INDIAN REPUBLICAN ARMY further declares that any person who will be able to produce any Englishman, woman or child to these headquarters, dead or alive, will be rewarded." (It is noteworthy that this is the only example which has come to notice in which women and children are mentioned as intended victims.)

Recruitment. In the early days of the movement the members were, before actual acceptance, put through a strenuous course of training and trial and were then admitted to the Society after a ceremonial initiation of a mystical and religious nature. Thereafter the members underwent further training in organised groups and were subjected to a very strict rule of life involving celibacy and, paradoxically, a high standard of morals. When, however, the movement spread beyond Bengal, while recruits were still strictly examined and tested before admission, the religious aspect seems to have been disregarded. Later, in Bengal itself, when terrorism, as the

*See Appendix 3.

result of political disturbances in the country, took deeper root and increased its hold, the old ideals were dropped and recruits were enrolled in large numbers with little reference to their character and antecedents. In the early days of the movement, the marriage of members had been forbidden, but in later years, young women and girls were not only enrolled as helpers but were actually enlisted as comrades. Terrorist groups were still formed from students' unions, physical training classes and the like, but provided that a youth was willing to assist in outrages there was no bar to his enlistment. In the main recruitment was confined to Hindus, generally of the better class, but outside Bengal and sometimes even in that Province Sikhs and Mussalmans were also admitted.

Naturally, the aims and objects of terrorism appealed in their crudeness to the immature student and throughout the history of the movement we find that the great bulk of terrorists has been drawn from schools and colleges. In some cases, teachers have preached sedition and revolutionary methods to their classes. Older men have, of course, appeared as important leaders but in nearly every case it is certain that they imbibed the principles of terrorism in their student days. The Mainpuri party of terrorists in the United Provinces in 1916—18 was led by Genda Mal, a teacher, and Yashpal, the notorious Punjab terrorist was once a master in the now defunct National School at Lahore, where he approached likely students and drew them into the fold. In Bengal especially the schools were badly affected ; a confessing revolutionary has stated that in Dacca town not more than two per cent. of the students were pro-Government and that about twenty per cent. had been recruited to his own party, which was only one of many groups in the town.

Brief Summary of Terrorism, 1917—1936. Before entering on a detailed account of terrorist activities during the past twenty years it will be convenient to review, briefly, the general trend of the movement. A general survey of conditions shows that the cult had very marked waves of intensity, which were fostered by political conditions in the country and in turn subdued by strong action on the part of the authorities. Profiting by the disturbed conditions prevailing everywhere, terrorism reached a high peak of activity in the early years of the War, but by 1917 had begun to show a marked decline as the result of the restrictions imposed by the Defence of India Act of 1915, which had been put into full use in 1916. The movement had been particularly violent in Bengal, but other provinces had not been free from its influence. In Upper India, Rash Bihari Bose had made extensive plans for a general uprising among Indian troops, but his scheme had been frustrated by the discovery of the plot at Benares, and the Benares Conspiracy Case followed. Bose was forced to flee the country and has since been living in Japan.

Thereafter, with most of their leaders in jail, all parties (except for a minor group in the Mainpuri district of the United Provinces), decided to desist from open activity, and the next few years show fewer crimes than any period since terrorism first raised its head. The release of the detenus in 1920 did little to stimulate revolutionary crime, as the released leaders realised that the time was not propitious and that preparations were needed before open violence could be resumed. In 1922, after two years of non-cooperation, at a time when the country was in a ferment and it was evident that Mr. Gandhi's non-violent ideals were impracticable, the terrorists were freed from restraint by the repeal of most of the special legislation introduced to supplement the Criminal Law, and immediately resumed a campaign of violence. At the outset, Bengal, the home and breeding-ground of terrorism, was most affected, and in 1923 suffered from a number of serious outrages. The United Provinces, which had received the attentions of two Bengali leaders, Sachindra Nath Sanyal and Jogesh Chandra Chatterjee, was not long in following suit, and a series of crimes ensued which culminated in the Kakori train dacoity. The resulting conspiracy case was a very serious blow to the United Provinces party, which was styled the Hindustan Republican Army. In Bengal the forces of law and order were strengthened to meet the revolutionary menace by the issue of an Ordinance in October 1924.

The effect of this action in Bengal and the U. P. was gratifying, and again there was a welcome decrease in terrorist crime, although plotting continued with even greater vigour than before. This was especially noticeable in the Punjab and the United Provinces. Chandra Shekhar Azad had escaped arrest when so many terrorists were tried in the Kakori Case, and he now united forces with the notorious Bhagat Singh of the Punjab and Phanindra Nath Ghosh of Bihar to form the Hindustan Socialist Republican Army with himself as Commander-in-Chief. This soon became a very powerful and active group which was to harry the Upper Provinces of India for many years; its example moreover reacted on the parent bodies in Bengal by inspiring the younger hot-heads to disregard the advice of their leaders and to form the New Violence Party. While in Bengal violence was discredited for a year or two, in the Punjab and the United Provinces several serious terrorist crimes were committed, notably the assassination of Mr. Saunders in Lahore in December 1928, and the throwing of bombs by Bhagat Singh and B. K. Datt in the Assembly at Delhi in April 1929.

In Bengal, in the meantime, all organisations were marking time and making great preparations for the expiry of the Bengal Criminal Law Amendment Act of 1925 which was to expire on March 21st, 1930. Early in 1930 Mr. Gandhi began his campaign of civil disobedience, thereby promoting a widespread wave of unrest. This was the hoped-for signal which had been awaited so eagerly by the younger revolutionaries who had chafed under the inactivity of their leaders, and the Chittagong group of the New Violence Party lost no time in bringing off their raids on the local Police and Auxiliary Force Armouries in April of that year. The remarkable success of this daring coup had an immediate effect on terrorists everywhere, but especially in Bengal, and the years 1930 to 1933 saw the most widespread activity that has yet occurred in the history of terrorism in India. In Bengal the number of terrorist crimes far exceeded anything that had been known before, and many of the most serious outrages characterising the movement occurred during that period. No less than nine British Officers were assassinated between August 1930 and

September 1933, while attempts were made on the lives of several others, including H. E. the Governor of Bengal.

In the Punjab, the United Provinces and Delhi, terrorism increased to an unprecedented extent, although, on the whole, the crimes committed were not of such a serious nature as in Bengal. The movement received severe set-backs when the two Lahore Conspiracy Cases and the Delhi Conspiracy Case were instituted. Although the publicity given to these cases and the open adulation of the accused by the press undoubtedly served as excellent recruiting propaganda to the terrorists, their leaders were removed from the scene of action and there was none to replace them in zeal, daring or in organising ability. Terrorism, therefore, although it became very widespread, deteriorated in quality, so that most of the activity found its expression in the inexpert making and throwing of bombs, which, though disturbing in their effect, did little or no damage to life and property. This activity was comparatively easy to deal with because the party organisation had become so much weaker and the connections between the various groups so fragile. Nevertheless, the situation was serious and needed long and stern efforts to combat it successfully. These efforts were aided by the issue of various ordinances and the passing of several enactments by the Government of India and in the several Provinces, which enabled the authorities to deal swiftly with suspected terrorists and to intern the more dangerous elements. Nevertheless, the process was long and trying to all concerned, and the endeavours of the authorities were not aided by the nationalist press, which cleverly vaunted terrorist atrocities in articles professing to deplore the outrages, or even openly canonising would-be assassins. However, legislation to prevent such abetment gradually had its effect, and slowly the general public came to realise that terrorists were more dangerous than useful. By 1934 there had been a distinct change for the better, and terrorist crimes for 1936 were the lowest for a long period of years. Another and important factor which made for this improvement was the gradual conversion of the terrorist to communism, a creed not in accord with the status of the average terrorist, who is recruited from the 'bourgeoisie', but one which he was persuaded to adopt as a path to his ideal of revolution, when he saw that the individualist methods in which he trusted only led to strong repressive measures whose success was ensured by the very nature of their methods. It is still too early to prophesy what form this unnatural alliance of terrorism and communism will ultimately take.

The Plan of this Book. One of the foremost objects of this account of terrorism has been the inter-provincial aspect of the movement, an aspect at once dangerous and difficult to detect. Stress has been laid on all inter-provincial cases, that is, cases in which the accused have been drawn from more than one province ; and to assist in assessing the comparative importance of the part played by accused in those cases lists of the convicted persons in each case with the sentences awarded to each, have been included in appendix 2.

For convenience sake, however, the history of terrorism during the last twenty years can best be dealt with by provinces and this plan has been followed, a separate chapter being allotted to each province, with the exception of the United Provinces, the Punjab and Delhi, where inter-provincial connections have been so marked, that these three provinces have been dealt with in a combined chapter.

The movement attained such large proportions that it would be impossible, in a compilation of this size, to deal with more than a small number of names. For the same reason an attempt has been made to confine the account to established facts, mainly those proved in courts of law. Much more is known to those acquainted with the subject, but C. I. D. records are the proper repository for such information, which would merely tend to blur the main features of the picture which it is desired to present. It is hoped that the index will serve as a useful guide for those seeking for references ; with this object in view the entries under 'Inter-provincial connections' have been made as exhaustive as the scope of this book permits.

CHAPTER II.

BENGAL.

The history of the first terrorist movement has been fully dealt with by Mr. Ker, I.C.S., in his " Political Trouble in India, 1907—1917 ", but in order to obtain a proper perspective of the years following, it will be convenient to review, briefly, the developments leading up to that year. For this purpose I have freely culled from the 'Memorandum on the History of Terrorism in Bengal, 1905—1933' and from periodical reports prepared in Bengal.

Brief review of the terrorist movement prior to 1917. The movement was started in 1906 through the newspaper 'Yugantar' in Calcutta, and in Dacca. Other newspapers then combined to pour forth a steady stream of sedition, abuse and incitement to murder. A heavy list of outrages was the result, and it became increasingly difficult to cope with the conspiracies under the existing law. In 1907, the Prevention of Seditious Meetings Act was passed to check the open preaching of sedition and violence but it was only extended to Bengal when its three years term had nearly expired, and was used more as a warning than as a purge. This was followed in 1908 by the Explosive Substances Act, and by the Newspapers (Incitement to Offences) Act. In the same year the Indian Criminal Law Amendment Act (XIV of 1908) was passed providing for trials by benches of three judges of the High Court without a jury.

These measures failed to check the steady stream of political dacoities and murders; there were 140 terrorist outrages between 1907 and May 1915, and the police found themselves powerless to cope with intimidation of witnesses. Even when conspiracy cases, prepared only with enormous labour and expense, were successful in Sessions Courts, more often than not the High Court reduced the sentences or acquitted the accused. The Indian Press Act of 1910 finally brought the newspapers under control, but the conspirators knew that so long as the Police had only the use of the ordinary law they could still expect to defeat them The Criminal Law Amendment Act of 1913 enacted that the offence of conspiracy might be committed even though no overt act in pursuance of its object accompanied the conspiracy, but even this was not enough, and by 1915, the situation had become one of unparalleled danger. Murderous outrages had reached an unprecedented frequency, and it was then recognized that the forces of law and order working through the ordinary channels were inadequate. Sir Reginald Craddock, in introducing the Defence of India Act, 1915, made clear that the framers of the Bill had in mind, especially, the revolutionary conspiracy in Bengal. The powers granted by the Act were both punitive and preventive. No committal proceedings were to be required and the trials were to be conducted by three Commissioners appointed by the local Government. The decision of these Commissioners was to be final. It was the preventive powers, however, which were by far the most effective. Armed with these powers the Police could place a terrorist under detention for 15 days, within which period the *dossier* of his case had to be prepared and submitted to Government. Charges were framed to which the *detenu* was required to reply. The Government order could take various forms ranging from custody in jail to compulsory home or village domicile. The *detenus* were to be given a substantial allowance and their relatives who were dependent on them were, likewise, to receive adequate monetary support. Subsequently it was arranged that, before Government passed orders, each case was to be examined *in camera* by two judges who would report whether in their opinion valid grounds existed for the issue of an order of detention under the Act.

Even after the enactment of the Defence of India Act of 1915, its provisions were not at once fully utilized, and although 233 persons were interned by June 1916, terrorist crime increased in violence. Following the murder of Deputy Superintendent of Police, Basanta

Chatterjee in that month, the need for extraordinary measures could no longer be denied, and the full use of the powers conferred by the Act was sanctioned by Government. From June 1916 to June 1918 there were 29 outrages in which 10 persons were murdered; from June 1918 to September 1919, there were only two outrages in which two persons were murdered; there were none in 1920 and 1921, and only one in 1922, in which one person was murdered. A total of 1,262 persons were interned in Bengal under the Defence of India Act, and 130 under Regulation III of 1818. With very few exceptions all the leaders in the Presidency of the Jugantar party and the Anushilan Samiti, the two branches of the revolutionary organization, were arrested.

The movement in 1917. The period with which we are dealing therefore opens at a time when the police, armed with special powers, were beginning at last to make an impression on the subversive movement which had prospered for so long. That, in 1917, there was still much to be done, is evident from the tale of terrorist crimes committed in that year. On the 5th January 1917, a plot to murder an associate suspected to have been giving information to the police nearly succeeded, but the intended victim made an excuse and telephoned to the police. In the same month a revolutionary was murdered by his comrades at Serajganj, but this was on account of immorality.

On the night of April 15th a typical political dacoity was committed by about 20 persons who stole a large amount of money and gold ornaments in the district of Rajshahi, after cutting the telegraph wires. In July two youths were arrested at Dacca station and a parcel of the loot and one of the Mauser pistols stolen from Messrs. Rodda in 1914, were recovered. From the scenes of four other dacoities Mauser cartridges and spent shells were recovered, and at the last a loaded Mauser pistol was also found. One crime took place in Dacca District in February and the second in Rangpur District in June, when an old man of

80 was dragged from his bed, his fingers were cut off with an axe and he was fatally stabbed. His son was also killed on the spot by a spear thrust. Dacca District again was the scene of the third dacoity, in October and the fourth took place in Tippera District in November, when one of the victims was shot through both legs.

Another dacoity was committed in a goldsmith's shop in Bara Bazar, Calcutta. On May 7th, two Bengalis who had asked to see jewellery were joined by four more who fired wildly with pistols, mortally wounding two brothers of the proprietor. After wounding two others, the dacoits decamped in a taxicab, and, as one of their number was also badly wounded, they shot him dead in a lonely place.

The Rowlatt Committee. The situation in 1917, was still sufficiently disturbing to warrant the appointment of a committee under the Presidentship of the Hon'ble Mr. Justice Rowlatt with the following terms of reference :—

(1) To investigate and report on the nature and extent of the criminal conspiracies connected with the revolutionary movement in India.

(2) To examine and consider the difficulties that have arisen in dealing with such conspiracies and to advise as to the legislation, if any, necessary to enable Government to deal effectively with them.

The committee, after a lengthy review of the events of the past years recorded the opinion that "the main reason why it has not been possible by the ordinary machinery of the criminal law to convict and imprison on a larger scale those guilty of outrages, and so put down crime is simply want of evidence .... this difficulty in obtaining legal evidence has been no doubt greatly enhanced by terrorism". The committee therefore recommended legislation conferring powers, with certain limitations, such as those conferred by the Defence of India Act. A

Bill was, accordingly, drafted and passed in the Assembly at Delhi in March, 1919, as the Revolutionary and Anarchical Crimes Act, 1919. The Act was still-born, but the accuracy of the findings of the committee has been proved by subsequent events.

The improved situation in 1918—20. The first part of the year 1918, saw a continuance of terrorist crime in the Presidency, but the second half of the year showed a welcome decrease which was to continue for some time, thus demonstrating the ability of the police to cope with subversive activity when given adequate powers. In 1919 there was only one revolutionary crime, and in 1920 no such crime was recorded. This great improvement was due solely to the grant of wider powers to the police in dealing with terrorist organisations. The police were now able to intern a terrorist before the crime that he was plotting could be committed, and also leaders, recruiters, and minor members as soon as they were mentioned by reliable agents.

The release of detenus and the Reforms. Early in 1920, after the Royal Proclamation of 1919, all those who had been interned under the Defence of India Act were released and the amnesty was extended gradually to most of the leaders of the revolutionary movements. Up to this time there had been no evidence of any connection between terrorists and the Congress Party; nor was there much sympathy for terrorists among the general population. In 1920 and 1921, the terrorists, who had begun to reorganise, exploited the Non-co-operation movement to the full for the purpose of recruitment, and deliberately set about capturing the Congress in Bengal. The Montagu-Chelmsford Reforms were formally inaugurated by H. R. H. the Duke of Connaught in February 1921, and were followed, in 1922, by the repeal of virtually all the enactments supplementing the Criminal Law except the Seditious Meetings Act, 1911, and Part II of the Indian Criminal Law Amendment Act of 1908. The Rowlatt Act, which had never been put into operation, and the Indian Press Act, were also repealed.

The Agitation which followed the Reforms. The impending Reforms, however, failed to meet the demand of the extremists and the destruction of the reformed system of government became the avowed object of all the extremist political parties. The period was one of great political and economic difficulty. The high prices prevailing as a result of the Great War had engendered a vague feeling of resentment against the Government, the religious sentiments of the Muslims had been greatly disturbed by the misfortunes of Turkey, and political feelings in general were stirred by events in the Punjab. Mr. Gandhi adroitly took advantage of all these factors to launch his non-co-operation movement in 1920. Schools and colleges and law courts were to be boycotted, titles renounced, national schools and arbitration courts started, and foreign goods, particularly cloth, boycotted, with a view to bring Government to its knees. It took a little time before the full effects of the furious agitation among the masses made themselves felt. Though Mr. Gandhi's ideas were non-violent, his followers gradually got out of control and the movement eventually led to the shocking tragedy of Chauri Chaura in the U. P. in February 1922. In Bengal the results of the movement were manifested in the mutiny in the Rajshahi jail, the exodus of tea-garden coolies from Assam, and a strike on the Assam Bengal Railway and the I. G. S. N. Co.'s steamer services. In the country districts the agitation was directed largely against the police including the village police, and in many districts there was a refusal to pay the chaukidari tax and the rents of Government and private landlords. Throughout this period, the press poured forth a torrent of propaganda and abuse, and kept the province in a ferment of excitement.

Terrorists reorganise. The terrorists, now freed from restraint, were content to watch developments while utilising every opportunity (such as the volunteer movement) for drawing their followers together and extending their influence. Endeavours were made to organise *ashrams* of a type similar to those which played so important a part in former movements. Leading members of the two main organisations were active in every form of propaganda particularly among the student class. Every cause of unrest was exploited and every centre of agitation utilised for the dissemination of terrorism and the winning of new recruits. Many of their leaders obtained responsible positions in district congress committees and used their positions to consolidate their followers. This penetration of the Congress machine had very important consequences, for it helped the terrorist party internally in the matter of recruitment and organisation, and externally in the matter of public sympathy. Penetration was so rapid that in 1924 the terrorists were in a position to compel the Bengal Provincial Congress to put through a resolution eulogising one Gopi Mohan Saha who was executed for assassinating a certain Mr. Day of Calcutta in mistake for Sir Charles Tegart, the Commissioner of Police. The time was to come when there would be few districts in the province where terrorists were not represented on local Congress committees.

Press propaganda. Being satisfied by Mr. Gandhi's arrest and conviction, in 1922, that his programme had definitely failed, the terrorists decided then to resume their campaign of violence. There is reason to believe that the Chittagong Congress of April 1922 was the occasion of the decision to resume violent methods. This second terrorist campaign was ushered in, like the first, by a resumption of terrorist propaganda in the extremist press. Within a short time of the repeal of the Indian Press Act in March 1922, mushroom vernacular journals like the "Atma Sakti", the "Sarathi", the "Mukti Kam", "Bijali" and others began to publish articles having a direct or indirect tendency to excite violent hostility against Government and the British. The commonest type of propaganda was to denounce the economic oppression of the British in India, to extol, in mystical and sometimes in poetic language, freedom and self-sacrifice, and to publish appreciative articles in praise of revolutionaries. This last was a new feature of revolutionary propaganda and its nature will appear from the following extract from the annual report on Indian newspapers in Bengal for the year 1923 :—

> "A noteworthy feature in the year under review was the large amount of writing in frank praise of old revolutionaries. The "Ananda Bazar Patrika" referred to them as selfless youths with indomitable resolution, who kindled the lamp of life by undergoing death. The "Prabartak" for March, in continuation of previous issues, extolled Kanai Lall Dutt (the murderer of the approver Narenda Lal Gossain in the Alipore Conspiracy Case). These are primarily narratives. Highly appreciative biographical notices of Jatindra Mukherjee and his three associates (killed at Balasore in an encounter with the police) now appeared in many papers. It was explained, however, that this laudation did not necessarily imply adoption of their methods. The justification was set forth by the "Sarathi", "The distrust of the people must be removed. To give them such a training, the life stories of self-sacrificing heroic patriots must be recited to them. We adopt their methods, but are we not on that account, to respect their renunciation, their heroism, and their patriotism"?

Resumption of crime. The Jugantar group was the first to strike. In May 1923, they committed a dacoity with double murder at Kona near Howrah; in the same month the Ultadinghi post office was looted. The same gang committed a robbery with murder at Garpar Road on the 30th July in which fire-arms were used. The murder of a postmaster at Sankaritola followed. The investigation in this produced full corroboration of the information already in the possession of Government, and showed that these outrages were all the work of a particular group of the terrorist party. Seven members of this group were put on trial in the Alipore conspiracy case, but many of the facts in the possession of Government could not be placed before the court and they were eventually acquitted; but Barindra Kumar Ghose was sentenced to death (though not executed) for the Sankaritola murder.

With the commission of these outrages, the situation became serious. It was clear that the terrorists had been encouraged by the belief that Government could no longer deal with their conspiracies effectively. It was clear also that unless immediate action were taken, Bengal would again be exposed to the dangers of the previous outbreak of revolutionary crime. Accordingly, several of the important leaders including Subhas Chandra Bose, the Chief Executive Officer of the Corporation, who was believed to have been behind the plot to assassinate Sir Charles Tegart, and who had given employment to a large number of Jugantar revolutionaries and *ex*-detenus under the Calcutta Corporation, were incarcerated under Regulation III of 1818. This action served, however, to check the movement only for the time being. New leaders were found and operations were resumed. In December 1923, a robbery of Rs. 17,000, the property of the Assam-Bengal Railway, was committed at Chittagong by four *bhadralok* youths armed with revolvers. Subsequent investigation showed that certain *bhadralok* youths were hiding in suspicious circumstances in a house in a village at some distance from Chittagong. The search of this house ten days after the robbery, led to the discovery of a number of weapons, and ammunition of a foreign make. The attempt to arrest the occupants of the house led to a running fight between them and a body of police and to the arrest of two youths with fire-arms. An attempt was made to decoy from his house one of the chief witnesses in the robbery case with the intention of murdering him; and on the next evening a sub-inspector who had arrested one of the accused in this case and knew the others by sight, was shot at Chittagong.

Plots to assassinate Police Officers. Some of the accused in the Alipore Conspiracy case stated subsequently that one of the immediate objects of the conspiracy was the assassination of police officers. In the early part of 1923, persons were found watching the movements and residences of these officers. The watchers were themselves placed under observation, and traced to places known to be haunts of the conspirators. In January 1924, Mr. Day was murdered in Calcutta, and the murderer, Gopi Mohan Saha, who was hanged for the crime, freely stated that he had intended Mr. (later Sir Charles) Tegart to be his victim. In March, a bomb factory, fully equipped with explosives and implements for loading and fitting bomb-shells (of which a number both loaded and unloaded were found) was discovered in Calcutta. The bombs showed a marked advance on anything which had previously come to light. In this case two youths were sentenced to seven years' transportation each. About the same time, a young *bhadralok*, Promode Kumar Nag of Dacca, was severely injured while handling explosives at Faridpur. Shells and chemicals were found in his house and he was eventually convicted to six years' rigorous imprisonment. In April an attempt on the life of Mr. Bruce was made. In July a well-known terrorist was arrested in the streets of Calcutta with a fully loaded revolver in his possession. At the end of July 'Red Bengal' leaflets made their appearance. The first issue announced the initiation of a campaign of assassination of police officers: the second impressed on the political leaders of Bengal the need for the existence of an active violence party. This was followed in August by the explosion of a bomb in Mirzapur Street in an attack on an informer, who escaped. One bystander was, however, killed and another injured. The man who actually threw the bomb was pursued and seized, and another arrest was made on the spot at the same time.

The above is a brief outline of the outward manifestations of the existence of a widespread conspiracy. Apart from these, Government were in possession of information to show that, during the year 1924, the conspirators attempted to assassinate police officers, high Government officials, and suspected members of their own organisations. No less than five such attempts were made between July and October, and the escape of the intended victims could only be regarded as providential. In some cases the would-be assassins suspected police vigilance, in others they were thwarted by the unexpected movements of their intended victims. In June 1924, the Bengal Provincial Congress at their meeting at Serajgunj passed a resolution expressing admiration for the spirit of self-sacrifice exhibited by Gopi Mohan Saha. The effects of the resolution were electrical. It became by far the most potent instrument for organisation, and a perpetual incitement to the youth of Bengal to take to violent ways.

Special Legislation to meet the menace. The situation towards the end of 1924 had, therefore, become one of considerable anxiety. The existence of a widespread revolutionary movement was hardly disputed; indeed it was admitted by Mr. C. R. Das, the Swarajist leader, himself. It was daily increasing in strength, and, as in the years before 1916, ordinary measures had failed to check it. The local Government felt bound, therefore, to meet the menace by obtaining from the Governor-General the issue of an Ordinance arming the executive with powers similar to those they had had under the Defence of India Act. On the early morning of the 25th October 1924, simultaneously with the promulgation of the Ordinance, action was taken against the more prominent revolutionaries under the Ordinance and under Regulation III of 1818. Sixty-nine persons were arrested that day and twelve others later, while searches were conducted at numerous places in Bengal. The raid yielded nothing in the way of arms, ammunition and explosives, but in thirty-three places revolutionary literature was found, and the immediate object of the raid was fulfilled. The revolutionary organisations and their campaign were for the time thoroughly dislocated and disorganised. While the secret parties were attempting to reorganise and recover from the effects of the blow dealt them, all Indian political parties, organisations and newspapers indulged in a systematic campaign of vilification or disapproval against the new weapon which the Government had brought into use.

By the end of November, 1924, no less than one hundred public meetings had been held in the Province and resolutions were passed condemning the ordinance as repressive and calculated to stifle legitimate political activities. A most pernicious feature of the agitation was the eulogy by prominent speakers, including Mr. C. R. Das, of the political murderers and assassins. The campaign was carried into the Legislative Council which had been specially called to consider a bill to pass the Ordinance into law in January 1925. The Council refused leave to introduce the Bill, which was, accordingly, in April, certified by the Governor to remain in force for five years.

The powers conferred by this measure were not as wide as those under the Defence of India Act. The definition of persons against whom section 11 (preventive arrest and detention by executive order) could be used was narrowed down to prevent the net being cast too widely and to avoid the criticism that it was aimed at the Swaraj party. The schedule, of offences in connection with which action could be taken, too, was shortened, and the net result was that it was possible to take action only against active terrorists as distinguished from recruiters or organisers. Nevertheless, prompt use of these powers, by placing leaders and active members under restraint, enabled Government to bring the movement under control. Between the issue of the Ordinance in 1924 and the end of 1928 only one murder by terrorists occurred. Only 187 persons were dealt with under the Act, and by September 1928 all had been set free, although a certain number remained for some time longer under restriction orders limiting their movements. When the Act expired in 1930, no use had been made of the special powers for the purpose of making fresh arrests for nearly three years. This result was made possible by the recognition on the part of the terrorist leaders that while the Act remained in force they were not sufficiently well organised to conduct a campaign against Government. It was not an indication that terrorist activities had ceased.

The effect of the Legislation. As a matter of fact, the information at the disposal of Government showed that after the arrests under the Ordinance of 1924, the leaders of the Jugantar and Anushilan groups, realising that they were not sufficiently organised, postponed the further execution of their terrorist plans. The policy of these leaders was to discourage violence for the moment, and, indeed, any isolated act of violence, and, instead, to use the consequent period of quiet for recruiting on a large scale, increasing the funds of the revolutionaries, and preparing, by laying in stocks of bombs and explosives, for an out-break on a national scale. The Dacca Anushilan Samiti, under Narendra Mohan Sen, was known to be engaged in forging notes for this purpose, and in fact Sachindra Chakravarti and Probodh Das Gupta were arrested in this connection in March 1925 and were later sentenced to 5 years' rigorous imprisonment each. At the same time, there were indications that some members of the party were attempting to obtain from communist sources money and help in their aims. Jogesh Chandra Chatterji, who was arrested in October 1924, and was later sentenced in the Kakori Conspiracy Case, had been seen to visit R. C. L. Sharmá, M. N. Roy's agent in Pondicherry. Sachindra Nath Sanyal also was in correspondence with known communist agents.

The younger members disapprove of non-violence. These two, Jogesh Chandra Chatterji and Sachindra Nath Sanyal, with other young hot-heads, did not approve of the leaders' policy. They had already incurred the displeasure of Narendra Sen and others by their independent work in the United Provinces, and Sanyal's issue of the 'Revolutionary' and 'Appeal to my countrymen' pamphlets in January 1925, further annoyed the leaders. During the year, some of these rebellious elements combined together to form what is sometimes known as the New Violence Party. Important members were Nalini Dutt, the head of a seceding faction of the Anushilan, and Nagendra Sen, the head of the Chittagong Party. Their aim was the immediate resumption of terrorism after collecting bombs, arms and ammunition. Sachindra Nath Sanyal was fortunately arrested in February 1925 and was later convicted in the Kakori Conspiracy Case, but planning went on throughout the year. Dacoities, robberies and attacks on police officers and others were discussed and arranged, but not one of the schemes was carried out Bomb-making was carried on, and on November 10th, 1925, houses in Dakhineswar and Sova Bazar Street, Calcutta, were searched. A bomb, revolvers, ammunition and chemicals were found, and, more important still, eleven known leaders of the party, which by now had also become known as the All-Bengal Revolutionary Party, were arrested. Rajendra Nath Lahiri, who was one of those arrested, was, after his conviction, sent to the United Provinces, where he was sentenced to death for his part in the Kakori dacoity. The others arrested were also convicted. An interesting recovery in the search at Sova Bazar Street was a copy of the official programme of this party. It quoted with approval the saying of Mazzini that 'actions are the book of the masses—ideas ripen quickly when nourished by the blood of the martyrs', and went on to say that revolution would arrive in India in the following stages :—

(*a*) Individual demonstrations, such as the murder of high officials, the capture of Government arms and ammunition, the destruction of Government institutions, jail outbreaks, the destruction of bridges, the wrecking of trains and the murder of spies and informers.

(*b*) Simultaneous demonstrations.

(*c*) Insurrection, including guerilla warfare.

(*d*) Revolution.

The programme shows that terrorists, profiting by their past experience, had come to the conclusion that it was necessary to have a plan of compaign on a much wider basis than an indiscriminate orgy of murders and dacoities. The party was preparing for a series of spectacular bomb outrages when the sudden arrest of the eleven leaders at Dakhineswar and Sova Bazar interrupted its plans and for a time dislocated its organisation. The desperate character of the gang was proved in May 1926 when these persons brutally murdered a distinguished police officer, Rai Bhupendra Nath Chatterji Bahadur, Special Superintendent of Police, Intelligence Branch, in the Alipore Jail. Their warder was overpowered, and the Rai Bahadur was battered to death with a crow-bar. For this crime Ananta Hari Mitra and Promode Chaudhri were hanged, and three others were transported for life.

Interim period. The next period was a difficult one for the revolutionary parties. Most of the important leaders were in jail, and those outside were not only disunited on the policy to be followed, but were continually bickering and striving for individual leadership. The Jugantar party was content to make preparations for a big event, but its Chittagong branch, now under the leadership of Surja Sen, who was then absconding, favoured the New Violence Party. This was the most active group, and it claimed connections with terrorist cells in the U. P., Punjab, Bihar and Orissa, and with Assam. The Anushilan party had lost many adherents when they joined the New Violence Party and the main bulk now became more interested in communist affairs and methods, which had been introduced by Gopen Chakravarti, an emissary of M. N. Roy. However, the programme of all branches was the collection of arms, bombs and other materials, and intensive recruitment. There were indications that arms were being smuggled into the country, partly *via* Burma, where a branch group existed. Indeed, in 1926 Sudhangshu Chaudhri was sentenced to imprisonment under the Arms Act and section 120-B., I. P. C., for having smuggled a revolver from Burma into Calcutta. Surja Sen was arrested in October 1926, and the leadership of the Chittagong group passed to Bijan Kumar Banerji, the Bengal leader of the Hindustan Republican Association, who infused new life into the party.

On the 6th January 1927, however, another blow was struck, when a house in Sukea Street, Calcutta, was raided, and bomb shells, revolvers and cartridges were recovered. In consequence, two terrorists were sentenced to seven years' rigorous imprisonment each and a third to 1 year's rigorous imprisonment. Then on 13th January, Bijan Kumar Banerji was arrested. These continuous set-backs prevented the New Violence Party from carrying out its numerous plans for committing outrages, but preparations still went on. In May 1927, a small group of the Calcutta Jugantar party, acting independently, committed an armed robbery in the Hooghly district; three persons were later convicted.

Deoghar Conspiracy Case. It seems that the leaders of the Jugantar and Anushilan parties attempted to form a coalition about this time, but in the circumstances, the scheme was short-lived. Other raids by the police in August and September removed bomb-making materials from the possession of members and resulted in some convictions. By July, however, a new leader had appeared, who claimed to have established touch with revolutionaries in Assam and the United Provinces. He was also in touch with Indra Chandra Narang, a Punjabi student in Calcutta, and Bengali members of the Hindustan Republican Association in Calcutta. This man was making rapid strides towards establishing his leadership, when he was arrested in Deoghar, in possession of two Mauser pistols and cartridges. He gave his name as Birendra Nath Bhattacharji of Kalagaria, Dacca. Amongst the papers seized was a notebook containing in cypher, group by group, names and addresses, with their code introductions and passwords, of 68 members of the revolutionary party in Bengal, Assam, Bihar and Orissa, the United Provinces, and the Punjab. The cypher book also contained the names of eighteen intended victims. This led to searches in many places. One of the most productive of these was at the house of Sailendra Nath Chakravarti at Allahabad, where two revolvers, two hundred cartridges, gunpowder, explosive substances, cypher addresses, a false beard, entrenching tools, three pairs of handcuffs and a mass of literature including military books, proscribed books and revolutionary pamphlets were found. Amongst these were copies of the 'Yellow' and 'White' leaflets which had figured so prominently in the Kakori

Conspiracy Case. Other searches produced similar finds, but not in such large quantities. Accordingly a case was instituted against nineteen Bengalis and one Punjabi at Deoghar, which ended in the conviction of eleven to sentences ranging from three to seven years' rigorous imprisonment. In addition Surendra Nath Bhattacharji and his brother Birendra were sentenced to three years' rigorous imprisonment under the Arms Act. The Punjabi, who had been studying at Calcutta, was acquitted on appeal to the High Court.

The Deoghar case was a very decisive blow to the revolutionary parties, and the break-up caused by the Criminal Law Amendment Act arrests, the successful bomb finds and this case, was now complete. The *detenus* under Regulation III of 1818, the 1924 Ordinance and the Bengal Criminal Law Amendment Act, were released, mostly in 1928, and all by the end of 1929, although some were still under restriction orders.

Resumption of crime. There was a slight recrudescence of terrorist crime in 1928, but in 1929, there was a fresh outbreak. Niranjan Sen Gupta and two others, realising that the discontented elements of both parties demanded sensational outrages, formed a new amalgamated party for immediate terrorism based on the methods, such as surprise attacks on armed police posts, and guerilla warfare, as described in Dan Breen's, 'My fight for Irish Freedom' The year opened with the murder in March of a Sub-Inspector of Police, Jyotish Chandra Ray, who was stabbed to death in Barisal by Romesh Chandra Chatterji. The murderer fled, but was captured by students, and was sentenced to death, although the High Court later commuted the sentence to transportation for life. This murder was the first committed by terrorists since the murder in 1927 in Alipore Jail.

Later in the year other crimes were committed by revolutionaries, notably an assault on an Assistant Sub-Inspector of the 24-Parganas District Intelligence Branch by Indra Chandra Narang and another, and an attempted mail robbery in the Rajshahi district by six youths, who damaged the headlights and tyres of the mail lorry and wounded one man with a revolver shot. The driver escaped with the mails by forcing his vehicle to proceed despite the damage which had been done. Three persons were convicted for this crime. There were two dacoities in December 1929. In the same month Niranjan Sen Gupta's quarters in Mechuabazar Street, Calcutta, were raided. Three persons including Gupta, were arrested, and new leaflets, a dagger and other articles were seized. Later a youth, Sudhangshu Lal Das Gupta, a nephew of one of the Rajshahi case accused, who entered the house was also arrested, and a bomb was recovered from a suitcase which he was carrying. Among the papers found was a list of the names of the members of the district organisation and a 'group for present action', consisting in all of forty-three persons. This was followed by numerous searches, throughout Bengal and later, from further information received, searches were made in Calcutta on 24th January 1930, and at Panchi Dhobani Lane, explosive materials, daggers, a wooden model of a bomb, and a wax cast of a bombshell, together with proscribed books, were found. More arrests were made and a case was instituted, charging twenty-seven accused with conspiracy. One of the accused became an approver, and one was tried separately. Eventually seventeen were convicted, but on appeal the sentence of Niranjan Sen Gupta was reduced from ten to seven years' rigorous imprisonment, and nine were acquitted. The sentences of the others ranged from three to seven years.

The young hot-heads demand action. Even this attack, however, was not sufficient to stem the aspirations of the hot-heads, who demanded immediate action, totally disregarding the advice of the older and more experienced leaders who realised that sporadic outbursts and minor outrages would merely call for strong Government action and a repetition of the arrests of 1924. It is noteworthy that by this time the old ideals of specially selected recruits of good moral character and exhibiting a loyalty to the cause, proved by a long period of probation followed by strict vows of initiation, had been relaxed, and any youth who professed sympathy with the aims of the revolutionaries and a willingness to help, was admitted direct to the party. The youth of the Presidency, especially the student class, was already sufficiently excited by the widespread propaganda of recent years to form a very large field for such recruitment, and there is no doubt that the old leaders were both embarrassed by the undisciplined new adherents and unable to control the desire for action. Events in the Punjab and the United Provinces must also have incited the youth of Bengal to action, stimulating their desire not to be in the background in a field which, hitherto, had been peculiarly their own.

The year 1930 was fairly quiet in the first three months, although in February a teacher was murdered in Mymensingh district and the body, severely mutilated by being run over by a train, of Bhupendra Raha Roy was found near Mymensingh. There were stab-wounds on the corpse and although the culprits were not detected there is every reason to believe that he was killed as a result of a quarrel. On April 12th five or six *bhadralok* youths armed with daggers and revolvers, raided a shop in Tala, Calcutta, and stole Rs. 15,000 in notes. Again the culprits were not detected but secret information pointed to members of the Madaripur branch of the Jugantar party.

The Chittagong raids. These events were, however, nothing compared with the amazing coup which was now brought off in Chittagong. The local group of the Jugantar Party had always held violent views, and it was the first to strike. One of the leaders there, Ganesh Ghosh, had been in touch with Niranjan Sen Gupta, who was, as we have seen, put out of action by the Mechuabazar case. It was therefore left to the group to work on its own, and on the night of April 18th, 1930, at about 10-30 P.M. the blow was struck. Preparations had been going on for several months. Money for buying equipment and arms was steadily collected by members of the party who stole it from their parents; khaki uniforms, badges, belts, leggings, and boots, were bought; arms were collected; bombshells were filled;

and members of the party were taught how to fire. Every detail of the attack had been worked out down to the synchronizing of the watches owned by members of the party who were to take part, and several mobilization lists were drawn up giving the constitution of the various groups told off for different branches of the assault. The mobilization scheme was so well thought out that when Ananta Singh and Ganesh Ghosh, two of the principal leaders, alarmed by indications that the police were meditating some action against them, decided to make their attempt earlier than they had originally planned, they were able to collect their force in one day, detail off the various batches under leaders, and proceed to the attack only one hour later than their scheduled time. Four batches set out from the Congress Office and Ganesh Ghosh's shop, one to capture the police armoury, one to capture the Auxiliary Force armoury, one to massacre the Europeans in the Club, and the last to destroy the Telephone Exchange and Telegraph Office. The delay caused the club party to find the building practically deserted, so that scheme was abandoned, but at the police armoury some 50 youths, all in khaki with the leaders dressed as officers, and in a taxi, the driver of which had been left trussed up in Ganesh Ghosh's house, took up a position and lay concealed until Ananta Lal Singh approached the police sentry and, after exchanging the usual challenges, shot him down and scattered the rest of the guard, two of whom were wounded. The pre-arranged signal "Bande Mataram" was then given and the remainder of the force swarmed into the lines, broke into the armoury and magazine, and armed themselves with muskets, revolvers, and ammunition. At the Auxiliary Force armoury a similar party drove up in a taxi, having chloroformed and dropped the driver. Loke Nath Bal dressed as an officer replied to the sentry's challenge and then shot him and another sepoy fatally. Sergeant-Major Farrell came out of his quarters and was shot dead. The armoury was then robbed of pistols, revolvers, rifles and a Lewis gun, but the ammunition which was in a separate room was overlooked. The building was then set alight with petrol and the raiders joined the party in the police lines; but in the meantime they had fired on passing motor cars and had killed a railway guard, the driver and the assistant driver of a taxi, a constable who was in the District Magistrate's car, and had wounded the driver of the District Magistrate's car and a villager who was in a passing taxi. They had therefore murdered seven persons and wounded two.

At the Telegraph Office a small party chloroformed the telephone operator, hacked the telephone board to pieces and then set fire to it. The Telegraph Master was fired at but he returned with a gun and drove off the party before they had succeeded in destroying the Telegraph Office. This party also joined the main party in the police lines where the assembled raiders were drilled and given instruction in firing. It must then have seemed that the rest of the programme, *viz.*, the seizure of the Treasury and the massacre of the Europeans of the station, would be easily accomplished, for the main Auxiliary Force armoury was gutted and the rifles and small arms removed, telephonic communication destroyed, the arms and ammunition in the police lines were in the raiders' possession, and the armed police were reduced to impotence. At about midnight, however, the Deputy Inspector General of Police, the Superintendent of Police, the Assistant Superintendent of Police and a member of the Auxiliary Force, opened fire on them with a Lewis gun, secured from a subsidiary armoury which by good fortune, the raiders had neglected. The raiders returned the fire and also threw a bomb which failed to explode, and they decided to retreat. In the meanwhile, one of the raiders had caught fire while saturating the guard-room with petrol and was so severely burnt that he subsequently died. Two of the leaders, Ananta Singh and Ganesh Ghosh, displaying unexpected humanity, carried this man off in a motor car with two others for treatment without leaving orders how to proceed. The result was that instead of returning to the town for the remainder of the programme, the party retreated to the hills north of the town, each, according to a statement, with a musket, at least one revolver or pistol, and a haversack full of cartridges. The raiders left behind three motor cars, some pickaxes, sledg-hammers and other tools, ten loaded bombs, four revolvers, two pistols, six shot guns, a number of cartridges, the Lewis gun which they had brought from the Auxiliary Force armoury, battered to pieces, and 39 riflos from the Auxiliary Force, all of which had been burnt. Meanwhile, two other parties, with the intention of cutting off all communication with Chittagong, had set out the day before to cut telegraph wires and derail trains. A goods train was derailed near Dhoom Railway Station and telegraph wires were cut there The second party made an unsuccessful attempt on the same night to derail the down mail to Chittagong some 70 miles away. The next day printed leaflets were distributed in Chittagong and in other districts of Bengal and other provinces. One announced that the Indian Republican Army had made an attempt to free India, and appealed to the students and youths of Chittagong to join in the fight. The other called upon the people of Chittagong for their allegiance and support. Both leaflets were issued by the President in Council, Indian Republican Army, Chittagong Branch.

The authorities in Chittagong were able to communicate the news of the raids by wireless from a ship in the harbour, and on the 20th April reinforcements arrived. On the 22nd April the main body of the raiders was tracked to Jalalabad Hill where an engagement took place before darkness put an end to the fight. Next day twelve of the raiders were found dead and twenty-three police muskets and nearly 2,000 loaded cartridges, a live bomb, a revolver and some revolver and pistol ammunition were found on the hill. The raiders had decamped during the night and divided up into several bands, and some actually managed to make their way back to Chittagong. One of these was tracked down and committed suicide. A revolver and a pistol with cartridges were found on his corpse. Another raider surrendered to the police. On the 22nd April, Ananta Singh, Ganesh Ghosh and two others were arrested by the police at Feni Station in Noakhali district, but effected their escape after wounding a sub-inspector and two constables although they lost a revolver in the struggle. On the 6th

May a party of six raiders opened fire on villagers who attempted to stop them, and killed three and wounded three others. A constable (although mortally wounded himself), seized Subodh Chaudhri and another raider was seized by the villagers. The remainder were found after an exhausting chase by the police party, and were shot dead after a short engagement. Each of them was found to be armed with a .450 Webley revolver. Later, acting on information obtained from a confession, two revolvers, four muskets, one gun and some ammunition were found in the hills.

Other crimes by Chittagonians. On the 28th June 1930, Ananta Lal Singh surrendered to the police after a quarrel with Ganesh Ghosh at Chandernagore where they were living with two others in hiding, and on the 31st August Ganesh Ghosh, Loke Nath Bal and Ananda Gupta were arrested and Makhan Ghosal was shot dead during a raid by the police on their shelter at Chandernagore. On the 8th October, Ambika Chakravarti was arrested in Chittagong district. Although 162 persons had by now been arrested only 36 were sent up in the first trial connected with the case. Girls had from the first been connected with the party and were now used to form links between those in jail and those still absconding. Kalpana Dutta was active in this way. Although so many of the gang had been accounted for the remainder did not cease to plot further outrages, and on the 1st December 1930, Inspector Tarini Charan Mukharji was shot dead at Chandpur Railway Station, while escorting the Inspector General of Police from Chittagong, by Ram Krishna Biswas and Kalipada Chakravarti, the first of whom was sentenced to death and the second to transportation for life. One revolver obtained from the Chittagong raid was recovered from them. On the 16th March 1931, two absconders were accosted by the police, but escaped after seriously wounding a sub-inspector.

On the 5th May while the gravel in front of the cells in the Chittagong Jail occupied by the accused in the Armoury raid case was being dug up, a cigarette tin containing two 12-volt electric bulbs was discovered. A thorough search of the jail yard ensued and resulted in the discovery of daggers, knives, explosive materials, a 450-bore revolver (stolen in the Chittagong Armoury raid case), some ammunition, and a dry cell electric battery. It was not found possible to prosecute any person in this connection, but the discovery indicated that a plot was being hatched by the Armoury raid under-trials for a jail outbreak

On the 2nd June, one Nibaran Chandra Ghosh was arrested at Chittagong while carrying a bundle which was found to contain a tin canister filled with explosives with two electric wires attached to it. Several houses were searched and three similar bombs were found in the shop of one Chandra Kumar Basu. Further investigation revealed a plot to blow up at several places the road round the Court buildings by which the members of the Special Tribunal were wont to pass on their way to Court to try the Chittagong case. Four tin canister bombs were found buried at a depth of one foot at different places in the road and an electric wire was unearthed, the end of which was under a drain. On the 4th June a man reported that he had noticed some wires leading into a vacant room of a house belonging to him. On a search being made three canister bombs were found buried at a depth of two feet in the mud floor. From the construction of these bombs it was clear that it was intended to explode them by electricity. The vigilance of the local police undoubtedly prevented a disaster. A case was instituted under the Explosive Substances Act and tried by a Special Tribunal. It resulted in the conviction of seven persons on the 29th September, 1931, three being sentenced to three years, two to two years and two to eight months' rigorous imprisonment. Another person was subsequently sentenced in the same case to five years' rigorous imprisonment on the 14th October 1931.

On the 30th August 1931, Khan Bahadur Ahsanullah, Inspector of Police, who had investigated the Armoury Case was shot dead with a revolver stolen in the raid, by Haripada Bhattacharji, a youth of 16, as the Inspector was leaving a football match. The assailant was arrested after a short chase and although the jury returned a verdict of not guilty, he was sentenced to transportation for life by the High Court. The murder of the Inspector was followed by serious rioting by the Muhammadans of Chittagong, who looted many Hindu shops. On the 1st March 1932, 12 of the accused in the Armoury Case were convicted of conspiracy to murder and other offences, and two to lesser punishment, while 16 were acquitted. Those who as yet remained at large, however, still continued with their designs, and on the 13th June 1932, when Captain Cameron was leading a search party at Dhalghat, shots were exchanged and he was killed, as were the terrorists Nirmal Sen and Apurba Sen. Suraj Sen and Pritilata Wadadhar, another girl who was in league with the gang, escaped. This girl then took a leading part in a raid on the Pahartali Institute when bombs were thrown into the main hall and shots were fired from guns and revolvers during a whist drive, at which some 40 Europeans were present. One lady was killed and 4 were wounded, but further casualties were certainly avoided by someone's presence of mind in turning out the lights. In the confusion the raiders escaped but Pritilata Wadadhar, clothed in male attire, was found dead outside. A statement was recovered from her person stating that the raid was an act of war. On the same day four types of pamphlets had been distributed exhorting teachers, students and the public to join in a campaign against British rulers and Europeans. On the 2nd of January 1933, the trial of Ambika Chakraverti and two other raiders began, ending on the 1st February 1933, with the conviction of Ambika Chakraverti who was sentenced to death, although the High Court commuted this sentence to transportation for life. Suraj Kanti Guha was sentenced to transportation for life by the Tribunal. On the 16th of the same month a military party surrounded a house at Gariala and, after an exchange of shots, Surja Sen and Brojendra Sen were arrested while trying to break through a cordon. The former was in possession of a revolver stolen in the Armoury raid. Kalpana Dutta and others escaped. Tarakeswar Dastidar now became the new president of the Chittagong branch, and active preparations were made to rescue Surja Sen. On the 20th March 1933, Sailesh Roy, who was arrested near the jail when talking to a warder, was found to be in possession of suspicious slips of paper which led to the recovery of a revolver and bombs from a granary, and on the 18th May 1933, a party of military surrounded the group's headquarters at Gahira. After an exchange of shots Tarakeswar Dastidar, Kalpana Dutta and others were arrested. Three stolen revolvers were recovered and later a tin box containing explosives and materials for bomb making were found. A third case was instituted which resulted in the conviction of Surja Sen and Tarakeswar Dastidar to death, while Kalpana Dutta was transported for life.

The effect of the Chittagong raids on the rest of Bengal. The series of outrages in Chittagong has, for convenience, been dealt with consecutively; and it is now necessary to return to the year 1930, and all that was happening in other parts of Bengal. The news of the Chittagong armoury raids was received by revolutionaries all over the province with amazement. Some could not believe that such a daring coup was the work of Bengali terrorists. When the truth was known the effect was electric, and from that moment the outlook of the Bengal terrorists changed. The younger members of all parties, whose heads were already crammed with ideas of driving the British out of India by force of arms, but whose hands had been restrained by their leaders from committing even an isolated murder, clamoured for a chance to emulate the Chittagong terrorists. Their leaders could no longer hope, nor did they wish, to keep them back, for the lesson of Chittagong had impressed itself on their minds no less than on those of their more youthful followers, and there seemed to be no reason why their over-cautious policy should be maintained. Recruits poured into the various groups in a steady stream, and the romantic appeal of the raid attracted into the fold of the terrorist party women and young girls, who from this time onwards are found assisting the terrorists as housekeepers, messengers, custodians of arms and sometimes as comrades.

Special Legislation. Another factor, which, too, had undoubtedly influenced the Chittagong group, was the fact that the Bengal Criminal Law Amendment Act of 1925 had expired on the 21st March 1930. The police had urged the retention of the Act as a permanent piece of legislation, but of all the alternatives considered the continuance for five years of the sections relating to trial by special procedure was all that was decided upon. After the Chittagong raid, however, the lost powers of arrest and detention were immediately conferred by ordinance. In July, the Bengal Government asked for the replacement of the Ordinance by permanent legislation, including the lapsed sections of the Bengal Criminal Law Amendment (Supplementary) Act, 1925, but was compelled to accept a five-year limit for the continuing Bill which was passed by the Legislative Council by a large majority, and became law as Bengal Act VI of 1930 on the 16th October 1930.

Increased terrorist activity. In the meantime, all parties and groups being fired by the example set in Chittagong, many plans for the emulation of that group's raid were made, although, fortunately, the authorities were able by making many arrests and taking various precautions to prevent any serious repetition of that coup. Nevertheless, acts of violence greatly increased in number during the year. In Calcutta, the main Jugantar Party, which had been preparing for many years, now became active under its leader Bhupendra Kumar Datta. Bomb-making was undertaken, and attempts were made to secure more arms. Bhupendra Kumar was arrested in June, and the leadership passed to Manoranjan Gupta. A detailed programme had already been drawn up, the principal features of which were :—

1. to attempt the lives of Europeans in hotels, clubs and cinemas, simultaneously in Calcutta and the mofussil, by throwing bombs ;
2. to burn the aerodrome at Dum Dum with petrol ;
3. to attack and destroy the Oriental Gas Works by using bombs and dynamite ;

4. to disable the Electric Supply Corporation by destroying two main stations in Calcutta;
5. to burn the petrol depot of the Burma Oil Company at Budge Budge;
6. to disorganise the tramway service in Calcutta by cutting the wires;
7. to cut the telegraph lines in the mufussil;
8. to blow up bridges and railway lines by using dynamite and hand-grenades.

The very magnitude of these proposals demonstrates the height to which the ambitions of terrorists had been raised by the Chittagong outbreak, and it is indeed fortunate that inter-party jealousies, the fact that the revolutionaries operated in small groups, and the counter-action of the authorities prevented these plans from proceeding beyond the proposal stage. Bombs were certainly prepared, arms collected and in some instances maps of sites had been made, but, although there were many outrages, nothing on a large scale was actually attempted.

Attempt to amalgamate parties. Manoranjan Gupta made strenuous efforts to amalgamate the Jugantar Party, the Anushilan Samiti, and the Chittagong rebels, but his negotiations with Rabindra Sen Gupta, the leader of the Anushilan, were fortunately cut short by Rabindra's arrest, although hopes of satisfactorily combining the groups were few, owing to Rabindra's dislike of Manoranjan's programme and their long-standing rivalry.

Attack on Sir Charles Tegart. One of the most-cherished plans of all revolutionaries was the murder of high officials, and Sir Charles Tegart, Commissioner of Police in Calcutta, was perhaps the most frequently named victim. We have seen that one attempt on his life miscarried in 1924. Now that violent activities had been resumed, this murder was again in the forefront of all anarchical proposals, and on August 25th, 1930, Anuja Sen Gupta and Dinesh Chandra Majumdar, who had been supplied with bombs and two revolvers, actually threw two bombs at Sir Charles' car in

Dalhousie Square, Calcutta. Luckily, the bombs missed their mark, although the driver of the car and four passers-by were struck by fragments ; but one bomb, which exploded close to the assailants, killed Anuja. As Majumdar, brandishing a revolver, attempted to escap he was pluckily captured by an unarmed constable, add was eventually sentenced to transportation for life.

More activities by Calcutta groups. On the same day, the 25th August 1930, Dr. Narayan Chandra Roy, a member of the Calcutta Corporation, was arrested. He later confessed that he had made bombs for the party, and produced from his house materials for making bombs. Still later, acting on the Doctor's confession, the police searched a house in Lal Madhab Mukharji Lane, which yielded two bomb-shells, gun-cotton and other materials. This led to the arrest of several persons. In the meantime, on the evening of 26th August, a bomb had been thrown into the compound of the Jorabagan police-station in Calcutta. No police officers were hurt, but three members of the public were injured. On the following morning another bomb was thrown into the compound of the Eden Gardens police station, killing a chaprassi, and wounding three others, including a police constable. As a result of the searches that followed, a case was instituted, in which the accused were charged with conspiracy to make bombs for murder, overt acts arising out of the conspiracy being the three bomb outrages, at Dalhousie Square, Jorabagan and Eden Gardens Two of the accused turned approvers, and finally two, including Narayan Chandra Roy, were sentenced to twenty years' transportation, while three others received sentences varying from two years' rigorous imprisonment to 12 years' transportation.

The Calcutta-Madaripur group of the main Jugantar party had been responsible for the dacoity at Tala, Calcutta, in April 1930, and on 17th October four youths of this group, armed with revolvers and daggers, raided some business premises in Armenian Street, Calcutta, and stole Rs. 2,500. The *darwan* of the firm struck one of the culprits, Suresh Chandra Das, a blow with a lathi while they were leaving, and was promptly shot dead by the others. Suresh was arrested by a constable, who pluckily held on to him, although the former stabbed him with a dagger. Suresh was tried and sentenced to transportation for life.

Another prominent group in Calcutta was that of the Dacca Sri Sangha. As we shall see, the Bengal volunteer group of the Sri Sangha had been responsible for the murder of Mr. Lowman in Dacca in August, but the actual assailant, Binoy Krishna Basu, had escaped. On the 8th December, three young men of this group, dressed as Europeans and armed with revolvers, on the pretence of seeking an interview, brushed past the chaprassi at the door, and shot Lt.-Col. Simpson, Inspector-General of Prisons, at his office table in Writers' Buildings, Calcutta. After this they went down the corridor firing into the rooms of other officials and wounded a Deputy Secretary and the Legal Remembrancer. They were trapped in the latter's room by the Inspector-General of Police and other police officers, and realising that escape was impossible, attempted to commit suicide. When the police entered the room they found three men; Sudhir Gupta had taken potassium cyanide and was dead, and Binoy Krishna Basu, the murderer of Mr. Lowman, and Dinesh Chandra Gupta had shot themselves. The former died a few days later, but Dinesh Chandra Gupta, who recovered was tried and sentenced to death. His execution was regretted by the Calcutta Corporation, which published his photographs on the front page of the Municipal Gazette.

Other groups in Calcutta were active in plotting crimes and making preparation, but arrests effected from time to time were mainly instrumental in preventing the numerous plans from being carried out.

Activities of groups outside Calcutta. In the districts, there were numerous groups, as in Calcutta, and like the parent groups, they maintained a feverish activity. Arms were collected and, where possible, bombs were made or obtained, and numerous plots were devised. In Mymensingh there was a particularly dangerous group. On the 1st April 1930, a member of the party, Bhupendra Kishore Raha Roy *alias* Pola, was stabbed and murdered (by members of the party it is believed), but the culprits were not detected. On the 14th May, the party was again suspected of having been responsible for the murder of an Assistant Sub-Inspector who died of stab wounds received in a riotous demonstration against police escorting excisable articles from a warehouse to vendors' shops. Again, on the 2nd of August Bidhu Sen, who was wanted in the excise looting case, fired twice at a constable who attempted to arrest him at Jamalpur, and escaped. The constable was unhurt. On the 7th August. Tarak Chandra Kar, Sisir Kumar Roy and a woman were arrested at Sarishabari with explosive materials which they were taking from Calcutta to Mymensingh. Other members of the party were arrested in Calcutta and six persons were tried, five of whom were convicted. On the 30th August, a bomb was thrown into the house of Inspector Pabitra Nath Bose, and two of his brothers were slightly injured. On the same day another bomb was thrown into the house of an Excise Sub-Inspector, but no casualty occurred. Again, on the 13th October, at Jamalpur, Nagendra Deb and Sudhindra Roy fired at a constable who was looking for these two absconders. They were arrested. On the 15th October, two young men entered the house of a Hindu lady and demanded ornaments at the point of the revolver; and, finally on the night of the 31st October, some fifteen persons, armed with a gun, a revolver, and knives, committed a dacoity in the house of a money-lender at Sealdah. Members of the Mymensingh Jugantar Party were arrested next day with a revolver and some of the stolen property.

Murder of Mr. Lowman, I. G. P. The Dacca branch of the Jugantar party was also at work with its nefarious plans. There were three groups here, the most active of which was the Sri Sangha, led by Anil Roy. On the 29th August, Binoy Krishna Basu, a member of the group, fired at close range at Mr. Lowman, Inspector General of Police, and Mr. Hodson, Superintendent of Police, and seriously wounded both. Mr. Lowman died of his wounds.

The assailant then escaped, to take part in the Simpson murder at Calcutta in December, when he shot himself. This group supplied four or five youths who, in December 1930, overpowered a peon of the Dacca Intermediate College, and relieved him of Rs. 2,000 which he was taking to the bank.

Another important group in Dacca was that led by Jiban Lal Chatarji. This group had planned with the main Jugantar Party a rising for the 23rd of June. On that night three persons were arrested in Narayanganj with wire-cutting instruments, and on the same night telegraph wires were actually cut in two places in the Munshiganj sub-division. Members of this group took part in a dacoity on December 18th, when twenty *bhadralok* youths, armed with *ramdaos* attacked a house in Paisagaon and stole property to the value of Rs. 2,145.

In Khulna, a group which had been fostered by the Daulatpur Satyasram, a notorious breeding-ground for terrorists, while taking part in activities connected with the Civil Disobedience Movement, was engaged in bomb-making and on 23rd September, an aluminium bomb was thrown at some police officers at Khulna Police-Station, wounding a sub-inspector and a head-constable.

It would be tedious to recount the activities of the many other groups, which existed in nearly every district of the Presidency. Suffice to say that Government became possessed of much information regarding the leaders, the more prominent members and their plans and machinations, and were able to arrest a number of the more active and dangerous spirits, thus undoubtedly preventing many more outrages.

We turn now to the other main party, the Anushilan Samiti. This, like the Jugantar, had groups in almost every district of Bengal, and all were excited by the success of the Chittagong outrages in April. This party, however, had not made such intensive preparations as the Jugantar, and had not reserved its strength for a big rising as its rival had done. Nevertheless, it was by no means backward, and rapidly gained in strength. The story of its activities in

1930 is similar to that of the Jugantar. Plans were evolved, preparations were set on foot, and then, generally because the police obtained news, their leaders were arrested. However, some crimes were committed, although there was none on the ambitiously large scale proposed. The Barisal group committed three armed dacoities, at Gopalpur on September 24th, at Nalchira on October 23rd and at Madhabpasha on October 29th, and pistols and revolvers were used on all three occasions. At Rajshahi on November 1st, a college peon was waylaid and robbed of a professor's salary which he was carrying, and at Mymensingh, in November, five *bhadralok* youths waylaid *darwans* who were escorting Rs. 15,000 to a business office, and made off with the whole amount.

The Anushilan Samiti had extra-provincial connections, and were certainly in touch with terrorists in Bihar, in the Punjab and in the United Provinces. In December on receipt of information to the effect that attempts would be made on the lives of the approvers in the Dalhousie Square bomb case, searches were made in Calcutta and in Patna, and two persons were eventually sentenced to short terms of imprisonment for conspiracy and illegal possession of arms. It was to one of the subsidiary groups in Calcutta, that of Bhowanipore of South Calcutta, that Jatin Das who died as the result of a hunger-strike begun while on trial in Lahore, belonged.

Although the police were able to frustrate, by the arrest of the plotters and consequent disorganisation of their groups, many of the plots for the assassination of officials, their powers were limited to what may be described as purely defensive action. These powers did not admit of wholesale attacks on various organisations, and although action taken was certainly successful in preventing further outrages on the lines of the Chittagong armoury raid, the terrorist organisation still remained comparatively intact.

The situation at the end of 1930. At the end of 1930, several of the most important leaders of all parties were under arrest, but the organisations, to all intents and purposes, were still unbroken. Press and platform propaganda in pursuance of Gandhi's Civil Disobedience Movement was arousing anti-British sentiment and a spirit of lawlessness in the province to a degree which would have been deemed incredible even in 1929. Seditious literature of the most violent description was being broadcast in the shape of pamphlets and books. It is true that the Congress formally dissociated itself from terrorism, but it was equally clear that if some of the workers and leaders of the Congress had been given a free hand they would not have been averse to giving their general support to terrorism.

The strain of 1931. The truce arranged between Lord Irwin and Gandhi early in March 1931, while it relieved the immediate strain on the Police owing to the cessation generally of civil disobedience activities, disheartened and depressed them and all other supporters of Government; for they believed they saw in the truce evidence of a lack of determination on the part of Government, in the last resort, to maintain its authority. Taken together with the expressed determination of His Majesty's Government to concede a great advance towards complete responsible Government in the near future, it was not surprising that many should wonder whether it was not better to make peace with those who were likely, within a short time, to obtain control of the machinery of Government, rather than risk suffering later for their loyalty to the existing form of Government. This general feeling of depression was enhanced by the manner in which the Congress acclaimed the truce as a victory, and openly and blatantly made preparations for a renewal of the conflict. These preparations were not in themselves illegal, and it was gall and wormwood to the officers of Government to have to remain inactive while the enemy consolidated their forces and perfected their organisation and plan. On the other hand, the terrorists were dissatisfied that the truce had not resulted in the release of political prisoners. They regarded themselves as the soldiers of India's freedom, and claimed the right to be released when a truce was arranged between the contending parties.

With the Gandhi-Irwin Pact, the Press Ordinance was withdrawn, and the Indian press at once reverted to its old habit of glorification of assassins and the propagation of the cult of murder. During March, the occasion for adulatory articles was found in the execution of Bhagat Singh and his two companions. When Mr. Peddie was assassinated at Midnapore on the 7th April 1931, the attitude of the press was far from satisfactory. Similarly, praise of Dinesh Gupta, the murderer of Colonel Simpson, and Ram Krishna Biswas, convicted of the Chandpur murder, was widespread and in some cases unrestrained, and demands for their reprieve were loud and persistent. Every acquittal of a terrorist was hailed with delight; everything that could be said in favour of them was printed in bold type. The culmination of this attitude of mind was the resolution of the Congress-managed Corporation of Calcutta recording its sense of homage to Dinesh Gupta, one of the murderers of Col. Simpson. It is small wonder that in the circumstances described, the terrorist cult should have found more votaries than even before, and that 1931 should have been one of the darkest years in the history of terrorist crime.

Terrorist crimes in 1931. No less than sixty-seven outrages, including nine murders, occurred during the year. It would be unprofitable to recount all of these crimes in detail, and only a few of the more dastardly and yet typical cases will be mentioned. By this time, when many leaders were in detention camps and 454 persons had been arrested under the Ordinance and the Bengal Criminal Law Amendment Act, the younger hot-heads had thrown off practically all control, and the old divisions of parties and groups were fast disappearing in the welter of numerous local parties owing little or no allegiance to any group or leader. All, however, were fired with the common desire to commit assassinations and outrages on the usual terrorist lines, although the lack of unity in organisation and leadership fortunately precluded the commission of any large-scale rising. This breaking-up into small fractions had, from the Police and administration point of view, one great disadvantage in that it was impossible, for the time being, to gain inside informations of the new formations and many crimes were committed by local groups which, until their acts brought them into prominence, had not hitherto been noticed. It is not surprising then, that in a period so fraught with excitement the 'patriotic' youth of the province should have indulged in an orgy of outrages, often with no other motive than the removal of the hated British official, merely because he happened to be British.

Of the outrages which occurred during the year it will suffice to mention the following:

On the evening of the 7th April 1931, Mr. Peddie, District Magistrate of Midnapore, walked over to inspect an exhibition of manual work in a local school, which he had himself arranged. While examining some of the exhibits by the light of hurricane lamps he was shot from behind and died next day. The assailants escaped, but Bimal Das Gupta, who later attempted to murder Mr. Villiers, confessed to the crime, although he was not punished owing to insufficient evidence. On the 27th July, Mr. Garlick, Sessions Judge, 24-Parganas, was shot through the head while sitting in Court. The assassin was immediately shot down by the sergeant on duty and committed suicide by swallowing potassium cyanide while lying wounded under the table. A note found on the murderer stated that the act was committed in revenge for the execution of Dinesh Gupta. Mr. Garlick had been President of the Tribunal which tried Gupta.

On the evening of the 21st August, at Tangail, a *bhadralok* youth fired at Mr. Cassels, Divisional Commissioner of Dacca, who was on his way to inspect a co-operative bank. The culprit escaped, but was later arrested and tried. He had made a confession to a magistrate, but, as was frequently the case, the evidence of eye-witnesses was meagre, and he was not convicted of the actual crime, although he was sentenced for illegal possession of arms.

We have seen that K. B. Ahsanullah, Inspector of Police, Chittagong, was shot dead on the 30th August by a Hindu youth, who was sentenced to transportation for life. On the 28th October, two *bhadralok* youths shot at and severely wounded Mr. Durno, District Magistrate, Dacca, while he was sitting in his car outside a shop in one of the main streets. The culprits escaped. The next day, in Calcutta, Bimal Das Gupta pushed his way into the office of Mr. Villiers, President of the European Association, and fired at him. Luckily, Mr. Villiers was only slightly wounded. Bimal Das Gupta was captured by three other Europeans who were in the room, and sentenced later to ten years' rigorous imprisonment.

On the 14th December 1931, Mr. Stevens, District Magistrate, Tippera, was visited by two girls, who presented him with a petition for a swimming exhibition to be arranged for them. He endorsed the petition to a local headmistress and as he handed it back to them on the verandah of his house, the girls shot him at point blank range. These girls, who were Santi Ghose and Suniti Chaudhri, were sentenced to transportation for life. Finally, on the 30th December, the principal witness in a political dacoity case was shot near his house in Calcutta. There were no eye-witnesses and the assailants were not traced.

As will be seen from the list in Appendix I there were several cases of bomb-throwing during the year, all except one being directed at the police. The exception occurred when a bomb was thrown on the lawn of the Royal Calcutta Golf Club, but as the missile did not explode, no harm was done. In fact, it is remarkable that although the majority of bombs were of a dangerous character, their effect on life and property were almost negligible.

The state of the Presidency was at this time particularly conducive to the commission of political dacoities and robberies, and, as will be seen from the appended list of crimes which occurred, the terrorists were not slow in making the most of their opportunities. These numerous crimes, emphasising the apparent ascendancy of terrorists, naturally cowed the population, of which a large proportion, inflamed by the press and agitators, already possessed decided terrorist sympathies, and evidence was extremely difficult to obtain. In fact, fearing reprisals which were often almost openly expressed by certain newspapers, witnesses frequently resiled from their statements, or, more frequently still, refused to give evidence of facts which must have been within their knowledge.

Supplementary Legislation. By the end of July 1931, it was evident that the existing legislation was not sufficient to cope with the terrorist menace. The way in which the press lent itself to constant and violent propaganda in favour of assassins has already been referred to. The murders which had taken place could be traced, in no small measure to incitement by the press, and the Bengal Government were convinced that action to control the press was a vital necessity. As concerning the powers of arrest and detention conferred by the Criminal Law Amendment Act, 1930, it was found essential to ask that its scope should be widened so that action could be taken not only against persons actually concerned in the commission of terrorist associations, but also against members or helpers of those associations. On the 9th October 1931, Act XXIII of 1931 (an Act to provide against publication of matter inciting to or encouraging murder or violence) was passed, and on the 29th October the Government of India promulgated Ordinance IX of 1931 conferring the powers asked for in regard to arrest and detention and widening the schedule of offences by the inclusion of sections relating to the waging of war against the King or the harbouring of absconders.

A month later on the 30th November the Bengal Emergency Powers Ordinance XI of 1931 was issued. Chapter I of the Ordinance provided for emergency powers which would apply immediately to the district of Chittagong. Military and Police were to combine in operations to round up terrorists and absconders in that district; and to render these operations effective, the District Magistrate was given powers, among others, to commandeer property, limit access to certain places, regulate traffic and transport, and impose collective fines upon recalcitrant inhabitants. Chapter II provided for special tribunals and special magistrates and a procedure designed to overcome delaying tactics.

Thus, though the situation at the end of 1931 was far from reassuring, the police were again armed with adequate powers. Civil disobedience was waning and they were, therefore, free to devote all their energies to the suppression of terrorism.

On the expiry of the ordinances, it was felt that the Bengal Government should continue to be armed with the legislative weapons necessary to grapple with the menace of the terrorist movement. Accordingly the Bengal Suppression of Terrorist Outrages Act, 1932 and the Bengal Criminal Law (Arms and Explosives) Act, 1932 were introduced and passed by the Legislative Council.

Crimes in 1932. During the first part of the year 1932, the air was thick with threats to carry out indiscriminate massacres of Europeans in clubs and cinemas, but, as before, the organisation of the terrorists was not such as to render an outrage on a big scale feasible. Nevertheless, the year resulted in an enormous crop of crimes, which again included murderous attacks on officials. On the 6th of February, while His Excellency the Governor of Bengal Sir Stanley Jackson, was addressing the convocation of Calcutta University, a girl graduate, Bina Das, originally of Chittagong, rose from her seat, walked up the aisle and when a short distance from His Excellency, took a pistol from her robes and fired three times. Luckily the shots went wide, and, before she could take another deliberate aim, she was overpowered by Sir Hasan Suhrawardy, the Vice-Chancellor, although she managed to discharge two more bullets which passed harmlessly over the heads of the assembly. His Excellency was unhurt, but a Bengali professor near him was slightly injured. His Excellency continued his address when order had been restored and it is noteworthy that he was loudly cheered when he later left the hall. Bina Das was sentenced to nine years' rigorous imprisonment.

On April 30th while Mr. Douglas, District Magistrate of Midnapore, was attending a meeting of the District Board Office, Midnapore, two youths came up behind and fired five shots, four of which hit Mr. Douglas, who died of his wounds on the same evening. Mr. George, Sub-Divisional Officer, Tamluk, armed guards and others chased the assailants and caught Prodyut Kumar Bhattacharji, who was in possession of a revolver containing five misfired rounds, and a written note in Bengali to the effect, "a slight protest against the Hijli oppression. Let Britain take note by the death of these people and let India awake by our sacrifice, Bande Matram" Prodyut Kumar Bhattacharji was sentenced to death.

On the 12th of June, when Rai Bahadur Suresh Chandra Bose, District Magistrate of Faridpur, and Mr. Habib-ur-Rahman, Superintendent of Police of the same district, were returning by train from Rajbari, a bomb was thrown at their carriage just after the train had started. No one was injured, and the culprits were not traced. Following this, on the 27th July, Babu Kamakhaya Prasad, Sub-Deputy Magistrate of Munshigunj, was shot dead in Dacca town. He had been sleeping in a room downstairs, and about 4 A.M. the Sub-Divisional Officer, with whom he was staying, was awakened by shots, and came downstairs to find him dead. Kalipada Mukherjee was sentenced to death for this crime. Two days after the murder of Babu Kamakhaya Prasad, Mr. E. B. Ellison, Additional Superintendent of Police, Tippera, was shot at Comilla by a youth and fatally wounded as he was returning home on his bicycle from his office. Mr. Ellison and his guard returned the fire, but the youth escaped, throwing away as he ran, a packet containing three manuscript pamphlets in red ink purporting to come from the Indian Republican Army, Chittagong, by order of Surja Sen. The leaflets advocated the cessation of isolated attacks on European officers in favour of indiscriminate attacks on all Europeans with a view to exterminating them. Mr. Ellison's assailant was not traced.

On August 5th, 1932, Sir Alfred Watson, Editor of "The Statesman", was returning in his car from the Bengal Club to his office, when a youth dashed forward, thrust his hand into the car, and fired one shot at Sir Alfred, who, fortunately, was not hit, although he felt the heat of the flame on the right side of his face. The youth dropped the revolver into the car, and was captured by a darwan and an armed constable. After a few steps the assailant collapsed, and a small packet of potassium cyanide was picked up on the spot. He died on his way to hospital, where his body was identified as that of Atul Chandra Sen, an engineering student hailing from Khulna district, and of the same village as Anuja Sen Gupta who attempted to assassinate Sir Charles Tegart in 1930.

Dacca was the scene of another outrage on August 22nd when Mr. Grassby, Superintendent of Police, while returning from office in his car was fired upon three times at short range, while the car was delayed at a level crossing. Mr. Grassby was hit twice, but not seriously, and he returned the fire, as did his orderly. The orderly, driver and a sergeant then pursued the assailant, who was stopped by a telephone linesman, but got away again. The orderlies then shot at and wounded him and he was captured. A bomb was also found on the car. Benoy Bhusan De Roy, the culprit, was sentenced to transportation for life.

The raid on the Pahartali Institute, Chittagong, on the 24th September has already been described. On the 28th September, a second attempt on the life of Sir Alfred Watson was made in Calcutta. While his car was proceeding slowly owing to a *gharry* in front, another came alongside and three shots were fired by its occupants, who were four Bengalis. These shots destroyed the glass on the right hand side of Sir Alfred's car near the back seat. The second car then ran into the first to prevent it from proceeding. Sir Alfred's Private Secretary, Mrs. Gros, who was with him threw an electric iron at the assailants, and then, before he could take up his revolver which was lying at his feet, she pulled him down. At this juncture a mounted sergeant hurried to the spot and fired at the assailants' car. Sir Alfred Watson, Mrs. Gros and the driver were all wounded. The assailants' car was found abandoned; two of the culprits, Manindra Lahiri and Anil Bhaduri, had committed suicide by taking poison. In this case, Sunil Kumar Chatterji was sentenced to transportation for life, Promode Ranjan Bose to 10 years' rigorous imprisonment and Amar Chandra Ghose to seventeen months' rigorous imprisonment, on charges of having joined in the conspiracy, and of having harboured one of the culprits, Biren Roy.

On the evening of the 18th November, Mr. Luke Superintendent of Rajshahi Jail, took his wife and daughter for a drive in his car, and while driving slowly, was attacked by three youths, one of whom threw a bicycle in front of the car. Three shots were fired, one of which hit Mr. Luke, and the assailants then made off, firing occasionally into the air. Bholanath Roy Karmakar was sentenced to seven years' transportation.

Terrorists also indulged in bomb-throwing, and there was a heavy list of dacoities to be attributed to them during the year, as will be seen from the appended table of terrorist crimes. It will be noted, however, that there was a welcome decrease in the second half of the year. This was due largely to the intensive activities of the police, who could now claim to have regained the upper hand. Plot after plot was discovered and foiled, and one leader after another was captured. A stage had at last been reached when in spite of dangerous conspiracies, which every now and then came to light, the situation was definitely under control so far as large scale organised outrages were concerned. But there was still a large number of individuals abroad who were prepared to commit or take part in isolated outrages, and had apparently no difficulties in securing arms. Hence, constant vigilance and continual action were required, not only against old members who were busy plotting, but also against new recruits who appeared still to be drawn into the movement in fairly large numbers and to be ready for any kind of "action"

The improvement in 1933. The situation continued to improve in 1933, when terrorists were responsible for only two murders in Bengal, although the Commissioner of Police in Chandernagore was one of the victims. He had gone with a party to search for three absconders who were reported to be in hiding there on the 9th March 1933, but the absconders ran out before the party arrived. One was chased and arrested by a head-constable. The Commissioner of Police and two constables followed the other two, when one fired three shots at the Commissioner, inflicting injuries from which he died next day. The fugitives then shot and wounded a boy who stood in their way, also a constable who tried to stop them, and made good their escape. The arrested man, Birendra Nath Roy was wanted in connection with the second attempted murder of Sir Alfred Watson, and, on being expelled by the French police, was dealt with under the Bengal Criminal Law Amendment Act, 1930. The other two were subsequently arrested in Calcutta, and convicted for another offence.

A comparatively long period of immunity from political murders was ended when, on August 23rd, shortly after he had interviewed a District Intelligence Branch Officer, Dhirendra De of Mymensingh District, was shot dead.

This was followed on September 2nd by the assassination of Mr. Burge, District Magistrate, Midnapore, who was to take part in a football match between two local teams. As he walked on to the ground, two persons who had mingled with the players closed in on him and riddled him with bullets. He died almost immediately. Mr. Norton-Jones, Additional Superintendent of Police, Midnapore, and Mr. Smith, Inspector of Police, who were both unarmed rushed at the assassins while they were still firing, brought them down and struggled with them on the ground until armed guards rushed up and shot both assassins dead. They were Mrigendra Datta and Anath Panja, both of Midnapore. The investigation which immediately followed this murder disclosed a deep-rooted conspiracy to terrorise Government officials by such insensate acts of brutality. Forty-seven persons were arrested, of whom six were ultimately discharged, two were externed under the Suppression of Terrorist Outrages Act and twenty-six were dealt with under the Bengal Criminal Law Amendment Act. Thirteen persons were tried by a Special Tribunal for the offence of conspiracy to murder and of these Nirmal Jiban

Ghosh, Ram Krista Roy and Braja Krishore Chakravarti were sentenced to death. Four others were sentenced to transportation for life and the remainder dealt with under the Bengal Criminal Law Amendment Act. One of the accused became an approver. In a supplementary case, Santi Gopal Sen, who had been absconding, was sentenced to transportation for life. All the convicted persons were of Midnapore.

Of the dacoities which were committed during the year the most inportant was that at Hili Railway Station on the main line between Calcutta and Darjeeling. On the night of the 28th October, fourteen or fifteen *bhadralok* youths armed with guns, revolvers, daggers and axes, and carrying torches, made the attack and looted the mail chest and the railway cash. They also damaged the telephone apparatus, but did not succeed in putting it completely out of action. While the dacoity was going on the dacoits fired at random and injured several people, one of whom, a postal peon, subsequently died of his injuries. The next day, after some brilliant work by a constable, seven of the culprits were arrested with a part of the loot, a loaded revolver, a loaded pistol, a gun, cartridges and three daggers. Six others were arrested later and more of the loot was recovered. The accused included Satyabrata Chakravarti of Dinajpur, an absconder in the Luke attempted murder case, and Pran Krista Chakravarti who had escaped after being sentenced in an arms case at Jalpaiguri to seven years' rigorous imprisonment. Four persons were sentenced to death by a Special Tribunal, and the others to transportation for life on various terms of imprisonment; but on appeal to the High Court, the sentences were reduced. Pran Krista Chakravarti and Hrishikesh Bhattacharji were sentenced to transportation for life; Satya Chakravarti and two others to ten years' rigorous imprisonment; and four others to lesser terms of imprisonment. A typical robbery took place on the 20th October 1933, when four *bhadralok* youths boarded a train as it was leaving Kurigram and robbed a passenger of Rs. 424 at the point of a revolver. Two other passengers in the compartment were threatened with daggers and relieved of their small cash. The culprits then jumped from the train, which was stopped. A chase ensued and four villagers stopped the accused, although one villager received a shot-wound in the face. Two of the assailants were captured, but the others escaped, for the time, leaving behind a shirt with Rs. 305 in a pocket. The two absconding youths were eventually captured and all four were convicted and sentenced to terms of imprisonment ranging from ten to seven years.

The arrest of Prabhat Chakravarti and the Inter-Provincial Conspiracy Case. These cases are but a few of those which occurred during the year, as the list of crimes shows, but it will be seen that there was a very welcome decrease, and that the work of the police was more successful. For some time it had been known that Prabhat Chakravarti and Jiten Gupta had been leading a very strong and active group of the Anushilan. Jiten had escaped from the Buxa internment camp in February 1932, but was re-arrested on 28th December 1932. Prabhat Chakravarti had absconded from his place of domicile in January 1932, and was arrested on the 14th January 1933. A loaded revolver and important papers, including cypher addresses of connections all over Bengal and other parts of India were found on him. The addresses found in the cyphers show a very wide distribution :—

Calcutta	32
Hooghly	1
Jessore	6
Faridpur	8
Rajshahi	2
Rangpur	3
Lahore	1
Patna	1
Purnea	1
Burdwan	1
Midnapur	14
Dacca	5
Chittagong	3

Malda	1
Cooch Behar	1
Benares	5
Gaya	1
Manbhoom	6
Berhampur	1
Khulna	6
Mymensingh	3
Noakhali	5
Jalpaiguri	1
Delhi	7
Bulandshahr	1
Jamshedpur	3
Hajipur	2
Birbhum	2
Nadia	2
Barisal	18
Tippera	8
Dinajpur	2
Amritsar	25
Shahjahanpur	2
Monghyr	1
Hazaribagh	2
Muzaffarpur	1
Madras	1
Waltair	1
Rangoon	4
Mandalay	1
Sylhet	3

Enquiries were made at all the addresses and many searches and arrests were made. A widespread conspiracy was revealed, with ramifications in many provinces, but especially in the Punjab, where a connection with the Hindustan Socialist Republican Army had been attempted. A mass of material was collected and eventually no less than forty persons were put on trial in what is known as the Inter-Provincial Conspiracy case. Two of the accused, Jitendra Chandra Naha and Hrishikesh Das Gupta on being tendered pardons became approvers, and many witnesses were examined who had been for a time revolutionaries or had, at some time or other toyed with the idea of becoming revolutionaries. This branch of the Anushilan was shown to have made extensive preparations for the enlargement and strengthening of the group and for the commission of outrages. In fact, some of the accused had already been convicted for their part in offences already committed : Naren Ghose had been convicted for his complicity in a dacoity which took place at Chhavali Charpara on 26th November 1932; and Pran Krista Chakravarti who, though arrested in possession of a loaded revolver, an automatic pistol and cartridges, and convicted, had escaped in November 1932 and had remained in hiding until he was again arrested for his part in the Hili dacoity, and again convicted. Outside Bengal the most important members of the party were Sitanath De, a resident of Faridpur district, and Dhirendra Nath Bhattacharji, who were both active in the Punjab. The former, who was the more dangerous, adopted the guise of a *sadhu* and visited many places, especially Amritsar and Lahore, in order to establish a strong connection with the Hindustan Socialist Republican Army, and to increase its following. His method was to excite youths with books, including *Bandi Jiwan* by Sachindra Nath Sanyal, then to encourage individual acts of terrorism as a means of organizing the party and increasing its funds and prestige, and ultimately to work for a general uprising. However, by 1932, finding the police too vigilant, he shifted to Madras with some youths from Amritsar, and there undoubtedly instigated the Ootacamund Bank robbery.

Dhiren Bhattacharji had made contacts in Lahore, but was arrested in mistake for another absconder in the Chittagong Armoury Raid Case on March 22nd, 1933. He was dressed as a Punjabi and gave his name as Ram Nath of Moradabad. He was confined under the Punjab Criminal Law Amendment Act and made a long statement to the police, implicating three persons, a Bengali and two Punjabis, who were all arrested in possession of arms and convicted on their own plea. The name of one of the Punjabis, Jagat Ram Joshi, occurs in the cypher list of addresses found with Prabhat Chakravarti.

To return to Bengal—much the same lines had been followed here, but on a far larger scale. In September 1932, the Anushilan party printed and issued all over India a large number of copies of a pamphlet, *Swadhin Bharat*, a typical piece of revolutionary literature. On the 14th September 1932, one of the accused, Abani Ranjan Sarkar, was arrested with a large bundle of these pamphlets. The consequent searches revealed a large quantity of revolutionary literature and the usual accessories, such as copies of military instruction books, books on chemistry and so forth, and several seizures of arms were made. There was also a large number of letters which proved conspiracy, the connexion of members, and the aims of the party, and the trial began in August 1933 before a Special Tribunal at Alipore. Sitanath De was then absconding, but was arrested at Benares on November 24th, 1933. He, however, managed to escape from Alipore Jail with two other accused, Purnananda Das Gupta and Niranjan Ghosal on July 31st, 1934, who were re-arrested before the conclusion of the case. Sentence was passed on Sitanath De in his absence. After a great number of witnesses had been examined and cross-examined at great length, the trial ended on May 1st, 1935, when thirty-one accused were sentenced. One had been discharged, and one had turned insane, while another absconder had died. The thirty convicted persons, excluding Sitanath De, appealed to the High Court, which acquitted one of them, Ajit Bose Prabhat Chakravarti, Jiten Gupta and Sitanath De were sentenced to transportation for life, three to fourteen years' transportation and the others to terms ranging from seven to one year's rigorous imprisonment. Sitanath De was arrested in Tippera district on the 4th May 1936.

The effect of this case was very damaging to this branch, which was one of the most active and widespread of the Anushilan party. Apart from those actually accused and sentenced, many persons who had been connected with the movement were called in evidence, and the result was that, apart from the leaders who were sent to prison, a large number of the more lukewarm sympathisers and dabblers, were discredited. This, combined with successes in other smaller cases and the ceaseless vigilance of the police, brought about an easier situation, although it was impossible to relax the extraordinary precautions for safeguarding the lives of officials and their families in Bengal, or to decrease the intensive intelligence organization which had been rendered so necessary by the events of the foregoing years. There was, however, a growing belief in some quarters, or perhaps little more than a hope that public opinion was slowly turning against terrorism and that in their efforts to crush it Government and its officers had earned a steadily increasing amount of sympathy and support from the community at large.

1934. The year 1934, however, was by no means free from outrages. True, there were no murders of British officials, but there were two attempts at murder, both on an ambitious scale. The first attempt took place at Chittagong on the 7th January 1934. Mr. Cleary, Superintendent of Police of that district, was returning to his bungalow after witnessing a cricket match when he noticed two suspicious youths advancing towards him. Stopping his car, Mr. Cleary ordered his armed orderlies to search the youths, but observing that this was being done perfunctorily, he was proceeding to search them himself when one of them hurled a bomb at him which burst doing no more than slightly wounding one of the orderlies over the eye. Mr. Cleary promptly grappled with his assailant and told his orderly to fire, which he did. Two shots were fired, the second hitting the assailant who succumbed shortly afterwards. The other youth attempted to escape and was pursued and shot dead. A live bomb was recovered from his person and another unexploded bomb was later found near the scene. Immediately after this incident, two other youths who had been taking cover near the cricket ground, suddenly appeared in the shamiana occupied by forty or fifty spectators, including European women and children, and threw two bombs among them, both of which fortunately failed to explode. One of the assailants, Harendra Chakravarti, then ran across the shamiana emptying his revolver indiscriminately amongst the spectators but injuring no one. He was pluckily disarmed and seized. The other, Krishna Chaudhry, an Armoury Raid absconder, was also pursued and seized, and a live bomb was taken from his pocket. Both the assailants were sentenced to death.

On the 8th May 1934, two Bengalis dressed in European clothes, succeeded in approaching unobserved the Governor's box on the Race Course at Lebong in Darjeeling. One of them, Bhawani Prasad Bhattacharji, advanced up the steps of the public stand, and, when opposite His Excellency the Governor, drew a revolver and opened fire. He was promptly seized and was almost simultaneously shot by both His Excellency's personal guard and by the Superintendent of Police, Darjeeling. Immediately afterwards the second Bengali, Rabindra Nath Banarji, opened fire with an automatic pistol at His Excellency from directly in front of the box. He also was seized and disarmed. His Excellency and party miraculously escaped injury, but a woman spectator received a flesh wound in the leg. The investigation which followed showed that the outrage had been planned in Calcutta and Dacca, and that eight persons, all residents of Dacca, were implicated in the conspiracy. The two assailants were sentenced to death, but His Excellency the Governor commuted the sentence on Rabindra Nath Banarji to fourteen years' rigorous imprisonment. Manoranjan Banarji, one of the conspirators, was sentenced to transportation for life ; others, Amiya Mazumdar, Madhusudan Banarji and Sukumar Ghosh received sentences of 14 years' rigorous imprisonment ; and Sushil Chakravarti 12 years' rigorous imprisonment.

Although these attempts to murder officials failed, there were four murders by terrorists in 1934. On January 8th, Netra Sen of Gariala, Chittagong, was hacked to pieces on suspicion that he was a police spy, which he was not. On the 10th April 1934, four Mohammedans who were seated on the verandah of a house overlooking the Deobhog-Baburail Road, Dacca, noticed three *bhadralok* youths proceeding at 2 A.M. down the Baburail Road. Their suspicions being aroused, they challenged the young men who were unable to give a satisfactory account of themselves. One of them was seized and a dagger which he was carrying under his arm fell to the ground. An attempt to apprehend the other two youths was made when one of them pulled out a revolver and fired, hitting one of the Mohammadans. Ramzan, another of the Mohammadans, was now picking up some 'monkey caps' which the youth had dropped when the same individual fired at him, hitting him in the neck. A third shot hit nobody. Ramzan gave chase to his assailant, but both the youths escaped and Ramzan collapsed and expired. Eventually one Motilal Malik was sentenced to death for the crime.

As usual, terrorists committed dacoities during the year. At about 2 A.M. on the 24th February, fifteen or sixteen persons armed with revolvers, daggers, iron rods and lathis, and carrying electric torches, broke into a house at Bathua in the Chittagong district and looted cash and ornaments to the value of Rs. 3,000. They assaulted the inmates and snatched away ornaments from the women, who were roughly handled. During their retreat they fired revolvers in order to scare away the villagers, but one of the latter attacked and seriously injured one of the dacoits with a sacrificial knife, before he could be rescued by his comrades. Two of the dacoits were recognised as a former servant of the victim and a visitor, and were arrested the following day. Acting on an anonymous letter, troops and police had surrounded the village of Fatehabad on the same night, and eleven of the dacoits were arrested at two points of the cordon as day broke. Much of the loot which the culprits had been attempting to bury was recovered. Another youth was arrested the same day, and all fourteen were sent for trial. Seven were sentenced to transportation for life, two to ten years' transportation ; three to ten years' rigorous imprisonment and the remaining two to seven years' rigorous imprisonment.

At about 11 P.M. on 2nd June 1934, at Hajiganj Railway Station, District Tippera, a gang of about twelve youths, dressed in khaki, after threatening the assembled passengers by firing shots, broke into a hut and removed a mail bag containing about Rs. 31,900. An old man who was in the hut with the peons was shot dead. The culprits were not traced at the time, but information was subsequently received to the effect that the Anushilan party was responsible. On the 6th May 1934, four bombs were thrown at Sibpur Police Station, Howrah, by two young men, who were both injured when a fifth bomb fell between them on the road and exploded. They were both arrested as they were running away One constable was hurt by fragments from one of the bombs. The investigation disclosed a conspiracy and led to a search which produced five more bombs. Bhola Nath Mukharji and Mohan Lal Nag, the two who had thrown the bombs, were sentenced to five years' rigorous imprisonment each, and Abani Kumar Mukharji, who was alleged to have instigated them, to six years' rigorous imprisonment.

A Great Improvement. Only the more important outrages and crimes have been described, but this is enough to show that terrorist activity still existed. That there was a great improvement, however, is evident from the fact that whereas in 1933 there had been an average of eight crimes a month, by September 1934 the average for the year had dropped to 1·5 a month. To quote from a report issued at that time, "this certainly indicates that the terrorist parties have been weakened by the action taken against them. It is necessary, nevertheless, to maintain the pressure if the improvement is to be maintained. Generally speaking, the parties in most districts lack competent leadership and are disorganized, but recruitment is going on and in many districts plots to commit dacoities and murders are being discussed. In some places it may be that some of this murder talk is indulged in by members merely in order to encourage recruitment and to keep up the spirits of the members, without any real intention of carrying out the projects ; in others, the plots are seriously discussed and would be carried out if police activity relaxed. The attack must continue, therefore, in order to prevent the groups developing and becoming dangerous. Apart from the searches for arms, literature and correspondence, opportunities to take action should be seized as often as possible, continued use must be made of section 2 (1) and section 2(*a*) of the Bengal Criminal Law Amendment Act. Free use of the latter section will undoubtedly have the effect of greatly reducing the numerical strength of the parties and discouraging recruitment." Later, at a dinner on St. Andrew's Day, His Excellency Sir John Woodhead, acting Governor of Bengal, said that the position showed a marked improvement on what it had been a year before. He proceeded, "the lack of success by the terrorists, the successes of the police in unearthing terrorist conspiracies and bringing terrorists to justice, the large mass of information now available in many districts, though as yet by no means in all, and the considerable finds of arms and explosives, all point their own moral. The steady and continuous pressure exerted during the last four years is proving successful. But do not misunderstand me, that does not mean that the pressure can be relaxed. It must be maintained till the terrorist movement has been brought completely under control." He suggested that the Lebong outrage was the turning point in the terrorist situation, and that thereafter the tide of public opinion definitely began to flow against the terrorists. Certainly the unequivocal and unqualified condemnation of this outrage by the nationalist press was unparalleled in the history of terrorism in Bengal.

It appeared that many persons who had been "sitting on the fence" now began to realise that terrorism was a dangerous two-edged weapon liable to get out of control. Parents were beginning to believe that the danger of their children being led astray was considerable and was not a figment of the imagination of the police. On the other hand, the number of irreconcilables was very large and youth as usual was loath to profit by the experience of others; terrorist recruitment, therefore, continued although its extent was difficult to estimate. Besides this, there was a very large number of persons interned under the Bengal Criminal Law Amendment Acts. The Act of 1932 had been extended without limit by the Bengal Criminal Law Amendment (Extending) Act of 1934, and from 1930 to the end of 1934 no less than 3,110 persons had been arrested under the Acts and the Ordinance. The majority of these were detained in camps at Buxa, Hijli and Deoli, the last named being in Ajmere and reserved for the more outstanding leaders and organisers. Other important *detenus* had been released, but were mostly restricted to their homes, villages, or districts.

It is therefore not surprising that terrorist crime, the concrete manifestation of terrorist activities, showed a very welcome decrease in 1935. There were only three murders during the year, all of a rather different type from those ordinarily committed by terrorists. On the 4th of June, Kalipada Bhattacharji of Faridpur district reported at the local police station that Amulya Chaudhri and Ashutosh Bharadwaj had stabbed him. He died on the 10th of June. The alleged motive of the crime—and this was borne out by the investigation—was that he was suspected by the local Anushilan gang to be a police informer. He was in fact an active helper of the police and a member of the Union Board. Ashutosh Bharadwaj was arrested and was sentenced to transportation for life. On the 15th of the same month, the sub-inspector of police in charge of Goalundo police station, Faridpur district, who had rebuked *detenu* Rohini Kumar Barua, a Chittagonian domiciled at Goalundo, for talking to an outsider that morning, was murdered in the evening by Barua who had hidden a *dao* under his dhoti and killed the sub-inspector with one blow on the back of the neck while the officer was writing at a table in the police station. The culprit confessed and was sentenced to death. On the 3rd of July, the Anushilan party (this time, of Dacca) made another attack on suspected police spies when Paresh Chandra Sen and Amulya Roy killed Hira Chakravarti, also of Dacca, by stabbing him. They were both sentenced to death. As will be seen from the list of crimes committed, there was only one dacoity during the year. This occurred on the 28th of January 1935, at about 7·30 P.M. in a goldsmith's shop at Kalitolla, Dinajpur town, only about 100 yards from the Kotwali police station. Five or six *bhadralok* youths who were armed with revolvers committed the crime, and there was reason to believe that they were working under the direction of Naren Ghosh, the then leader of the local party. One of the men arrested became an approver and three persons, all of Dinajpur, were convicted and sentenced to terms of rigorous imprisonment.

The Titagarh Conspiracy Case. During the year 1935, a very decisive blow was struck at the Anushilan party in Bengal and Faridpur by the investigation and subsequent trial of what is known as the Titagarh Conspiracy case, which at the time of writing, has only just been concluded. On the 27th December 1934 a house in Belgharia, Calcutta, was searched and a young *bhadralok* of Sylhet was arrested with suspicious letters and other documents in his possession. A watch on the house resulted in the arrest on the 30th December of a much wanted absconder Debaprasad Sen Gupta of Faridpur district and Hill Tippera, who was known to have connections with Barisal, Faridpur, Agartala, Tippera and Sylhet. From his possession notebooks and cyphers were recovered. Later, on information given in an anonymous letter that some suspicious youths and a young girl were staying at a house at Titagarh, the house was raided and the inmates arrested after a struggle. One of those arrested was Purnananda Das Gupta who had escaped from the Alipore Jail with Sitanath De during the trial of the Inter-Provincial Conspiracy case. A pistol, cartridges and a mass of documents including formulæ for explosives and much cypher material were recovered together with a large quantity of chemicals suitable for the preparation of explosives. A protracted and careful investigation followed, in the course of which no less than 171 persons were arrested. Of these, 33 were sent for trial before the special tribunal which began hearing the case in November 1935. Purnananda Das Gupta has been sentenced to transportation for life, Prafulla Sen to twelve years' rigorous imprisonment, and fifteen others to various terms of imprisonment. Apart from instituting this important case, which deals mainly with members of the Anushilan Party in Calcutta and Faridpur, the police continued their campaign against the possession of arms by terrorists and made many recoveries during the year ; it is estimated that the losses of arms incurred by terrorists in this way far exceeded the number that they were able to obtain either by smuggling or other underground means. Nevertheless, there were as usual continual rumour of plots, though this was not surprising in view of the usual methods followed by terrorists and especially as the main parties had been so seriously disorganised and split up into small groups. Even in the most favourable conditions, only a very small percentage of the terrorists' plots which are discussed are converted into action, and this particular party was most averse to translating such plots into action. The speech of the acting Governor of Bengal at the St. Andrew's Day Dinner in 1934 has been quoted. In his speech at the 1935 function, His Excellency the Governor said, "Without being over-confident, I may fairly say that the main onrush of that wave (the last wave of terrorism) has been broken, and I gratefully acknowledge the manner in which, during the last year or two, public opinion has come to our aid. Let me, however, utter a word of warning. The history of terrorism shows that it always has come in waves, and that if it is neglected when one wave has spent its force, the next wave is bigger and more violent. There still remain in Bengal materials for the reorganization of terrorist activitiy and would-be leaders who are only biding their time. Our vigilance cannot be relaxed, and unremitting search must continue both for the secret organisers and the hidden apparatus of mischief. But at the same time it is our duty to spare no effort in the task of reclaiming to useful avenues of employment those who have been misled and are prepared, if given the opportunity, to return to saner ways." This very satisfactory state of affairs continued in 1936 as is evident from the list of crimes committed during the year. For the first time since 1920, terrorists committed no major outrages during the year, although Himangshu Bhaumik when surrounded fired at the police party but was himself shot in the legs and arrested at Feni, district Noakhali. This great improvement is to a large extent due to the change of the public attitude to terrorism. The man in the street is always activated by a natural desire to back the winning horse, and the principle has not been belied in the case of the Bengal public and terrorism. The year 1936, however, clearly shows that the spread of Communist ideas is an important factor in the future policy of terrorists. The infusion of communistic doctrines into the terrorist ranks had been noticeable since the early days of the Hindustan Socialist Republican Army, the very name of which shows that Bhagat Singh and his associates had been tainted with these principles. Most of the *detenus* in detention camps in recent years have been intensively studying Communism and Socialism and have been impressed by the value of an armed mass revolution as a means to obtaining independence. It must not be understood that terrorists have embraced the Communist doctrine as a whole, for the very creed is aimed at the elimination of their own particular class, the *bhadralok*. They do, however, see in Communist principles, and especially in those principles which relate to action, a great resemblance to their own, and they are unduly engaged by the hope that through Communism they will approach nearer to a mass rising than they ever did by their old terrorist methods. On the other hand there is no reason to believe that the Communist Party accepts or will ever accept the *bhadralok* terrorist at his face value; but there exists in communism the obvious basis for the fusion of both schools of revolutionary idealism.

CHAPTER III.

THE UNITED PROVINCES, PUNJAB AND DELHI.

The revolutionary party in the United Provinces and in the Punjab was, in 1917, quiescent. Rash Behari Bose, following the failure of the projected uprising in Benares, Lahore and elsewhere had in 1915 fled from the country, having handed over the leadership of the party in these provinces to Raghendra Nath Dutt, *alias* Girja Babu, who, however, was arrested in October 1915 and sentenced to 5 years' R. I. for his part in the Benares Conspiracy Case. Vinayak Rao Kaple, who had been one of Rash Behari Bose's lieutenants, and had escaped from Lahore in 1915 when arrests and searches were made, was active in the United Provinces and the Central Provinces, and was endeavouring to enlist recruits for the party. In this connection he visited Agra College, and the Central Hindu College at Benares also received his attention. Another active figure was Sushil Chandra Lahiri, and letters in his handwriting from Lucknow and Aligarh were intercepted in Bengal and in the Central Provinces.

Party Discipline. On the 9th February 1918, the murdered body of Vinayak Rao Kaple was found in an unfrequented lane in Lucknow. The crime was traced to Sushil Chandra Lahiri and Nripendra Nath Chakravarti, the former of whom was hanged, while the latter escaped arrest. The motive for the crime is interesting as it illustrates a fundamental principle of the society, that of the death penalty for treachery. Vinayak Rao Kaple had been responsible with one Tejendra Mohan Ghosh for a political dacoity at Abdullapur in Bengal on October 27th, 1917. For this crime he had been given a Mauser pistol by Atul Ghosh, one of the Bengal leaders, but after the dacoity he and Tejendra had absconded with Rs. 6,000 of the loot and the pistol.

On being arrested Sushil Chandra threw away a box containing two revolvers and 219 rounds of Mauser ammunition. A search of his room produced a formula for making bombs, in which picric acid, ammonium picrate and gun-cotton were to be used.

As the result of this further set-back, the activities of the party in Northern India were not important for some time, but an independent organization, with its headquarters in the Mainpuri district of the United Provinces and with members in other districts, flourished between 1916 and 1918. As usual, the members of the party were mainly students, and many of them had been coached by one Genda Lal who had been headmaster of the D. A. V. School in Auraiya, Etawah. The society, which was known as the Matravedi Sanstha or the "Society of those who are prepared to sacrifice their lives for the motherland", was divided into four branches to deal with propaganda, military aspects, secret service and industrial activity. The oath which members of the society were required to sign is interesting and runs,

"Bande Matram.

Shrimanji, I bow to you. To-day I enlist myself as a member of the "Gupta Sanstha" (secret society). By the omnipotent and omnipresent God I do hereby promise that I will never be a traitor to the cause of the society. By the name of mother Bharat I declare that I will free her from the yoke of foreigners and thus become a true and dutiful son. I will not turn back from the service of the country till I die. I will always be ready to sacrifice my body, mind and property for the sake of the Motherland. I am a true son of the Mother and I will never cause any obstruction in the work of the society. The sun might forego his heat and the moon her coolness, howsoever difficult troubles might confront me, I shall never turn back from the call of duty, and if need be, shall not care for family ties. I swear by the Mother that I will not fail to carry out the orders of the society, and in case of my failure the society will have the right to pass the death penalty upon me."

Many of the members were given society names, and in pursuance of the objective of the society a quantity of arms and ammunition was collected, including guns, rifles, pistols and daggers. Some 25 members of the society committed a dacoity with fire-arms in the Mainpuri district on November 11th, 1917, and although only a few ornaments were obtained, the owner of the house was slashed with a sword while making his escape, and a woman was tortured by being pricked about the head with daggers. Bicycles and a typewriter were stolen for the use of the society. In January 1918, a number of the members assembled with the object of looting the house of a *bania* in Etawah, but the idea was abandoned. Their attention next turned to raiding a sub-treasury at Auraiya, but the unexpected return of the Tahsildar caused the abandonment of this scheme. Some of the members, however, succeeded on the 21st January 1918 in robbing a *sarraf* of a box containing about Rs. 600 worth of gold and silver ornaments. About the same time, some of the conspirators in Lucknow who required money impersonated C. I. D. officers and extorted money from a man who had run away from Delhi. In June 1918, a leader's quarrel prevented the commission of a dacoity in Shahjahanpur district, but a few days later, on the 23rd June, the house of a well-to-do Brahmin widow was looted in village Pareli in the Hardoi district. On this occasion the maid-servant was shot dead and the mistress of the house was tortured by pricking her shoulder with a dagger and burning her fingers with a torch until she gave up her keys. Loot valued at Rs. 10,000 was taken away, but not before the conspirators had shot two villagers. Meanwhile, the society was publishing revolutionary leaflets which were posted up in many towns in the United Provinces. Finally, many members of the gang were arrested, and although some of the leaders escaped from jail during the trial, the conspiracy was effectually broken up when 10 youths were convicted in 1919.

There was a slight recrudescence of activity in 1922 when, taking advantage of the confusion occasioned by riots in Bareilly, old members of the Mainpuri conspiracy shot at and wounded three constables in various parts of the town, fatally wounding one. All three were sentenced to transportation for life.

Revival. The main party in Northern India was revived in 1920, when Sachindra Nath Sanyal, a Bengali domiciled in Benares, who in 1916 had been sentenced to transportation for life for his participation in the Benares Conspiracy, was released in 1920 by Royal Amnesty. His methods were to choose likely youths and interest them in his book 'Bandi Jiwan', which gave an account of terrorist movements and activities up to 1915 in such a way as to arouse their immature minds to similar action. The book was eventually proscribed by the U. P. Government in 1931, but not before it had been translated into Hindi and Gurmukhi, and had been widely distributed. An authority has said of this book, 'It is one of the best known gems of terrorist literature'—and another, 'The author has sent more young men to the gallows or to prison for terrorism than any man who has lived in India'. By 1923, Sachindra Sanyal had made considerable progress, and in 1924 he went into hiding in Bengal, having passed on the work of organization to Jogesh Chandra Chatterji, another Bengali, who had come to Benares in 1923. Jogesh stayed in Bengal for some months, actively enrolling members for the revolutionary society, and then extended his sphere to embrace Allahabad, Cawnpore and other districts of the U. P. He had, it seems, completed his mission by October 1924, when he returned to Calcutta. Here he was arrested and interned under the Bengal Ordinance.

Formation of H. R. A. The result of these activities was the formation of the Hindustan Republican Association, the rules of which were recovered, and are reproduced in Appendix 3. These rules are wide in their scope, but a paper recovered from Jogesh Chandra Chatterji when he was arrested showed that some progress had been made with the original programme, and that the organisers were adapting their methods to the times. Organisers were acting in 23 districts of the U. P., and the remaining districts were grouped. About 100 members were acknowledged. The intensive duties of (apparently) district organisers are shown in another paper recovered, the "Twelve Points", in the handwriting of Rajendra Nath Lahiri, who was the Benares district organiser. The number of non-co-operators was to be ascertained and their current mental attitude was to be studied; the population, villages, roads, railways, etc., with maps, hospitals, police, army strengths, arms, clubs, schools, factories, motor vehicles, and even bullock carts were to be enumerated, while practically all Government servants, down to the army sepoy were to be noted by name and address.

By the end of 1924, the organization of the party in the U. P. was complete enough for the commission of dacoities a method of raising funds in full accord with the principles and traditions of the revolutionaries. Three of these dacoities, at Bamrauli on Christmas Day, 1924, at Bichpuri on the night of March 9/10th, 1925, and at Dwarkapur on May 24, 1925, went untraced and unconnected with terrorists until the daring hold-up and looting of a train just after leaving Kakori station near Lucknow on the evening of August 9, 1925, raised suspicions that terrorists were responsible. At Bamrauli, the house of a well-to-do Brahmin was attacked and about Rs. 4,000 worth of loot was carried off. The dacoits, who were well armed, shot in cold blood a villager who dared them to come out and fight. At Bichpuri, a house was ransacked and the dacoits again exhibited extreme callousness. An approver later stated that Quicksilver', the society name for Chandra Shekhar Azad, who by now was an important member, laid a *kukri* on the neck of a child in order to force its mother to show where her valuables were hidden. He was dissuaded from murdering the child by Ram Prasad 'Bismil' who was in charge of the gang Another woman had burning rags placed between her legs to make her speak and, once more, a man was shot dead. About Rs 2,000 was looted from a house in the Dwarkapur dacoity, in which, as usual, arms were freely used and in which, again as usual, professional '*badmashes* formed part of the gang. Here too, a man was shot dead.

Having been successful in these crimes, the party then aimed at bigger game and, following a general principle, turned their attention to Government moneys as on previous occasions, professional dacoits were enlisted, and a large party lay in ambush near Kakori on August 9th, 1925, for a train which three other members (who had insinuated themselves into the guard's van at the last stopping station) halted at the appointed place by pulling the communication chain. The guard was overpowered and the passengers were warned not to leave the train. One passenger who braved the firing and alighted was promptly shot dead. Meanwhile, a safe containing the earnings of various stations up the line was removed, and was later found broken open and rifled, the total loss being over Rs. 4,500.

Various considerations, notably a similarity of cartridge cases picked up on the spot to those used in Bengal dacoities, led to suspicion falling on terrorist party members, who were rounded up. Many arrests and searches were made, and from the mass of information gleaned, a conspiracy case was instituted. Two accused confessed and were pardoned; four were hanged, including Rajendra Nath Lahiri and Ram Prasad; five, including Jogesh Chandra Chatterji and Sachindra Nath Sanyal, were sentenced to transportation for life; and eleven received sentences for various terms of imprisonment. Unfortunately, one of the most important members, Chandra Shekhar Azad, was not caught.

The course of the proceedings in the courts was exceptional, and was distinguished by the obstruction of the accused, who frequently relinquished or re-engaged their counsel, while some resorted to hunger-striking. The final judgment was announced in August 1927, the committal court proceedings having begun in December 1925.

Gathering up the threads, and extension to Punjab. After the Kakori trial, the U. P. branch of the revolutionary party was left considerably weakened, but the party was by no means dead. Phanindra Nath Ghosh, of Bettiah Bihar, who had joined the Bengal Anushilan Party in 1916 and had organized parties in Bihar in 1926, met Jatindra Nath

Sanyal, whose two brothers (Sachindra and Bhupendra) had been convicted in the Kakori case, and in 1927 was receiving revolvers from him. Of these, one revolver was later used in the Punjab. At the end of the year, Ghosh took a revolver to Benares, where it was subsequently used on November 13th, 1927, by a Bengali youth in an attempt to murder Rai Bahadur J. N. Banerjee, Deputy Superintendent of Police, who had taken a prominent part in the investigation of the Kakori case. This youth was a member of a Bengali 'cell' at Benares, which was in close touch with the New Violence Party of Bengal. He was seized on the spot, and later was sentenced to transportation for life.

In the meantime, Sukh Dev of Lyallpur, Punjab, had been busy from 1926 enlisting recruits with Lahore as his headquarters. He was helped by Yashpal, a master of the National School in that city, who introduced him to one Jai Gopal. Sukh Dev also enlisted Hans Raj Vohra, who, like other recruits, was shown the pamphlet on the constitution and aims of the Hindustan Republican Association. Bhagat Singh was also in touch with Sukh Dev at the time. In 1928, Hans Raj began to organize a Students' Union with political propaganda as its object.

The early months of 1928 were spent in Rawalpindi by Hans Raj Vohra, who was joined there by Jai Gopal and was visited by Bhagat Singh and Sukh Dev. He endeavoured to create a local centre there.

In the United Provinces, J. N. Sanyal, Lalit Kumar Mukharji and Ajoy Kumar Ghosh were discussing the resumption of active work when, in July 1928, Gaya Prasad, Sheo Varma and Sukh Dev met, and as a result Gaya Prasad opened a pharmacy at Ferozepore under the name of Dr. B. S. Nigam. This pharmacy was later used by members travelling between the Punjab and the East, and here they used to change their clothes according to their destination. It was also to be used in obtaining materials for the manufacture of explosives and was besides expected to be of some pecuniary benefit. In August 1928, Sukh Dev rented a house in Amritsar and this and the pharmacy at Ferozepore became meeting places for the party.

The formation of the Hindustan Socialist Republican Army. Towards the end of August 1928, Phanindra Nath Ghosh was invited by Bijoy Kumar Sinha to join a new party proposed to be formed by the amalgamation of the Provincial parties in the Punjab, U. P., Bihar and Bengal. Subsequently, on the 8th and 9th September meetings took place at Feroze Shah Tughlak's Fort at Delhi, as a result of which an amalgamation was made, with the exception of Bengal, as the party there was reported to be opposed to terrorism and violence. A central committee of seven was formed composed of Sukh Dev, Sheo Varma and P. N. Ghosh, who were to be in charge of the Punjab, U. P., and Bihar respectively, Chandra Shekhar Azad (who was not present) head of the military department, Kundanlal Vidyarthi the proposed head of the central office located at Jhansi, and Bhagat Singh and B. K. Sinha, who were to act as links. Terrorism was adopted as the policy of the party, and dacoity, murder and other acts of violence were included in the programme. It is significant that the new name selected for the party was the 'Hindustan Socialist Republican Army'. The immediate programme included the rescue from jail of Jogesh Chandra Chatterjee, and S. N. Sanyal, Kakori case convicts, and action against the Simon Commission; it was further decided that bomb-makers from Bengal should be invited to instruct members of the party in their art. Other resolutions were passed for the murder of the approvers in the Kakori Case, and the commission of a dacoity in order to raise funds. Party names were also assigned.

Dasehra Bomb Outrage at Lahore. In the meantime, on October 23rd, 1928, a bomb was thrown into a crowd of people returning *via* the Roshnai Gate into Lahore city from Dasehra celebrations, killing 10 and injuring 50 persons. In 1930, the offenders were traced; of them one had died in the interim, and another turned approver. Abdul Ghani was hanged for the crime, but no connection with the main revolutionary party was shown. No less than 14 bombs of the Mills type were unearthed from a cunning hiding-place when the accused were arrested.

Preparations. For the next month or so, members of the H. S. R. A moved about constantly, and Bhagat Singh visited Phanindra Nath Ghosh at Bettiah, where a proposed dacoity was discussed without a decision being reached. Bhagat Singh, however, obtained certain revolvers which he arranged to send to Agra. There were later, in November and December 1928, various meetings in Lahore, at which plans were discussed and members of the party were given instruction in loading and unloading pistols by "Panditji" (another party name of Chandra Shekhar Azad) Azad also unfolded a plan to raid the Punjab National Bank; two members were to deal with the chaprasi, another to cut the telephone wires, Sukh Dev was to disarm the chaukidar, and "Panditji" was to overpower the cashier, while two others, who were given bags, were to collect currency notes The whole operation was to be conducted in three stages marked by whistle blasts to be given by "Panditji", the final stage being the flight in a taxi which was to be waiting in readiness. The failure of a member to drive this taxi ruined the whole plan, although the other members had taken up their positions ready for action.

Murder of Mr. Saunders. The next proposal was to murder Mr. J. A. Scott, Senior Superintendent of Police, Lahore, who was charged by the party with having struck Lala Lajpat Rai. The death of L. Lajpat Rai on November 18th, 1928 was falsely alleged by the party to be the result of his having being beaten by the police during disturbances on the occasion of the arrival of the Simon Commission in Lahore some weeks earlier. This allegation was widely made at the time but in point of fact L. Lajpat Rai received no injury at the hands of the police. An unmarked member of the party watched Mr. Scott's movements for several days, and then the 17th December was fixed for the outrage. On that day, Mr. Saunders, Assistant Superintendent of Police, went to office on a red motor cycle and was mistaken for Mr. Scott. The conspirators made elaborate plans for their escape on bicycles, and when Mr. Saunders left his office Shivram Rajguru fired at him, causing him to fall from his machine. Thereupon Bhagat Singh ran up and fired several shots into Mr. Saunders as he lay on the ground. The culprits then made good their escape, but not before "Panditji" had also mortally wounded Head Constable Chanan Singh who joined in the chase through the D. A. V. College, Lahore. Posters, in the handwriting of Bhagat Singh, were later affixed to various public places in Lahore, 'Saunders is dead, Lalaji is avenged'.

On the 31st of December 1928, Sukh Dev and two other members saw Mr. Scott pass a canal bridge in his motor-car, but refrained from shooting, as Sukh Dev remarked that as he had escaped once, it was useless to fire at him again.

Intensive bomb-making. Towards the end of this month, Bhagat Singh went to Calcutta, where he made enquiries about bombs and endeavoured to arrange for someone to teach the party how to make explosives. By the 14th February 1929, several members of the party had foregathered in Agra, and bomb-making began under the direction of Jatindra Nath Das, a Bengali, the materials employed being picric acid and potassium chlorate, as an attempt to make ammonium picrate had proved unsuccessful. It was now decided to rescue Jogesh Chandra Chatterjee on his transfer from Agra to the Lucknow Jail, and seven members of the party, the leaders being Bhagat Singh and "Panditji", actually went to Cawnpore, but deferred the attempt as they considered the lock-up there to be too difficult to attack. Sukh Dev then went to Lahore in order to have copies made of bomb-shells received from Calcutta, and it was proposed to bomb the Simon Commission. More bomb-shells were procured and filled, but this proposal was rejected owing to the expense of travelling, and it was decided instead to throw a bomb in the Legislative Assembly. One bomb was taken to Jhansi and was there exploded in an unfrequented place as a test. Bomb-making at Agra continued until the house there was abandoned at the end of March, when the party headquarters were shifted to Saharanpur.

Sukh Dev and Kishori Lal were meanwhile busy making bombs in Lahore, where they ordered a number of cast-iron bomb-shells and plugs from a local moulder.

Assembly Bomb Outrage. On April 8th, 1929, Bhagat Singh and Batukeshwar Datt each threw a bomb in the

Legislative Assembly hall at Delhi and scattered red warning leaflets. Bhagat Singh also fired two unaimed shots from a pistol. Six persons were injured and the two culprits were arrested. The pistol was afterwards proved to have been used in the Saunders murder. Bhagat Singh and Datt were both sentenced to transportation for life under section 307 of the I. P. C. and 3 Expl. Substances Act, on the 12th June 1929.

Round up of conspirators and the first Lahore Conspiracy Case. On April 15th, a police party raided the Lahore headquarters and arrested Sukh Dev (who had a loaded revolver in his possession), Kishori Lal and Jai Gopal. A live bomb, eight bomb-shells and a large quantity of chemicals was recovered, together with notebooks containing formulae, and numerous other books and documents. The headquarters at Saharanpur was raided on May 13th, when Sheo Varma and Jai Dev were arrested, and six bombs, three shells, three loaded revolvers, ammunition, books including 'Manufacture and use of Explosives', and a large quantity of chemicals and apparatus were recovered. Two days later, Gaya Prasad, not knowing of the raid, returned to the Saharanpur house and was arrested. Shivram Rajguru was arrested in a garage in Poona, in possession of a revolver and ammunition, on 30th September 1929.

In all, twenty-four persons were arrested in various places; five accepted tenders of pardon, three were discharged, and one, Bhagwan Das, died after a hunger-strike. After a lengthy trial, characterised by the unruly behaviour of the accused in court, which ultimately necessitated the appointment of a Special Tribunal under Ordinance No. III of 1930, Sukh Dev, Bhagat Singh and Shivram Rajguru were sentenced to death, seven others to transportation for life, and two to shorter terms of imprisonment, while three were acquitted. Chandra Shekhar Azad again evaded arrest, and the other absconders were Kailash Pati *alias* Kali Charan, Bhagwati Charan, Yashpal and Satgurdayal Awasthi.

Attempts on lives of an approver and an informer. In August 1929, Benarsi Lal, who had been an approver in the Kakori case, and was now living at Shahjahanpur, received a bomb by registered post, the parcel being franked by supposed 'biri' merchants of Fatehgarh. A few days later Sheo Charan Lal who was then at Agra, and was suspected of being an informer received a re-directed parcel also containing a bomb, the parcel being as before franked as from the same bogus merchants at Fatehgarh. No arrests were made in these connections but it was later learnt from a statement made in the course of the Lahore Conspiracy Case that the plot had been hatched by Chandra Shekhar Azad and his associates.

Ahmadgarh-Kup Dacoity. On October 15th, 1929, a gang held up a train between Ahmadgarh and Kup in the Malerkotla State in the south of the Punjab, and having overawed the train staff and passengers with pistols and guns, demanded the surrender of the Government money. The gang endeavoured to break open the train safe, but were unsuccessful and, fearing exposure if they delayed longer, abandoned the attempt. The crime was eventually traced to six youths led by Sher Jang and Harnam Sing who were endeavouring to obtain funds for the 'Kirti' newspaper of Amritsar, a journal which was in difficulties owing to its having been more than once proscribed. Three persons, including Sher Jung and Harnam Singh, were sentenced to 10 years' rigorous imprisonment each, and two more to seven years' rigorous imprisonment each, while one accepted a pardon. No connection with other revolutionary parties was found to exist, although Kailashpati stated later that Bhagwati Charan had told him that his own men had committed the crime. The crime, however, goes to show how far the principles of terrorism had spread among the youthful intelligentsia.

The arrest and trial of the main leaders of the party in the Punjab and U. P. weakened the movement considerably and removed some of the best organisers, but the revolutionary virus had been widely spread in both provinces and there were still left several enthusiasts to keep the ball rolling and enough sympathisers and underlings to supply workers. Public opinion, unsettled by the Civil Disobedience

Movement, ran wild and was further excited in favour of the revolutionaries under trial by most of the nationalist newspapers, which painted the accused as oppressed martyrs placed on their trial by an Imperialistic Government for purely patriotic acts. Bhagat Singh especially became a national hero, and his exploits were freely lauded in the nationalist press, so that, for a time, he bade fair to oust Mr. Gandhi as the foremost political figure of the day. His photograph was to be met with in many houses, and his plaster busts found a large market.

Further activities by remnants of party. Yashpal, who had early been connected with the party but appears to have remained in the background, now came to the fore with Bhagwati Charan, and these two decided to wreck the Viceroy's train. They used Indar Pal, who had been enlisted by Yashpal, to watch the railway line near Delhi in the guise of a *sadhu,* and persuaded Hans Raj 'Wireless', who had a reputation for great skill in electrical matters, to arrange a mine to be exploded by electricity. The mine, which contained T. N. T., was laid under a sleeper and connected by over 300 yards of 'flex' wire buried three inches in the ground, to a battery and switch hidden near the Purana Qila, Delhi. Yashpal, dressed for this occasion in a military uniform complete with breeches and gaiters, and accompanied by Bhag Ram, exploded the mine on December 23rd, 1929, but fortunately no loss of life occurred, although two feet of rail were blown out and some fragments were forced through the floor of a coach to find lodgement in its roof. A motor-cycle purchased by Yashpal for his escape after the crime could not be made to work and was abandoned after the offence.

After this, the main activities of the Lahore group were directed towards an attempt to rescue Bhagat Singh and his co-accused. Hans Raj first attempted to introduce stupefying gas into the court room, but was unsuccessful. It was then decided to rescue only Bhagat Singh and Datt, who, as convicts, were taken from the jail to the court in a separate van. For this purpose a party armed with revolvers and bombs was arranged, and headquarters were established in a house on Bahawalpur Road, Lahore.

About this time, Bhagwati Charan and Sukh Dev Raj took some bombs out into waste land near the Ravi in order to test them. Apparently one bomb exploded prematurely, for Bhagwati Charan was killed and his companion received injuries in the left foot. The body of Bhagwati Charan was hidden, and the rescue plans were abandoned. The party dispersed when another bomb exploded, this time in the Bahawalpur Road house, on June 6th, 1930. Hans Raj Wireless' was now made Provincial Organiser for the Punjab with Indar Pal as his assistant, and in order that the party should not be identified with the H. S. R. A., the name was changed to the 'Atishi Chakar', or 'Fire Ring' party.

Simultaneous bombs in various towns of the Punjab. Hans Raj now conceived his most diabolical plot. He rented houses and rooms in various cities of the Punjab, and on the morning of June 19, 1930, small decoy bombs were exploded by means of candle fuses. The police, who rushed to the spot, found a neat black box fitted with handles resting on the top of obviously revolutionary literature. The box was a powerful 'booby trap' bomb designed to explode when lifted. These traps were arranged at Lahore, Amritsar, Gujranwala, Sheikhupura, Lyallpur and Rawalpindi. At Gujranwala a Head Constable was fatally injured and others were wounded, and at Lyallpur one officer sustained rupture of his ear-drums which led to his death two months later, while another lost the sight of an eye. In the other four places the plan fortunately miscarried.

The Lahore branch of the party was more or less quiet after this, but on the 20th July 1930 some chemicals exploded in a suitcase which one of the members, Amrit Singh, was carrying in the Said Mitha Bazar. The next plan was to rob the Octroi Office at the Railway Goods Shed, Lahore, but nothing had been done up to the time when the conspira tors were arrested at the end of August.

The Rawalpindi Centre. In the meantime, the Rawalpindi branch decided to raise funds by robbing the cashier of the office of the Controller of Military Accounts on the 1st of August, but, although the party actually set out, slipshod methods of organization led to failure. There was, however, great activity in bomb-making, which was facilitated by the fact that a number of the conspirators were metal-workers. Another attempt to obtain the salaries of the office of the Controller of Military Accounts was made on September 1st, 1930, but this also miscarried. One member of the gang, Hari Ram, was arrested on the 4th September, and three others then decamped. A few of the less efficient members who were left made futile endeavours to commit robberies and burglaries in Rawalpindi and the neighbouring villages, and on September 27th, 1930, they threw a bomb at a Police guard stationed on the shop of a Hindu who had refused to comply with the request of the Congress Party to close it. This bomb failed to explode. The remnants of the gang were arrested early in October.

In November 1930, the trial of the second Lahore Conspiracy case opened, as the outcome of the cases briefly sketched above. Four of the accused were, after another lengthy trial, sentenced to transportation for life, and eleven others were sentenced to various terms of imprisonment. Yashpal, Hans Raj 'Wireless' and Chandra Shekhar Azad were among the absconders.

By this time the bomb cult had spread very extensively in both the United Provinces and the Punjab. There were many minor outrages, explosions and recoveries of bombs in both provinces for the next few years ; but not all these occurrences can be laid at the door of the terrorist party, the organization with which we are mainly concerned, although in some cases terrorism, not always of officials, was the motive of the crime. For instance, on the 22nd February 1930, a bomb was thrown on to the dais at a students' meeting in the Khalsa College, Amritsar. The Principal of the college, for whom the missile was intended, had incurred the displeasure of some students by interfering with "Independence Day" celebrations. Three students were arrested, of whom one turned approver, and although one other was sentenced to death, he was later acquitted by the High Court. It is suspected that in this case the actual bomb thrower was the approver. In Jullundur, a raid on the night of March 2nd, 1930, disclosed a bomb factory and resulted in the trial of six persons. It was shown that a secret society had been formed by the leader Mani Ram Dhanda, who had been in Delhi. Three persons were sentenced to imprisonment, including Mani Ram who was sent to jail for 10 years.

Activities in Delhi. During this period, the main headquarters of the H. S. R. A. was in Delhi, where the leading spirits were C. S. Azad, Bhagwati Charan, Yashpal and Kailash Pati. In the summer of 1929, Gwalior had been the scene of meetings, and there picric acid and guncotton had been prepared. In November 1929, a meeting was held in Cawnpore when provincial representatives for the U. P., Delhi and Rajputana were appointed and arrangements were made for liaison with the Howrah group of revolutionaries. At another meeting at Cawnpore in February 1930, Yashpal was appointed Provincial organiser for the Punjab, and it was then decided to make Delhi the headquarters of the Central Council of the H. S. R. A. At this meeting, a plan to rescue the accused in the Lahore Conspiracy Case and to murder four who were considered to have been unfaithful was drawn up, but, as we have seen, the Lahore group failed to carry out the scheme. There were also proposals to form local centres at Ajmere, Jaipur and Jhansi. In January 1930, Bhagwati Charan drafted the H. S. R. A. Manifesto, 'The Philosophy of the Bomb', and Azad had it printed at a press near Cawnpore. The leaflets were brought to Delhi and distributed from there on 'Independence Day', January 25th, 1930. At this time, large purchases of cartridges for rifles, automatic pistols and 12 bore guns were made from a dealer in Delhi through an associate who possessed a license.

In June 1930, the party decided to commit a robbery, as funds were low and money was required for the proposed rescue at Lahore. An attack on the lorry conveying the salaries of the Delhi Railway Clearing Accounts Office from the Imperial Bank was arranged, but fell through as on the 1st July 1930, the day fixed, a hartal in the city resulted in intensive police patrols which frightened the plotters. Five days later, Azad, Kailashpati, Dhanwantri, Lekh Ram and Kashi Ram committed an armed decoity at the Gadodia Stores in Delhi City, and carried off some Rs. 14,000 in cash in a motor-car, firing in the street as they left in order to discourage pursuit. This loot was distributed to various centres and, with the Delhi allotment, a bomb-factory disguised as a soap factory was opened. There large quantities of explosives were prepared in the next few weeks, until, disturbed by the arrests in August in Lahore, the members of the party decided to close down the factory. The explosives were moved to another house, and were recovered by the police in November 1930, when an expert estimated that there was enough material to make 6,000 bombs.

Kailashpati was arrested in October 1930, and made a full statement; in December, Dhanwantri wounded a policeman before he, too, was arrested in the Chandni Chauk. Other arrests followed, and after a lengthy investigation a conspiracy case was instituted in Delhi before a Special Tribunal, with Kailashpati as an approver. Owing to the delaying tactics of the accused, the trial dragged on for seven months, and the case was then withdrawn. Of the 14 accused, two were interned under Regulation III of 1818, four were released, and eight were charged with specific offences. Azad, Yashpal and some others again escaped arrest.

The break-up of the main party organization. With the conclusion of these cases, the main organization of the H. S. R. A. was broken up, and the more energetic and imaginative leaders were now either in jail, under trial, or in hiding. Gradually these important absconders were accounted for, and the movement degenerated into small local conspiracies and numerous, but isolated, cases of bomb-throwing. It would be to little purpose to recount these petty cases in detail; the list of cases in the appendix shows how wide-spread was the cult. Some cases, however, deserve at least passing mention, and for some incidents we must retrace our steps for a few months. While the main groups had been working in the bigger towns such as Delhi, Lahore and Amritsar, smaller groups showed signs of activity elsewhere. For instance, on May 19th, 1930, a bomb was thrown at the police in Multan. The investigation revealed a small local conspiracy and resulted in the conviction of eight persons. Bombs were thrown into the compound of the Chenab Club at Lyallpur on June 6th, 1930, and ten days later into a police post at Jhang. On August 8th, 1930, information having been obtained that one Lakshmi Kant had obtained a revolver from Gwalior in order to assassinate the Commissioner at Jhansi, a trap was laid, and the would-be assailant was arrested, in possession of a revolver and a bomb, just as he approached for an interview with his intended victim. Lakshmi Kant was sentenced to transportation for life. On September 9th, 1930, a bomb left lying outside a police post in Benares was picked up by an old woman and exploded, blowing off her hands and causing her death. Subimal Roy and Mrinalini Dasi were convicted for this offence. On October 4th, 1930, an attempt was made on the life of Khan Bahadur Abdul Aziz, Special Superintendent of Police of the C. I. D., Lahore. As the Khan Bahadur was being driven along a canal bank near Lahore, his car was fired at. The driver pulled up, thinking that a tyre had burst, whereupon a fusillade of shots was fired, fatally wounding an armed personal guard and injuring the driver. The Khan Bahadur and a companion returned the fire, but the assailants escaped. Eight days later two shots were fired through the lighted door of a police sergeant's room in Lahore. That the revolutionaries were possessed of courage is shown by the resistance of Tehl Singh and Basheshar Nath at Lahore on November 4th, 1930, and of Salig Ram Shukla at Cawnpore on December 1st, 1930. These persons fired at the police parties deputed to arrest and search them, and Shukla wounded no less than three police officers before he was himself shot by the Superintendent of Police. He was encountered in the early morning and circumstances indicated that he was about to accompany friends outside the town for revolver practice.

On the 20th October 1930, a gang, headed by Devi Chand of Gujrat, Kathiawar, committed a dacoity with murder at Manauli in the Ambala district. In December 1930, the members collected in Delhi in preparation for another crime at Etah in the United Provinces, but they were arrested in possession of country-made arms obtained from Alwar and Jaipur. Chanan Singh became an approver and stated that other crimes proposed included the murder of the Deputy Commissioner, Delhi, and of a Mahant at Nankana Sahib. Devi Chand was arrested nearly a year later. In the trial which resulted, one person was sentenced to death, and two to ten years' rigorous imprisonment each, but three others were acquitted.

A more noteworthy event was the attack on His Excellency the Governor of the Punjab as he was leaving the Convocation at the Lahore University Hall on December 23rd, 1930. Hari Krishan, of Mardan, fired at short range, but fortunately only injured His Excellency in the arm, although an Assistant Sub-Inspector, Chanan Singh, was shot dead. An Inspector and a lady doctor from Delhi, who was at the time talking to the Governor, were both wounded. Hari Krishan and another were arrested on the spot. The former was sentenced to death and, subsequently, Ranbir Singh, Durga Das, and Chaman Lal, his associates, were convicted of conspiracy and also sentenced to death.

Continued operations. The year 1931 opened with a series of bomb explosions in Benares. On December 12th, 1930, a constable stirred a round object with his *lathi* at the Chowk Police Station, and it exploded with the emission of much smoke. On January 5th, 1931, some youths who attempted to rob a mail-van in Benares, ran away, throwing a bomb at their pursuers during their flight. Five persons were sent for trial, of whom one was an approver, but all were acquitted. On the same date, a bomb was found in front of Police Station Dassaswamedh, Benares; on the 8th January 1931, a bomb exploded at the same place; and on the 11th of the same month a boy found behind Police Station Chowk a bomb which exploded and injured him. The same gang was suspected in all these cases, but the crimes were not brought home. Meanwhile, at Cawnpore, on January 2nd, 1931, Asok Kumar Bose attempted to assassinate an Inspector of the C. I. D., but his pistol misfired. He escaped, but was later arrested at his home, in possession of a revolver. Bose was sentenced to 5 years' rigorous imprisonment for attempted murder and illegal possession of arms.

An important event took place in Allahabad on the morning of February 27th, 1931. The police received information that the notorious absconder, Chandra Shekhar Azad was in the Alfred Park. Mr. Nott-Bower, Superintendent of Police on special duty joined Thakur Bisheshwar Singh, Deputy Superintendent of Police, in the Park, and approached Azad and his companion, who were sitting under a tree. Azad and his companion drew revolvers and began firing, whereupon a revolver duel took place at short range between Azad and Mr. Nott-Bower, both of whom were wounded before they took shelter behind trees. Azad's companion had run away. Thakur Bisheshwar Singh tried to outflank Azad, and fired at him, probably wounding him in the head, but he himself received a bullet in his lower jaw. Azad fell back dead. Meanwhile, many students had collected and were urged by Azad to help him before he died, as he was selling his life for his country.

The removal of this leader resulted in the breaking-up of the main party of the H. S. R. A. and the scattering of its members, so that inter-provincial connections increased. At this time the Cawnpore branch, which was the most active was known to have links with the Punjab, Delhi, Bihar, Bengal, Gwalior, Bombay and even Karachi.

About the same time communist ideas began to penetrate into the terrorist circles of the United Provinces, where the leaders were not slow to appreciate the lessons of the Lahore Conspiracy cases and to realise that the Communist programme would serve their purpose equally well without necessitating self-immolation.

Nevertheless, these considerations did not immediately penetrate to the rank and file of the terrorists and there was no cessation in the numerous cases of bomb-making and bomb-throwing, as will be seen from the appended list of outrages. The police were successful in both the United Provinces and the Punjab in securing arms from revolutionaries, and it is fortunate that the bomb explosions which occurred caused but little harm to life and property, although in some instances, experimenters and would-be revolutionaries were hoist with their own petard when efforts to prepare explosives and bombs resulted in premature explosions and the death of, or injuries to, the dabblers. The bomb cult spread so widely that bombs were used not always for terrorist purposes but as the weapon for prosecuting party or family feuds. Congress members also used bombs to supplement their threats and to impress on foreign cloth merchants the error of their ways in disobeying Congress commands. These circumstances, coupled with the fact that it was often difficult to trace the throwers of bombs, made it almost impossible to distinguish between cases of terrorism and those of purely private or Congress connexion. The bombs used also degenerated in efficiency, and could more usually be described as 'crackers'. It is a known fact that, in some areas, villagers have used crackers composed of a mixture of explosives contained within some edible substance as a means to capturing wild animals, such as pig; on picking up the tempting morsel, the unfortunate animal had its head blown off. Nevertheless, the widespread use of the bomb became a very disturbing factor, calculated seriously to unsettle the official, especially the police officer, who might expect to become a target at any time or place.

At the same time, other serious crimes of violence did not wholly cease. On May 7th, 1931, two men who were being brought from Kashmir to Sialkot on a charge of having forged a cheque attacked their police escort as the train neared Suchetgarh and shot one constable dead. In addition, a Sub-Inspector and a head constable were wounded. The culprits then escaped, but one was arrested the same day in possession of a revolver and cartridges. The investigation disclosed a terrorist conspiracy of small extent but with ramifications in Quetta and elsewhere. Prabha Khan was sentenced to death for the crime; Hans Raj, who was not arrested until 1933 in the United Provinces, to transportation; and Kasturi Lal and Jagdish Chandra Pandit to three years' rigorous imprisonment each. On June 6th, 1931, a constable in Cawnpore arrested Kashi Ram, an absconder in the Gadodia Stores Dacoity case, Delhi; he was fired upon by three companions of Kashi Ram, whom they rescued. The constable was wounded. Hans Raj and Rajendra Narain Nigam, two of the culprits, were apprehended and convicted, and Kashi Ram was ultimately sentenced to seven years' rigorous imprisonment. On the 20th June 1931, three armed men committed a robbery in the shop of a cloth merchant in Cawnpore and shot the cashier dead. The crime went unpunished, but two members of the local branch of the H. S. R. A. were suspected to have taken part. In the same month, on the night of the 22nd/23rd, two men held up an ekka carrying a cloth merchant and two of his friends on the outskirts of Lucknow, and threw two bombs. They then made off on bicycles, firing shots as they went. Five days later, Hazari Lal and Suraj Nath Chaube were arrested after a struggle in Patna, and Hazari Lal confessed that they were responsible for the Lucknow outrage. On the 18th July 1931, two unknown persons fired three shots at Birbhaddar Tiwari, who was not injured. Tiwari was suspected in revolutionary circles as having given information which led to the death of Chandra Shekhar Azad. Three days later, on the 21st July, Ramesh Chand Mehta, a revolutionary suspect, was fired at and hit in the back by Raja Ram *alias* Zalim, as they were returning from a Youth League meeting. This also was probably a case of reprisal on a suspected police informer. A bill-collector in Cawnpore was attacked on August 6th, 1931, and when two passers-by attempted a rescue, one was seriously wounded by the assailants and died later. The crime was traced to Debi Dayal, who had been recruited to the terrorist ranks by Satgurdayal Awasthi; he was sentenced to death. Another terrorist Raja Ram Zalim was himself shot at in Cawnpore on August 11th, 1931, and killed, it is believed, in pursuance of an internal party feud, although there were some indications of his having committed suicide. A second attempt on the life of Birbhaddar Tiwari was made on November 24th, 1931, at Jalaun, Orai. A youth in the crowd placed the muzzle of his pistol at Tiwari's back and pulled the trigger, but the cartridge misfired. Tiwari's companions seized the assailant, Ramesh Chandra, who fired twice, but did no harm. Ramesh was sentenced to ten years' rigorous imprisonment.

The extent to which terrorism had gained a hold, and in turn had been fought by the police, can be gauged by the following figures, collected in the Punjab at the end of 1931, which include also the figures for the two Lahore conspiracy cases. At that time, three Hindus and two Sikhs had been hanged, while four Hindus and one Sikh were awaiting execution for terrorist crimes. No less than 163 persons had been charged with bomb-making or bomb-throwing, the collection of arms for murderous purposes, the dissemination of leaflets inciting to murder, conspiracy to murder, murder and similar crimes. Of these, forty-six persons had been sentenced to an average sentence of two and a half years, and fifty-seven were still under trial. In addition, eighteen persons had been outlawed and were living hunted lives, while eleven had become approvers. With the exception of forty-five Sikhs and five Mohammedans, all were Hindus.

A meeting of the H. S. R. A., which had gradually been built up again after the disorganization following Chandra Shekhar Azad's death, was held in Meerut in December

1931, and was attended by representatives from the United Provinces, Delhi, the Punjab and Bengal groups. A rough plan of action for the reopening of hostilities was mapped out, the first step in the campaign being the advertisement of the existence of the party as a means to attracting fresh recruits. A leaflet was widely distributed on 'Independence Day' (January 26th, 1931) throughout the whole of Northern India, although only a few copies reached Delhi and the Punjab.

The first major event of 1932 was the arrest of Yashpal who was absconding from the Lahore and Delhi Conspiracy cases. It was learnt that he was spending the night of January 22/23rd, 1932 at the house of an Irish woman named Mrs. Jafar Ali *alias* Savitri Devi, and early on the morning of the 23rd January, a police party raided the house. After a revolver duel in the semi-darkness Yashpal was captured, and was later sentenced to seven years' rigorous imprisonment for attempted murder. This capture seriously hampered the activities of the central body, and the arrest of another important leader, Daryao Singh, in Meerut struck another telling blow. The local group in Meerut was further disorganised by arrests and searches resulting from information gleaned after Daryao Singh's arrest, and the group's channels of communication were cut. The chief members of the party scattered again, leaving local formations to work on their own lines. In Cawnpore, a group led by the Pande brothers (Surendra and Virendra) formed a dangerous organisation, but action against the leaders under Section 110 (*f*), C. P. C., proved successful and open activities and propaganda gave place to a kind of guerilla warfare and secret plotting. Bomb outrages continued, and between February 23rd and April 8th, 1932, no less than eight such incidents happened in Allahabad. The first bomb, on February 23rd, exploded behind Bahadurganj Police outpost; the next was found in one of the reserve lines barracks on February 27th; that night a third bomb exploded on the roof of P. S. Muthiganj; and on the 28th February another exploded on the roof of the Station Officer's house at P. S. Kydganj. The fifth bomb was found inside the grounds of P. S. Kydganj, and this, of the same cigarette-tin type, contained six live revolver cartridges in addition to the usual missiles. This first batch appeared to be in connection with the celebration of 'Azad' week, held to commemorate the anniversary of the 'hero's' death. Another cigarette-tin bomb exploded in Allahabad on March 28th, 1932, and on April 8th a bomb of the same type was thrown at a constable, who received slight injuries. Unfortunately it was impossible to bring home the crime, although the local revolutionary group headed by Mahabir Prasad Banga was strongly suspected. In April and May, 1932, telegraph wires were cut in several places in the Allahabad, Lucknow and Agra districts, but again the crimes were untraced. In May, Ludhiana district also suffered from this form of mischief.

On the 27th May 1932, as the result of a house search in Cawnpore, several weapons, two bombshells (one bearing the initials H. S. R. A.), cartridges, acids and revolutionary literature were seized. The stock was the remains of Azad's armoury and magazine. On the night of July 4/5 1932, bombs, guns, pistols and cartridges were recovered in Gurdaspur. The investigation led to the disclosure of a small local conspiracy, the participators in which were all Sikhs. Fourteen persons were sentenced to terms ranging from three to thirteen years. When the judgment was delivered the convicted persons hurled abuse at the police, shouted revolutionary slogans, used insulting language to the Judge and called on Indians to expel the British from India. Another local conspiracy was unearthed in Agra in the same month, following an armed dacoity on July 13th, 1932, when some seven or eight persons threatened a cashier with a dagger in the course of looting a cloth dealer's shop in the city. The gang was also suspected of a dacoity which had taken place in March 1932, when a *darwan* was seriously injured but nothing was stolen. Bacha Babu, the leader, and ten others were arrested. On a search of Bacha Babu's house on August 5, 1932, four revolvers, two pistols, some acid and a dagger were recovered. For this offence Bacha Babu was sentenced to seven years' rigorous imprisonment. Meanwhile, on July 27, 1932, at Delhi, two Bengalis and two others attacked a police constable in the Qudsia Gardens in order to steal his revolver. They were arrested and Harbandhu Samajdar was sentenced to seven years' rigorous imprisonment, while Ganpat Lal and Bhagwan Sahai were sentenced to five years' rigorous imprisonment each.

On the August 12, 1932, in consequence of information received, the police raided several houses in Cawnpore and in one of them arrested Rajendra Prasad Nigam, an absconder, who was known to have been in touch with the H. S. R. A. leaders in Delhi and in the U. P. From his belongings were recovered a revolver, an automatic pistol and some ammunition. At another house, resistance was offered and Haldhar Bajpai fired five or six shots, slightly wounding a sub-inspector and narrowly missing the Superintendent of Police. In this house, two revolvers and cartridges were recovered as well as other arms and ammunition; a quantity of H. S. R. A. leaflets and other literature was recovered in other searches. Further searches were carried out in Dehra Dun, and many arrests were made. There was a slight lull in terrorist outrages in the provinces of Upper India from August to November 1932, but on November 22, 1932, two youths stopped the Dehra Dun express between Lucknow and Hardoi by pulling the communication cord and, alighting from the train, fired three shots at the guard, whom they wounded. They then ran away, but were arrested next day in possession of a gun and a revolver. They were sentenced to 7 years' rigorous imprisonment each.

On January 1933, Prabhat Chakravarti was arrested in Calcutta and a cypher obtained from his possession gave, among many others, addresses revealing his connections in Allahabad, Benares, Bulandshahr, Shahjahanpur and the Punjab. Searches were carried out in all of these places, but the only success obtained was in Allahabad where documents were recovered establishing the existence of an organisation for revolutionary propaganda in the U. P. under the direction of the Bengal group. The U. P. organiser proved to be Sitanath De *alias* Brahmachari, who had long been wanted by Bengal and had spent many years in the United Provinces and the Punjab.

The year 1933 opened with increased activity in the United Provinces, but the outrages were of local importance only. On January 4th, 1933, three youths of St. John's College, Agra, attacked a postman in Agra who was carrying Rs. 4,475, but were surprised and diverted. On the 5th January, Chandrama Singh, who was wanted for attempted murder in Bihar, was arrested in Cawnpore after a revolver duel with the police. He was sentenced to 2 years' rigorous imprisonment under the Arms Act and later to five years' rigorous imprisonment for attempt to murder. On February 2nd, 1933, at Sitapur, a postman was robbed of Rs. 633 by two youths armed with a revolver and a spear. The youths were arrested and sentenced each to 3 years' rigorous imprisonment and a fine of Rs. 325. On February 20th, 1933, a brutal dacoity was committed by six persons in Lyallpur. The leader, Kirpal Singh, confessed that his gang, which was composed of four Sikhs, a Hindu and a Musalman, was in league with the local terrorist party, which had intended to commit political dacoities, had not one member disappeared with the funds. On the 25th February 1933, Nand Kishore Nigam, an absconder in the Delhi conspiracy case, was arrested at Cawnpore. He was sentenced to two years' rigorous imprisonment for being in possession of an unlicensed revolver. On the 15th March another absconder, Vishwanath, who was wanted in Gaya for robbery and conspiracy, was arrested, also with a loaded revolver in his possession, at Benares.

Thereafter, outrages ceased with almost startling suddenness, but the police made frequent captures of bombs and arms during the year, and not a few leading terrorists were arrested on one charge or another. Hans Raj, who was wanted in Sialkot, was arrested in Muzaffarnagar on April 17, 1933, and Swami Satyanand was arrested when his house was searched for absconders on May 6th. He was sentenced to 2 years' rigorous imprisonment for the illegal possession of arms, a box containing two revolvers, one automatic pistol, one country-made pistol, a gun and cartridges having been recovered.

Thus by the middle of 1933, the Punjab Government could say that, with the help of the Special Powers Ordinance of July 1932, and the Punjab Criminal Law (Amendment) Act of November 1932, terrorism was definitely under control. While there was reason to apprehend that there was still much overt sympathy with the movement, the attitude of the Legislative Council to the bill enacted as the Punjab Criminal Law (Amendment) Act of 1932, was encouraging, in that terrorism and violence were openly condemned. Nevertheless over 3,000 names were by then indexed in the terrorist records of the Punjab C. I. D., the majority of whom were potential organisers, so that constant vigilance and unceasing preventive action were still necessary. In the United Provinces it was recognised that the terrorists had decided to call a halt in face of the strong Government action directed against them. Here there was exhibited a tendency to accept Communist doctrines and the Communist argument that individual terrorism merely leads to the strengthening of Government measures for resisting political change.

On October 29th, 1933, the Punjab Police, acting on information received, searched a tonga which was being driven along the Mall, Lahore, and recovered a country-made bomb designed to be exploded by electricity, but it was found that the informer was the real culprit. In the United Provinces, the notorious absconder and inter-provincial organiser from Bengal, Sitanath De, was arrested in Benares on November 24th, 1933, in connection with Prabhat Chakravarti's party of Bengal. The investigation following the arrest did not disclose any deep-rooted organisation of the party in the United Provinces ; it was acknowledged that there were sympathisers in a number of districts, but it could not be said that the organisation had gained a firm foothold anywhere else than in Benares where it was under control. Benares, and especially the Hindu University, continued to be a forcing house for seditious instruction and propaganda and a harbourage for revolutionaries from all provinces. The town also contained the only United Provinces branch of the Rashtriya Swayam Sewak Sangh, organised by Dr. Hidgewar of Nagpur, the chief objects of which were to infuse a military spirit into Hindus and to impart physical training, including the use of *lathis*, spears and daggers.

Although the Punjab was quiet in 1934, there were several minor outbreaks in the United Provinces, but none of the cases was sent to court. Two crude bombs were thrown in Cawnpore causing no damage as they did not explode. The suspects were dealt with under section 110, Cr. P. C. A more serious case was a dacoity in Ballia district on December 25th, 1934, but terrorists only formed a minor part of the gang. The prosecution of terrorists found with arms in their possession continued ; and further indications were found that Communist methods were being adopted and that the terrorist plan of individual outrages was being replaced by preparation for mass action. Attempts were made to link up parties, and in October 1934 a meeting was held in Bombay with a view to forming a Central Party consisting of terrorists, communists and the left wing of the Congress Party.

In January 1935, Sudhir Adhikari, the Benares leader of Sita Nath De's party, was arrested for the Bengal police in Allahabad, where he had made his headquarters and was attempting to organise, and two ciphers were recovered from his possession. One of these ciphers contained names of the party members, and searches were carried out in Bengal and the United Provinces. On January 11, 1935, Desraj Singh of Banda was arrested at Benares in possession of 25 rounds of revolver ammunition. The following day a revolver was found in Ram Lachan Tiwari's room at Ballia, and Tiwari and Gokul Das, the leader of a party, were arrested. A note book in cipher was recovered from Desraj Singh which gave the names of 67 members of his party. Searches were made in fourteen districts of the United Provinces, in the Punjab, C. P. and Bihar, and a pistol, ammunition and a mass of revolutionary literature were obtained.

In the United Provinces, Kesho Prasad Sharma, a Bihari ex-student of the Benares Hindu University, who had been arrested with Sita Nath De in November 1933, but had not been prosecuted for want of evidence, was the most important organiser. During the year 1935 he toured extensively, visiting Calcutta, Patna and Delhi besides several centres in the United Provinces, and on being arrested in Allahabad on December 9, 1935, was sent to Bengal to be dealt with under the Bengal Criminal Law Amendment Act.

Towards the end of 1934 an individual described as Rajendra Narayan Sharma of Lahore came to notice in Lucknow labour circles. He established close touch with known communist suspects, and in February 1935 formed contact with a member of Sita Nath De's party at Benares. He was arrested at Lucknow in May 1935 and was identified as Ram Nath, a terrorist absconder from the Punjab and a member of Shambhu Nath's section of Sita Nath De's Anushilan Party. He was wanted for harbouring Prem Kumar, a revolutionary absconder, and was sent to Amritsar to stand his trial.

Delhi was the scene of two acts of bomb-throwing during 1935. On September 30th, a bomb exploded in the New Delhi Post Office, and on October 20th a bomb was thrown from the over-bridge on the New Delhi Railway Station and exploded close to two Europeans who were standing near the Frontier Mail. A small gang, with no outside connections was found to have been responsible for these two crimes. Shiv Shankar was sentenced to four years rigorous imprisonment, but the other accused was acquitted. Two others of the gang had become approvers.

In 1936 there was an outbreak of explosions in the United Provinces, but none was of such a nature as to be alarming, and connections with terrorists were not apparent or proved. On October 12, 1936, in Cawnpore, when a Dr. S. Sen was called to a house, he was suddenly surrounded by twelve armed and masked men who stated that they were members of a revolutionary society and forced him to write a letter to his father asking for payment of Rs. 5,000 as ransom. Dr. Sen was rescued by his father and friends, the kidnappers having fled. Investigation in this case has not been completed at the time of going to press, but one Shekhar Nath Ganguli, a previous convict and an externee from Bengal, has been arrested. He had come from Barisal, where he belonged to the Jugantar group, to Allahabad and subsequently proceeded to Cawnpore, where he joined the 'Nav Chetan Sangh', a revolutionary organisation recently formed by a local suspect, Sheo Kumar.

No cases of open terrorism occurred in the Punjab and Delhi during 1936, except that, as in the United Provinces, revolutionary leaflets appeared from time to time. These leaflets showed a distinct communist bias, illustrating the general inclination of terrorists to forsake, at least for the time being, individual terrorism, and to follow a safer, but none the less effective, path towards mass revolution.

CHAPTER IV.

ASSAM.

Despite its proximity to Bengal, Assam was not, in the early years of terrorism, seriously affected by the cult. In 1913, a Bengali was killed at the gate of the house of Mr. Gordon, the Sub-Divisional Officer of Maulvi Bazar in the SylhetDivision, when a bomb which he was carrying, exploded. From that date until 1931 there was no terrorist crime in the province, but there was a constant infiltration of Bengalis with terrorist leanings. In 1926, information was received that revolutionaries were working a bomb factory in a tea-garden in Sylhet, although no further clue was discovered.

In October 1927, the Bihar Police arrested Birendra Nath Bhattacharji, a Bengali who claimed to be reorganising the H. S. R. A., and from his possession recovered a book in cypher containing many names and addresses. As a result, simultaneous raids were made in the provinces concerned and various incriminating articles and documents were seized from the houses searched. Five names appeared in the cypher list with addresses in Assam. Upendra Chandra Dhar, of Hailakandi, Cachar, who had read for a time in the Chittagong Medical School and had subsequently visited Agra, Allahabad, Cawnpore, Gaya, Calcutta and several other places, was arrested. He admitted that he was a member of the terrorist party and that his leader, Birendra Nath Bhattacharji, had deputed him to Assam to recruit members for the party. Upendra was one of the accused in the Deoghar Conspiracy Case which had been instituted in Bihar, and was convicted there. A conspiracy case was launched at Hailakandi, but was withdrawn after a long investigation had been made in view of the fact that the principal conspirators in the meantime had been dealt with in Deoghar. It is known that early in 1929, Probhat Chakravarti, a prominent terrorist of Bengal, left for Assam, where he spent some months trying to organise a party in Sylhet, before he returned to Bengal. Thereafter, various leaders held sway for short periods, but the party did not come prominently to notice, and, in fact, the activities of the members appear to have been directed more towards Bengal than to Assam.

Terrorism resumed. In the first few months of 1931, the long immunity from terrorist crime which the province had enjoyed, was broken by a series of mail robberies and dacoities in Sylhet district, but there was no definite evidence to show that terrorists were responsible for the outrages, except in a train robbery which occurred in the Surma mail train on the night of 13th November 1931, when an assistant manager of a tea estate was robbed of Rs. 270 at the point of a revolver. The victim changed his statement before a magistrate and was successfully prosecuted for having given false information, although it was later learnt that the robbery had actually been committed by four youths of the Jugantar party from Comilla, Bengal.

On the 3rd January 1932 two clerks were robbed of Rs. 15,000 by four armed youths in a running train between Shahjibazar and Chatian railway stations. Terrorists were strongly suspected but the crime could not be brought home. On January 31st, 1932, three persons broke into Shamsernagar post office but were disturbed by the Post Master who fired off a gun. The culprits escaped. Another serious crime took place on February 27th, 1932, when four masked men entered the mail-van of a train travelling between Duliakhal and Paikpara, held up the mail peon at the point of a revolver and looted the bags of some Rs. 4,000. When the train stopped at Paikpara the culprits made good their escape. In September of the same year, a dacoity at Dughar, Sylhet, believed to have been committed by some 25 terrorists, resulted in a loss of Rs. 15,000. On November 7th, 1932, Kazaldara post office was attacked by armed dacoits, who were disturbed before they could manage to secure any loot.

On January 12th, 1933, four *bhadralok* went out in a taxi to Chandpur, in Sylhet district, chloroformed the driver and handyman, and assaulted two mail runners. Shots were fired and the robbers made off in the car with some Rs. 6,000 in insured covers and cash, to Kuighat, where the vehicle was abandoned. This crime was followed by a daring dacoity in the Sylhet district on February 7th, 1933, by men dressed in European style and armed with revolvers and rifles. A boy was shot dead and Rs. 3,000 were stolen. On March 13th, 1933, a mail peon who was taking bags from Itakhola Post Office to the railway station was attacked by six youths, one of whom Ashit Chandra Bhattarcharjee, defied interference from the crowd by brandishing a pistol. The post bags were torn open and insured articles valued at about Rs. 2,000 were stolen by the gang, which fired at its pursuers as it made off, killing one man and wounding two. Bhattarcharjee was apprehended on the spot by the infuriated crowd and three others were caught in a nearby village. The remaining two absconded with the booty. One of these was arrested on June 29, 1933. Bhattarcharjee was sentenced to death, and three others to transportation for life. Bhattarcharjee and two others were residents of Bengal, but the fourth was of Sylhet. On September 2, 1933, at about 4·30 A.M., another mail dacoity was committed, this time at Shamsernagar railway station. The Surma mail had just left when a man assaulted the peon who was about to take away the bags. The peon closed with his assailant, upon which five other persons came up and carried off the bags which contained Rs. 2,130 in cash and notes. Shots were fired, but no one was injured. The terrorist party at Maulvi Bazar organised by Anil Das was strongly suspected of this crime, but searches of the houses of the members produced nothing of value to the investigation although some proscribed books and suspicious correspondence were found.

The authorities in Assam had already realised that the subversive actions of terrorists in the Province were becoming dangerous, and that connections existed with the dangerous Sri Sangha of Dacca, with Tippera, Calcutta and other important centres of revolutionary activity in Bengal. In order to obtain more information and so be armed for the combat with the movement a special force was sanctioned in 1933. The subversive elements were mainly imported from Bengal, either when matters became too hot for terrorists there, or as deliberately planned attempts to infuse the cult of terrorism into Assam and to raise funds for the parties in Bengal, by the commission of crimes and by the collection of subscriptions. In the course of the investigation of a fraud case on Messrs. Grindlay and Co.'s bank in Calcutta, several arrests were made of terrorists in Assam, including Tara Kishore Bardhan. Information then came to light that this man had been the leader of a strong party in the Sylhet district with connections with the Calcutta Jugantar group, members of which had been responsible for several of the terrorist crimes committed there, including the Chandpur mail robbery. Another important leader was Anil Das. Another mail-dacoity was committed on 5th December 1933 when five *bhadralok* youths armed with a crow-bar, a toy pistol and a hockey-stick, attacked the runners carrying the mail at Sonaru, between Habiganj and Ajmiriganj in the Sylhet district and escaped with insured covers worth Rs. 7,680.

The Sylhet Organisation. In February 1934, the Assam Police recovered the rules and regulations of the Sylhet District Revolutionary Organisation. It is one of the most elaborate sets of terrorist rules that has been seen, the translation covering no less than twenty-three pages of typed foolscap. After dealing with the organisation which, incidentally, specifies that members should never be recruited from any community other than Hindus, it proceeds to deal with the future programme. It admits that individual terrorism may have to be put into effect against 'police officers, spies, magistrates, judges, Governors, and other high officials', but it recognises that after such activities, 'Government takes recourse to severe measures' which interfere with the progress of the *Samiti* and bring about a demoralisation in the revolutionary organisation, though it may kindle fire to some extent. The main objective, which is the overthrow of the existing Government, is therefore to be attained by mass revolution. In pursuance of this object it is specified that a list of arms licence-holders should be obtained and efforts made to acquire their arms by all possible means, that full information must be obtained of the dispositions of troops and police, and that maps must be prepared of the district showing all roads, railways, telegraph lines, etc. The need of recruiting signalmen and other railway employees as members is recognised, as is also the need of a spy department to gain the confidence of C. I. D. officials or to acquire their secrets by obtaining employment with them as servants. The immediate necessity is the acquisition of money which 'must be collected by any means whatsoever as early as possible', dacoity being specifically mentioned as one of these means.

Another serious crime was committed in the province by terrorists when, on the night of February 13th, 1934 a rich money-lender's house in Sardabaz, a village in Sylhet district, was attacked by a gang of armed *bhadralok* youths who broke open a chest and made off with Rs. 450. On March 2nd, 1934, four *bhadralok* youths, armed with deadly weapons, entered the shop of a Marwari at Kalighat in Sylhet town, raided the 'gadi' where the day's takings were being counted, and ran off with as much money, some Rs. 2,000, as they could grab. They were chased and three were arrested. The magazine of an automatic pistol was found on the 'gadi' and the pistol itself in a drain close by. The case was tried by Special Tribunal and Ajit Kumar Chakravarti and Benoy Bhusan Laskar were sentenced to seven years' rigorous imprisonment each, and Motilal Roy to 5 years' rigorous imprisonment. The approver, Benoy Bhusen Deb Roy was pardoned. This was followed, on March 20th, 1934, by an attack by two armed youths on the mail-runners of the Ajmiriganj-Baniachang line at Umednagar. Rs. 9,585 were stolen, but one of the youths was caught after a chase and Rs. 6,785 were recovered from him. The other youth surrendered a few days later. The two accused, Satyendra Chandra Ray and Gopendra Nath Ray, both of Sylhet district, were sentenced to six years' rigorous imprisonment each. The threat of terrorism had now become so pronounced in Assam that in March 1934 special legislation in the form of a Criminal Law Amendment Bill was introduced into the Local Assembly and passed. Still, outrages did not cease for on June 11th, 1934, the communication cord of a mail train was pulled shortly after leaving Tinsukia in the Lakhimpur district. Armed *bhadralok* youths then attacked the mail van and robbed the bags of over Rs. 3,000. Arrests were made subsequently and some of the loot was recovered, together with a revolver, gun and dagger. Seven youths were sent for trial and Sachindra Kumar Das and Bipulananda Kar Chaudhri were sentenced to seven years' rigorous imprisonment each; the approver was discharged and the rest were given the benefit of the doubt and acquitted. On September 18th, 1934 yet another mail dacoity was committed near Jalsuka in the Sylhet district, when the boat carrying the mails was fired upon by six armed *bhadraloks* from another boat. Four youths then boarded the mail-boat, threw the two runners into the river and decamped with articles worth Rs. 16,135. The dacoits were chased by police and villagers in boats and twenty miles away, near Sarmangal, shots were exchanged. The Assistant Sub-Inspector in charge of the pursuit party and a runner were both wounded.

An improvement. In the meantime, action had been taken under the special powers provided and the more prominent terrorists had been interned. Vigorous action in the recovery of arms also had its effect, and, in 1935, there was only one attempted terrorist crime, on May 31st, when two youths, Paresh Chandra Chattarji, of Dacca and Habiganj, and Pradyumna Nag of Habiganj attacked a mail-runner, tried to gag him and threatened him with daggers. Help, however, was at hand, and the culprits made off, but were pursued and Pradyumna was actually speared by the runner. Both were arrested and were subsequently sentenced to 7 years' rigorous imprisonment each.

Since that date no terrorist crime has been committed in Assam, where terrorism is on the wane. It has been possible to release some of the *detenus*, but a constant watch is still necessary over the potential hot-bed in Sylhet.

CHAPTER V.

BIHAR AND ORISSA.

Until 1936 these provinces were united, but so far as terrorism is concerned, Orissa has not been affected to any great extent. The remarks which follow will, therefore, be mainly confined to Bihar.

Situated as it is between Bengal and the United Provinces, it is not surprising that Bihar has, from time to time, been the scene of terrorist activities and crime. There are considerable differences of race and language between the inhabitants of the Province and those of Bengal, although many Bengali settlers and Hindus of Bengal descent reside in Bihar. Intellectually keener, as a rule, than the true natives of the province, these have become prominent in Government services, in offices of all kinds and at the Bar.

Prior to 1917, Bihar had been the scene of two of the most abominable crimes in the whole history of terrorism. In 1908, two Bengali youths of the Calcutta Anushilan Samiti, who had been deputed to murder Mr. Kingsford, Judge of Muzaffarpur, who, as Chief Presidency Magistrate, Calcutta, had become distasteful to terrorists, hurled a bomb at a carriage outside Mr. Kingsford's house, and murdered two ladies who were driving in it. One shot himself dead on arrest and the other was hanged. No further crime occurred until 1913 when three Mahratta youths who had been studying in the school of a notorious revolutionary in Jaipur State, murdered a rich Hindu priest as well as his unfortunate boy-servant. The object appears to have been to collect funds for revolutionary purposes.

Early Activities. Thus, prior to the period with which we are dealing, Bihar had not greatly suffered from internal terrorist activity, although Phanindra Nath Ghosh, of Bettiah, who had joined the Bengal Anushilan Party in 1916 had attempted to organise parties in Bihar. He was interned for one year under the Defence of India Act in 1918. After his release he again engaged in organising the party at

Bettiah and in 1925 organised a band of volunteers known as the Hindustani Sewa Dal for the purposes of political activities. In 1926 he went to Benares and there met some of the members of the United Provinces revolutionary party, which had been greatly weakened by the Kakori case arrests. Later, Ghosh met Jatindra Nath Sanyal, whose two brothers had been arrested in the Kakori case and were later convicted, and by 1927 Phanindra Nath Ghosh was active in the traffic of arms between Bengal and the United Provinces. Towards the end of the year Sheo Varma, who had been sent to Bettiah by J. N. Sanyal, and Bijoy Kumar Sinha, visited him to obtain a revolver, but Ghosh himself took the weapon to Benares where it was subsequently used in the attempt on the life of Rai Bahadur J. N. Banerjee in 1928.

The Deoghar Conspiracy Case. Meanwhile, during the year 1927, a new figure had appeared, first in Calcutta and later in Bihar, in the person of Birendra Nath Bhattacharji, of Dacca, who claimed to be in touch with revolutionaries in Assam and the United Provinces, and who was endeavouring to resuscitate the Hindustan Republican Association which had been stunned by the Kakori case. He was making rapid strides in establishing his leadership, when he was arrested in Deoghar, in possession of two Mauser pistols and cartridges. A note book in cypher was recovered from his room, which, decoded, gave the names and addresses of 68 members of the revolutionary parties in Bengal, Assam, Bihar, the United Provinces and Punjab, and the names of eighteen intended victims. Searches were made in many places, and one in Allahabad was productive of much incriminating material, including two revolvers, explosives, and literature. Eventually a conspiracy case was instituted which led to the conviction of twelve Bengalis at Deoghar.

The Hindustan Socialist Republican Army. Phanindra Nath Ghosh spent the first few months of 1928 in Calcutta, but his activities there appear to have been of no importance. During these years, Ghosh had enlisted, among others, Man Mohan Banerjee and Kanwal Nath Tewari. In August 1928, Ghosh was visited by Bijoy Kumar Sinha, who suggested the formation of a new party to be composed of the existing parties in the Punjab, United Provinces, Bihar and Bengal, and proposed a secret meeting at Delhi on the 8th and 9th September 1928. Accordingly, on the 4th September, Ghosh and Man Mohan Banerjee went to Delhi and on the 9th September, having seen the place on the previous day, they went to the appointed rendezvous in the Feroz Shah Tughlak Fort, and were joined by Kundan Lal, a member of the Punjab party. A short distance away, Bhagat Singh, Sukh Dev, Jai Dev, Sheo Varma, Bijoy Kumar Sinha, Brahm Dutt and Surindra Nath Pande were holding a meeting. Next day, Phanindra Nath Ghosh and Man Mohan Banerjee attended another meeting with Bhagat Singh, Kundan Lal, Bijoy Kumar Sinha, Sukh Dev, Jai Dev and Sheo Varma, and it was agreed to form an amalgamated party to be known as the Hindustan Socialist Republican Army; with a central committee on which Phanindra Nath Ghosh was to serve as the member for Bihar. One of the resolutions passed was that bomb-makers from Bengal should be invited to teach members of the party how to prepare bombs, and for this purpose Phanindra Nath Ghosh and Bhagat Singh arranged to meet in Calcutta during the Congress to be held in December. Dacoities were proposed and Bihar was selected as a suitable venue, with Bhagat Singh and Ghosh again as the members to arrange the actual crimes. After the meeting Ghosh went to Meerut and then to Amritsar and Lahore before returning to Bihar, where in September he was visited by Bhagat Singh, but the proposal to commit a dacoity was abortive. Phanindra Nath Ghosh did, however, make over a revolver to Bhagat Singh.

Other Workers. Another active organiser in Bihar was Rambinode Singh of Malkachak, district Saran. This man, like Phanindra Nath Ghosh, had been interned under the Defence of India Act, and after his release had founded, in 1921, at Malkachak an ashram as the Gandhi Kutir. By 1929 the ashram had been ruined by the peculations of its founder and a Congress Board was formed to investigate misappropriations amounting to nearly one lac of rupees, connected with the manufacture and sale of khaddar. A mutual friend of Phanindra Nath Ghosh and of Rambinode Singh was Satnarayan Singh of Karhio, district Muzaffarpur, but by 1928 a much more important person came to the fore, in Jogendra Shukul of Jalalpur, district Muzaffarpur. This man had spent many years in the Punjab and the United Provinces and had earned a reputation amongst revolutionaries for his part in the smuggling of arms in Bhopal. He now returned to Bihar and made the Hajipur Gandhi Ashram his centre. Under his leadership the gang committed a series of dacoities and other crimes, ostensibly with the object of collecting money for political and revolutionary purposes, but in reality to satisfy the cupidity of the members of the gang.

The first crime which has been traced to this gang of terrorists was a dacoity with murder at Bazidpur on November 9th, 1928, when a party armed with guns, revolvers, kukris and steel chisels, shot one of the inmates of the house and looted nearly a quarter of a lac s worth of property. No clue was obtained for many months, but it was strongly suspected that Rambinode Singh, Jogendra Shukul and Satnarayan Singh were the leaders. Jogendra Shukul was also strongly suspected to have led local criminals in a dacoity at Bahlolpur in Muzaffarpur district on January 11th, 1929 when a revolver was fired and Rs. 400 in cash was stolen. In this case, some of the dacoits drove to the scene in a motor-car. In a third instance, when cash and property worth Rs. 2,800 were stolen in a house-breaking case at Garaul, district Muzaffarpur, on 5th April 1929, Jogendra Shukul was named as a culprit by an accused who confessed before a Magistrate, but the case was not sent for trial.

Two months later, a dacoity was committed at Maulania in Bettiah district on June 8th, 1929, and ornaments valued at Rs. 1,200 were stolen. In the course of the crime one man was killed by a spear-thrust. While the investigation was proceeding, Phanindra Nath Ghosh and Manmohan (*alias* Manohar) Banerjee had been arrested in connection with the Lahore Conspiracy Case, and in the course of lengthy confessions detailing their activities all over the north of India, Manohar disclosed that this Maulania dacoity had been committed at his instigation by Jogendra Shukul and a mixed band of revolutionaries and ordinary dacoits, the object being to collect funds for the Punjab cases, and for absconders such as Chandra Shekhar Azad. As a result the two revolvers used in the crime and most of the stolen property was recovered, and Manohar's servant, Raghuni Chamar, was made an approver. Upon this, Jogendra Shukul went into hiding, but was still visited by youths from all over Tirhut, some of whom were trained by him, the training including practice in revolver shooting on the banks of the Ganges. In December 1929 three participants in the Maulania dacoity were sentenced to ten years' rigorous imprisonment each.

For the time being the party did not indulge in open acts of violence but in May 1930, Jogendra Shukul led his gang in the commission of two dacoities. On the 29th May, a car containing six people drove into a village, Jhajhra, in Darbhanga district, and its occupants fired a number of shots. After threatening a householder with torture the floor was dug up, and the dacoits, some of whom were dressed in khaki shirts and shorts, decamped with Rs. 6,500 in cash. Two days later a larger party, similarly armed with guns, swords and kukris, and using a car, as at Jhajhra, looted property worth Rs. 4,000 at Dheluaha in the Champaran district. Some of the inmates of the raided house were wounded by gun-shots. In the course of the ensuing investigation, the Gandhi Kutir at Malkachak was raided on June 11th, 1930, and after a desperate struggle Jogendra Shukul was arrested. A loaded revolver was found under his pillow. Ten days later another revolver, many shot-gun cartridges and several kukris were recovered from Rambinode Singh's house. Other recoveries included maps of the scenes of both the Jhajhra and Dheluaha crimes. Cases were instituted and in what is known as the Tirhut Conspiracy Case, Jogendra Shukul was sentenced to ten years' rigorous imprisonment and seven others to lesser terms. Jogendra Shukul was later convicted to serve 10 years' rigorous imprisonment for his part in the Maulania dacoity and Rambinode Singh was sentenced to two years' imprisonment for having harboured

Shukul. While still under trial determined efforts were made for the escape of the leaders. Letters were smuggled out of Jail, asking the gang to supply revolvers, ammunition, ropes, swords, chloroform and money. The plan became known and it was found that an iron bar in Shukul's cell had been filed through. A saw was recovered from a warder, a revolver, ammunition, daggers and a bomb from a near-by temple, and ropes and chloroform from a member of the gang.

In the absence of the leaders the gang was inspired by Ramdeni Singh, who had escaped from jail, and who conspired to murder one Bageran Singh whom the party suspected of having betrayed Shukul. The plan fell through on two occasions, and then Ramdeni plotted his last adventure. Accompanied by four other members he attacked the railway staff at Hajipur Railway Station on June 15th, 1931, while they were transferring a bag containing over Rs. 600 to a train. The station-master was shot dead with a revolver, a clerk was shot in the leg and a menial was slashed with a kukri. The culprits then made off with the money, but quarrelled over the division of the spoil. Ramdeni was arrested three weeks later and his notebook showed how the money had finally been distributed. He was hanged in 1932 for the crime.

Meanwhile two youths, Ram Bhawan Singh and Ramjanam Singh, leaders of local volunteers, who, whilst serving sentences for civil disobedience, had been corrupted by Jogendra Shukul, Rambinode and Ramdeni, were busy organising a local branch of the Hindustan Socialist Republican Army in Chapra town. Starting as an association of high-souled patriots this soon developed into a gang of thieves and robbers. They began with threatening leaflets to police officers and liquor dealers, and in April 1931 are believed to have hurled a bomb at a house in which an Indian Assistant Superintendent of Police was staying. But funds were running short, and the members of the party decided on a robbery. The first attempt was abortive, and to assist their plans, many ordinary local criminals were enrolled. No less than four attempts were made to rob a Math of Phulwaria, the magnet being three gold bricks and Rs. 30,000 in cash which the priest was said to possess. On one of these occasions they arranged to get help from Ramdeni Singh but the arrangements went wrong. At the fourth attempt, on 22nd August 1931, they carried arms and bombs, one of which Rambhawan threw, causing injuries to an inmate of the house, so that a leg had to be amputated. A second bomb exploded in Rambhawan's hand, completely severing a portion of the limb. This catastrophe frightened the party, which fled from the scene. The recovery of the severed hand led to the exposure of the gang, most of the members of which hailed from Chapra town or Saran district, but one was Surajmal Singh of the Sultanpur district of the United Provinces. In the subsequent conspiracy case which was instituted, Rambhawan Singh received sentences totalling ten and a half years and six others were convicted to lesser terms.

Just before the Phulwaria event took place, Ram Naresh was arrested on Chapra Railway Station in illegal possession of a revolver and a phial of chloroform. It was known that he intended to join the Chapra party in some dacoity. He was sentenced to two years' imprisonment. Two other revolvers intended for the party were recovered in Lohardaga in August 1931.

That during this period, the Bihar terrorist party was in touch with other branches of the Hindustan Socialist Republican Army is shown by events which took place in June 1931. Hazari Lal, a resident of Patna City, had run away from home in 1925, and, while in Bengal, had been converted to the revolutionary cult. He had returned to Patna and in 1928 was receiving visits from Chandra Shekhar Azad and other terrorist leaders. Azad then took him to Delhi in that year and thereafter Hazari Lal was frequently on the move, paying frequent and long visits to such places as Delhi, Benares, Agra, Lucknow and Ambala. He learnt to drive a car at the last place. He was one of the accused in the Delhi Conspiracy, and, while absconding, had been in Alfred Park, Allahabad, with Azad, when the police surrounded the party and shot Azad. Hazari Lal escaped and then, on June 22, 1931, he and Bhawani Sahai held up a cloth merchant on the outskirts of Lucknow. Pistols were fired and a bomb was thrown, slightly injuring the merchant. Hazari Lal then fled with Suraj Nath Chaube, a student of Patna, to their home town, Patna. Their arrival became known and they were ambushed in Patna City on the night of June 28th, 1931. Chaube was rendered incapable of resistance by a blow from a lathi, but Hazari Lal attempted to escape after throwing his cycle at a police officer. He threw a bomb as he ran away, which seriously injured a Sub-Inspector, a Head-Constable and himself. The Sub-Inspector died an hour later. Both Chaube and Hazari Lal were armed to the teeth. Chaube had two bombs, an automatic pistol and several cartridges and Hazari Lal had another bomb besides the one he had thrown and a loaded service revolver with forty-seven cartridges. Chaube was eventually sentenced to ten years' rigorous imprisonment and Hazari Lal to fourteen years' transportation, but the latter made a valuable statement covering many of the activities of the H. S. R. A., and ten years of his sentence were remitted.

Chaube had already been suspected in a case in which a student, Ramlalit, had been murdered. Besides a long account of his connections and activities with the United Provinces and Delhi branches of the H. S. R. A., Hazari Lal admitted that he had suspected Ramlalit of being a police spy, and that he and Chaube had made an unsuccessful attempt to murder him. Ramlalit was eventually shot, by either Kanhai Missir or Hazari Lal.

On the information thus obtained, a conspiracy case was instituted in Patna. Among the incidents which were included were four bomb explosions which had taken place in Patna district in the preceding eight months and an attempt at armed robbery which had been made at Maharajganj on December 14th, 1930. Hazari Lal was made an approver, and Phanindra Nath Ghosh, who had been approver in the Lahore Conspiracy Case, also gave evidence. Chaube was sentenced to death by the Sessions Judge, but on appeal the sentence was reduced to transportation for life. Three others, including Kanhai Missir were also transported for life and two others were sentenced to seven years' rigorous imprisonment each.

Such vigorous action by the authorities, unassisted by any special provisions of law, was successful in preventing the formation of any strong vigorous party in Bihar. Nevertheless, in common with most other provinces of India during this period, the terrorist virus and the cult of the bomb could not be completely eradicated, and small parties appeared in several districts of the Province from time to time. In accord with the general habit of terrorist parties in Bihar these small parties usually embarked on crimes of violence which led to their detection and punishment.

On the 26th December 1931, a dacoity was committed in a monastery in Champaran district, but the culprits, who were armed with revolvers and crackers, were able to obtain only the meagre contents of an iron safe. The investigation brought in news of a very amateur revolutionary organisation in Gobindganj and eight live bombs and chemicals were recovered. In Patna, the remnants of the gang, which had been dispersed by the Conspiracy case, derailed a train on two occasions, at Sadisapur on January 25th, 1932 and at Futwa two days later. That there was no death on either occasion can only be described as a miracle. The outrages were traced to a Behari Sikh, Ram Partap Singh and three friends, one of whom became an approver. Ram Partap Singh and Sakaldip Gope were sentenced to imprisonment for life and Bhagwan Singh to seven years' rigorous imprisonment. On February 5th, 1932, Mohit Chandra Adhikari, an old revolutionary suspect, led a party which raided the house of a rich Mahant in Amarpur, and murdered their victim. They failed to open a safe, but made off with some Rs. 200 in cash. Mohit and a companion were apprehended that night, and with another were eventually convicted and sentenced to transportation for life. In June, crackers were used in a dacoity at the Sabour Post Office, and information was received that a raid on the Bihpur Post Office had been planned. Two

Congress workers in possession of bombs and daggers were arrested at Bihpur railway station on June 23rd, 1932, and one made a statement showing that a gang of Congress workers and professional criminals had been responsible for the Sabour dacoity besides several thefts and burglaries. Six persons were convicted in the case which was instituted.

A much more serious crime was committed on November 9th, 1932, when Phanindra Nath Ghosh, who had been approver in the Lahore Conspiracy Case and in the Maulania Dacoity case, was stabbed in Bettiah Bazar, and died a week later. His companion, who attempted to catch the murderers, was also wounded and died later. Chandrama Singh and Baikunth Shukul, both absconders, were suspected and eventually arrested, the former after he had fired at the police. He was sentenced to two years' imprisonment for illegal possession of arms, but was acquitted in the murder trial. Baikunth, who was arrested in possession of a dagger and a bomb, was eventually hanged. Both were members of Jogendra Shukul's organization.

There were indications that this gang was still organising under the leadership of Rambinode Singh and on November 24th, 1932, the Local Government declared over forty members to be members of a criminal tribe, the foremost being Rambinode Singh and Satnarayan Singh of Hajipur. The rest consisted mainly of those convicted in the Tirhut conspiracy, the Hajipur dacoity, the Chapra conspiracy, the Patna conspiracy and certain Arms Act cases. There had also been persistent rumours that Jogendra Shukul would attempt to escape from jail, and once at least he nearly succeeded in doing so: to prevent such an occurrence, he and two friends were transferred to the Andamans in December 1932.

Other manifestations of activity in 1932 were the usual crop of revolutionary leaflets and recoveries of arms by the police. A more disturbing factor was the use of the Province as a sanctuary by Bengalis anxious to avoid the special measures in force in their own Province. The coalfields at Jharia were a favourite resort for this purpose. At the same time it was known that Bengalis were in touch with terrorists of Bihar, and this received striking confirmation when Prabhat Chakravarti was arrested by the Calcutta police in January 1933. A list of addresses in cypher which was recovered, included the names of eighteen persons in Bihar the majority of whom were already known, although the connection had not been fully realised. As in other provinces, searches were carried out. In Bihar these resulted in the exposure of a revolutionary group in Gaya. From confessions many hitherto unknown facts were elicited and it was found possible to institute a conspiracy case against nineteen persons, three of whom were made approvers, although one of them retracted in court. The investigation showed that Shyama Charan Barthwar, Sathrughna Saran Singh and Biswanath Prasad were the leaders of the Jubak Sangha which had been started in 1929. Having become dissatisfied with the policy of non-violence, they decided to commit overt acts in order to obtain money for the overthrow of Government Early in 1930 a plan was made to derail the Imperial Mail, but, although a suitable spot was visited, nothing tangible was done. On the 8th March 1930, four of the members headed by Shyama collected at Palmerganj railway station in order to steal the post office cash, but the police, who had been warned, frightened off the gang. This was followed, on the 11th May 1930 by a dacoity in Daltonganj Town when more than five men robbed some cash and half-notes from a mail-runner. This case was undetected until January 1933, when, following a confession, Shyama and Promotho Nath Mukharji were identified. On the 1st August 1930 there was another mail dacoity in Daltonganj Mofussil and Rs. 200 in cash were stolen. This case was similarly undetected until 1933. On the 16th September 1930, Promotho Nath Mukharji stole a sub-inspector's revolver in Daltonganj, and attempted to fire the weapon as he was being chased, but he did not know how to release the safety-catch. For this crime he was sentenced to three years' rigorous imprisonment. Among suspicious correspondence recovered from his possession was a map of the district with a track to Netarhal, a hill-station, marked in red, and instructions for the cutting of telegraph wires. At this time, too, revolutionary pamphlets were being distributed in trains. On the 7th October 1930, Shyama Charan Barthwar was apprehended in Benares State with arms, ammunition and explosives, but escaped with a fine. Members of the party sent threatening letters to officers in Gaya in October of that year, and were also discussing the committal of dacoities at the time. 1931 was quieter, probably because Satrughna Saran Singh was in Jail under the Criminal Law Amendment Act, but in 1932 red H. S. R. A. leaflets of a very inflammatory nature were distributed in Gaya town, and by this time the party was in possession of several weapons. Members of the organisation also paid visits to Calcutta to get in touch with revolutionaries there, but beyond discussions and proposals to murder officials and some traffic in arms, the party was inactive until the end of the year when a serious proposal to commit a robbery was made, but even this came to naught. In the meantime the party had lost some weapons to the police. One of the absconding accused, Biswanath, was arrested in Benares on March 15th, 1933 with a revolver and cartridges in his possession, which he attempted to use. Three formulae for the preparation of bombs and a letter to a co-accused were also recovered. The hearing of the case began on April 3rd, 1933, and seventeen of the accused were committed for trial. Two of the accused went on hunger-strike until they were afforded legal defence, and then, towards the close of the prosecution evidence, thirteen filed petitions confessing their guilt under section 121-A, I. P. C. Eventually sixteen were convicted and sentenced to terms ranging from 1 year's rigorous imprisonment to seven years' rigorous imprisonment with a fine of Rs. 200 for the three principals, Shyama Charan Barthwar, Dr. Kesho Chand and Biswanath Prasad. The High Court upheld the orders. Of those convicted, Barthwar and Prasad had residences in the United Provinces at Benares and Darbhanga respectively, and three others were residents of those provinces.

This case was a very decisive blow to terrorists in Bihar and subsequent activities were very mild. Irreconcilables still plotted and threatened mischief, but they were never able to organise a strong party capable of indulging in the outrages so typical of terrorists in other provinces. An important, but isolated, feature came to light in the Monghyr district, where for some time it had been suspected that arms were being made. On the 6th March 1933 a mistri was caught red-handed just as he had finished making a ·380 bore revolver and was later sentenced to two years' rigorous imprisonment and a fine. In May of the same year other mistries were found making a ·450 revolver. Connections were found with groups in Bengal but it was not shown that the parties in Bihar had procured any weapons from the Monghyr district. In March 1933, following a confession by a chaprassi of a colliery in Jharia, three serrated brass bomb shells were recovered. Three Bengalis, Bhabesh Chandra Hazra, Jyotirmoy Roy and Promotha Nath Ghosh, were found guilty under section 6 of the Explosive Substances Act read with § 120 B., I. P. C., and were sentenced to seven years' rigorous imprisonment each.

On the 17th May 1933 one Doublai Keori, who had been converted to Sikhism and had been given the name of Teja Singh was found dying after an explosion, but although he accused a neighbour of having thrown a bomb at him, his wounds tended to show that he was himself carrying a bomb and that it had exploded in his pocket. This view was strengthened when another bomb was later discovered in his garden. Another explosion took place in a house rented by Malay Krishna Brahmachari who had toured about as a missionary. He was rendered unconscious but was not otherwise hurt. A list was found in his room of 384 names and addresses. Brahmachari was sentenced to seven years' rigorous imprisonment under the Explosive Substances Act. More serious incidents were two attacks on police officers. On December 4th, 1933, Chandrika, an absconder in the Hajipur Dacoity case of 1931, attacked and seriously injured a Sub-Inspector outside Madhupari railway station. He was chased and captured by the police and members of the public and the kukri he had used and some explosives were recovered from him. He was sentenced to transportation for life.

On the 17th December 1933 a constable was assaulted by Sheobachan Singh at Sonepore in Saran district, but the culprit escaped.

On the 15th January 1934, the northern portion of Bihar suffered from a severe earthquake, and, taking advantage of the numerous relief schemes initiated, terrorists trooped into the Province. Although serious results were feared, and it is known that attempts were made to re-organise, no untoward events occurred, except that two boys found a bomb near the temporary hut of a Police Inspector at Madhubani in Darbhanga district on the 23rd April 1934, and were slightly injured when it exploded. A Hindi revolutionary leaflet was found on the spot.

On the 23rd August 1934, the lodgings of Lekh Narayan Lal of Simri, Darbhanga, were searched and explosive substances, pieces of iron and a packet of needles were recovered. He was sentenced to six years' rigorous imprisonment. Recoveries of arms continued to be made and vigorous action sufficed to keep terrorist organisations under ground. The original gang formed by Jogendra Shukul was still hampered by the restrictions of the Criminal Tribes Act, and even the leader, Rambinode Singh, became more reconciled to his enforced inactivity. Action was taken where possible against troublesome organisers and propagandists under the Bihar and Orissa Public Safety Act, and comparative peace obtained for many months. There was a small outbreak on June 1st, 1935 when, forewarned of a planned dacoity, the police waylaid a party in Dhanbad which proposed to rob a Marwari. Four youths were arrested of whom three were sentenced to four years' rigorous imprisonment and a fine, and the fourth was ordered to produce security for good behaviour. This gang was the remnant of the old Jharia party. Following this on July 6th, 1935, an explosion took place in a village Gandhwar, of Tirhut, which caused the death of one Asharfi Thakur, and injured five others, all of whom were arrested. One of the accused, Kameshwar Jha, confessed, and stated that Suraj Narayan Singh, who had been interned had taught them to make bombs. One bomb had been prepared when it exploded. Shibkant Missir, Dayanand Jha and Brahmdeo Thakur were each sentenced to transportation for fourteen years in this connection and Chandrakant Missir was sent to jail for five years. Another explosion took place a year later, on July 5th, 1936, in Patna, when a youth was injured. He admitted that he and five others had been experimenting with bomb ingredients. Still later, on October 5th, 1936, an explosion occurred in Patna in the court-room of the Chief Justice. Some damage was done to the furniture but no injuries resulted. Two days later Harinandan Kahar surrendered and admitted that he had taken a bomb into the High Court and had ignited it there. This case is still under trial at the time of writing.

Apart from these comparatiyely minor outrages which were, for the most part, nothing more than the poorly planned and generally abortive attempts of misguided youths to imitate terrorist activities elsewhere, Bihar has been free from dangerous terrorists. True, the province has suffered from invasions, especially from Bengal, but the police by means of prompt and vigorous action have been successful in curbing serious outward manifestations, and, in fact, the lot of the terrorists in Bihar is by no means an easy one. In the last few years there have been signs, as elsewhwere, of an infusion of communistic ideas not only among Bengali revolutionaries in the province, but also among the indigenous terrorist.

CHAPTER VI.

BOMBAY (excluding SIND).

The first leaders of terrorist thought in India made Bombay their headquarters, but outward manifestations, especially in the form of outrages, were few but spectacular. In 1909, Ganesh Savarkar was sentenced to transportation on a charge of abetment of waging war against the King. Within a few days his brother, Vinayak Savarkar, made a most seditious speech at the India House in London; this speech was followed within twelve days by the murder of Colonel Sir William Curzon Wylie, Political A. D. C. at the India Office. In December of the same year the District Magistrate of Nasik, who had committed Ganesh Savarkar for trial, was shot dead. Three men were hanged and in a conspiracy case which followed, twenty-seven were sentenced to imprisonment. In the same year, two coconut bombs were thrown at the carriage in which Lord and Lady Minto were travelling in Ahmedabad. These serious crimes were followed by a long period of quiet and no major crime was traced to terrorists until 1928, but on October 8th of that year a powerful explosion took place in a third class bogie compartment of an express train from Allahabad as it approached Manmad. Three passengers were killed and eight others injured, among the latter being Harendra Dev Bhattacharji of Benares. This youth made a confession implicating Manmohan Bireshwar Gupta of Benares and stating that he was carrying explosives with the object of attacking the train in which the Simon Commission was to travel. Gupta pointed out a room in Benares which had been used as a factory for explosives. Both were tried and sentenced to seven years' rigorous imprisonment each.

This outrage was followed almost a year later by another again committed by persons who also hailed from outside Bombay Presidency. While passengers and luggage from the Allahabad express were being examined for contraband at Bhusawal railway station on September 11th

1929, Bhagwan Dass and Sadashiv Raghunath, both of Jhansi objected to their trunks being opened. When, at last, Sadashiv's trunk was examined, and a pistol was seen by the Excise Head Constable, the men were told to accompany the police. Bhagwan Dass drew a revolver and fired point blank at a police head-constable, but missed his aim, whereupon Sadashiv picked up the box containing the pistol and bombs and ran away some distance before he was caught. Meanwhile Bhagwan Dass again opened fire, but he was also secured after a chase. Two revolvers and three bombs with many cartridges were recovered. Identifications showed that Bhagwan Dass had been in Lahore with the other conspirators when the plot to murder Mr. Scott was hatched, and which resulted in the murder of Mr. Saunders, and that both Bhagwan Dass and Sadashiv were connected with the bomb factory at Agra. From a statement made by Sadashiv it was learnt that they had been staying in Gwalior and were going to Akola to meet Shivram Rajguru, *alias* 'M' originally of Poona, and another important absconder in the Lahore Conspiracy Case. During the trial of Sadashiv and Bhagwan Dass and when Jai Gopal, an approver in the Lahore Case, had been taken to give evidence, Bhagwan Dass, who had obtained a revolver, suddenly attacked the approver and a Punjab Sub-Inspector of Police, injuring both. For the incident at Bhusawal railway station Sadashiv was sentenced to transportation for fifteen years and Bhagwan Dass to nine years' rigorous imprisonment. For the attack on Jai Gopal and the Sub-Inspector, Bhagwan Dass was sentenced to transportation for life.

Further information was obtained of the movements of Shivram Rajguru in the Bombay Presidency and on September 29th, 1929, this absconder was arrested, with a companion, in Poona. A revolver and cartridges were recovered from the room where they had been sleeping. The garage of an associate, D. B. Karandikar, was also searched and Karandikar was found with a loaded pistol in his pocket. He was arrested, and a search of his house produced a revolver and cartridges. Shiv Ram Rajguru was hanged in the Lahore Conspiracy case.

There were no further outrages in Bombay Presidency for over a year, but, on October 9th, 1930, as Sergeant Taylor of the Bombay Police, his wife and two friends drew up outside Lamington Road Police Station, Bombay, at about midnight, they were fired upon by assailants in another car which was standing on the other side of the road. Both Sergeant Taylor and his wife were injured. The assailants' car was driven away and was later found abandoned near Andheri. The driver of the car was found and he confessed, stating that one Swami and Vaishampayan, members of a local revolutionary party, had fired the shots, and that the act was in pursuance of a conspiracy on the usual terrorist lines. The driver was made an approver but, after a long trial, the case collapsed in court with the acquittal of all the accused.

In common with other provinces, bomb-making was now indulged in by the youths of Bombay Presidency. On December 28th, 1930, a powerful explosion took place in a tailor's shop in Ahmedabad. The tailor and his friend, a Congress picketer, were injured, the latter seriously, and while in hospital this man stated that they, with two others, had been preparing bombs for use against the local Deputy Superintendent of Police. Babubhai Madhaval Patel, the picketer, was made an approver and the tailor, Dahya Dullabh was sentenced to five years' rigorous imprisonment, but successfully appealed to the High Court. On January 13th, 1931, a primitive bomb was thrown into the sub-jail compound at Ahmadnagar, and a day earlier, on the 12th January, a bomb had been thrown near Maharbardi police station, Bombay, while the police were dispersing a crowd. No injuries were caused in either case. On the 29th April 1931, at Rander, Surat, a boy of fourteen years of age, who was experimenting with bomb materials, received injuries in his arms and legs when an explosion took place. There were also explosions on the 16th and 18th June 1931, at Reay, Mazagon, Bombay, when a Hindu boy and a Mohammedan boy were injured.

In May and June, 1931, there were several thefts of arms by young boys in Poona who had formed a revolutionary group there, with a branch at Kolhapur. Ambitious schemes had been prepared, but the only theft attempted produced two rupees when a school was raided. Nine boys were sent for trial, and five of them were convicted and sent to the Borstal School at Dharwar for two years each; Bendale, the oldest, was sentenced to four years' rigorous imprisonment; another was sent to the Borstal School for six years; and two were given the benefit of the doubt and released on security for good behaviour.

Poona was also the scene of one of the most serious terrorist crimes which have been perpetrated in Bombay Presidency. Sir Ernest Hotson, the acting Governor, was making an informal visit to the Ferguson College, Poona, on July 22nd, 1931, when a student, Vasudev Balavant Gogate, suddenly took out a revolver and fired two shots at him. The first bullet was deflected by the stud of a notebook in His Excellency's pocket and the second went wide. Sir Ernest was not hurt and immediately tackled and secured his assailant with the help of his A. D. C., who found another revolver on Gogate. The ensuing behaviour of the other students was far from satisfactory, cries of 'Shame' were made when Gogate was removed by the police, and the rear window of Sir Ernest's car was smashed. Gogate stated that he had acted on his own initiative and had obtained the revolvers and ammunition from Hyderabad, Deccan. He gave his motive as a personal hatred of Sir Ernest Hotson in being appointed to officiate as Governor in preference to an Indian. Gogate was sentenced to eight years' rigorous imprisonment.

After this outrage Bombay was spared from further terrorist crime until March 1933, but in the meantime, signs that the terrorist spirit was alive were visible in the leaflets and posters which frequently appeared, and the tone of the newspapers which, in common with those of other provinces, lauded any 'patriotic' crimes. On March 25th, 1933, a bomb was thrown in the Empire Cinema,

Bombay, slightly injuring one person. Again, on the 6th April 1933, a bottle containing chemicals and pellets was thrown in the same cinema, but the missile did not explode. On the 7th April, a schoolmaster was relieved of the pay of his staff. The investigation of this last crime led to the disclosure of a terrorist group which had been newly organised by Janardhan Balkrishna Bapat, who had been concerned in the Lamington Road shooting case of 1930. A programme to acquire money for the purchase of arms by the commission of crime against property had been drawn up, but the ambitions of the party led to the throwing of the crude bombs at the Empire Theatre before sufficient technique had been acquired. Finally, three persons were charged with manufacturing bombs with the object of endangering public life, but they were not convicted.

Students in Poona were apparently still infected with the terrorist virus for when His Excellency the Viceroy visited that town in July 1933, a revolutionary leaflet in Marathi was found pasted on a wall of the Sir Parashram Bhau College. Nearby was a small glass bottle containing a mixture of potassium chlorate and arsenic sulphide and labelled, 'a simple bomb'. Unfortunately there was insufficient evidence to prosecute the person whom the police were satisfied was the perpetrator. In April 1934, the Presidency, which had been so free from intense revolutionary activity, and had suffered only from sporadic and isolated outbursts, was the scene of a number of bomb explosions, when, during a textile strike at Sholapur, no less than five explosions took place between April 23rd and 26th. The motive appears to have been to terrorise loyal workers. Two types of bottle bomb were used, one designed to explode on concussion and the other by means of a fuse. On April 30th, 1934, a student, Vithal Dasapant Sukhantar, while cycling in Poona, was injured when a package on the handle-bar of his machine exploded. Investigation showed that he and Shridhar Purshottam Limaye, a local Communist, had conspired to obtain explosives, probably with the object of utilising them at Sholapur to terrorise loyal mill-workers. The two accused were sentenced, Sukhantar to 2½ years' rigorous imprisonment and Limaye to 1½ years' rigorous imprisonment.

In the meantime, another indiscriminate attack on a European was made on the 27th April 1934, when Mr. Sweetland, a warrant officer attached to the Auxiliary Force, India, and who was cleaning his motorcycle in the A. F. I. quarters, was attacked by Waman Baburao Chawan, a Mahratta of Ratnagiri, who threw a dagger at Mr. Sweetland, striking him in the cheek. The assailant then attempted to fire a revolver, but the round misfired and Mr. Sweetland threw back the dagger which only hit a wall. The latter then picked up his two children who were playing nearby and rushed up a staircase, followed by Chawan, who fired repeatedly, missing every time. Chawan then ran away but was chased by Mr. Sweetland and two Pathan watchmen and was caught by two policemen. The revolver used was very old with primitive hand-made cartridges. Chawan stated that his motive was a desire to revenge Bhagat Singh's death. He had been staying with Gajanan Vishnu Damle, a revolutionary of Benares. W. B. Chawau was sentenced to seven years' rigorous imprisonment for attempted murder but the case of conspiracy against Chawan and Damle was withdrawn.

On June 22nd, 1934, a bomb of the fuse type was thrown at the bed of a European spinning-master of the Old Mill, Sholapur, but no injury was caused. On June 25th, 1934, shortly before Mr. Gandhi was due to arrive at the Vishram Baug, Poona, another car drove up and Mr. L. B. Bhopatkar alighted. Apparently he was mistaken for Mr. Gandhi, for the band in attendance began to play, and then a bomb exploded violently on the pavement, slightly injuring some twelve persons, including four policemen. Another bomb case occurred on July 9th, 1934, when a boy, Ramchandra Harihar Govani, was severely injured at a caste dinner in Arale while playing with a package which exploded The owner of the room, Janardhan Daji Kshirsagar, wrote to Anant Laxman Bhonde asking him to remove certain articles from a bag in the house of Ramchandra Daji Kshirsagar in Arale, and to throw them into the river. Bhonde handed the letter to the police who found a mixture of potassium chlorate in a tin inside the bag. Janardhan Daji Kshirsagar was subsequently sentenced to eighteen months' rigorous imprisonment under the Explosive Substances Act. Sholapur was again to the fore in August 1934, when two informants told the police that a carpenter of the Old Mill had concealed bombs in his house. A search produced nothing, but the informants then showed where four bottle-bombs of the fuse type were buried. This led to suspicions of a 'plant', and the informants confessed. They were both sentenced to five years' rigorous imprisonment.

Since these cases occurred, there have neen no terrorist outrages in the Presidency, where the movement has never reached serious proportions.

CHAPTER VII.

SIND.

The newly formed province of Sind, which, geographically and ethnographically is widely separated from Bombay, was until the last few years untouched by terrorism, but it was perhaps inevitable that when the cult was at its height in the neighbouring province of the Punjab, some infiltration should occur. The first indications were a number of bomb explosions at Karachi. On September 16th, 1930, a bomb was thrown at the City Police Station, Karachi, but no damage was done except to stain the roof yellow. On the 29th September 1930, an explosion occurred in Rewa Chand's building, Karachi, which blew out a small piece of plaster from a wall. In the first case, two persons, Jethanand and Khairatram, were convicted of a conspiracy to make bombs to destroy Government buildings, but were acquitted on appeal. Ishwar Chand, an approver, stated that they were members of a local revolutionary party which had been formed by one Senji, a Bengali who had visited Karachi in April 1930. In the second case Yagdutt was tried, but the case against him was withdrawn. On November 7th, another bomb was thrown at the City Police Station, Karachi. On November 25th, 1930, some bomb-making materials were found in a house in Karachi, and on November 28th, a bomb was thrown into the compound of the Superintendent of Police, Hyderabad. Meanwhile, revolutionary leaflets were found and threatening letters were received, most, however, bearing signs of having emanated from irresponsible school boys.

An isolated case of dacoity occurred in Nuthio village in the Thar desert on July 23rd, 1931, when three zemindars, two *ex*-convicts and another, entered the village, fired off guns to scare the inhabitants and then looted the houses of two Hindus, carrying off over Rs. 4,500. Investigation showed that the culprits, who were all Sikhs, were collecting money to avenge Bhagat Singh, and that they had been incited by Meng Singh of Kapurthala State who had visited their village shortly before.

Sind was untroubled by terrorists for some time but in 1932, Hans Raj 'Wireless', who had devised the mine which exploded beneath the Viceroy's train at Delhi, and the 'booby-trap' bombs in Lahore, Amritsar and other towns in the Punjab, took refuge in a village near Hyderabad. Information was received and the mill where he was hiding was raided on June 3rd, 1932. Hans Raj was found sleeping with a loaded automatic pistol under his pillow, but he was arrested before he could use the weapon. A search of the premises produced cartridges, two bombs, a hand-made country pistol and dies for making counterfeit coins, seven counterfeit rupees and a minting machine. Hans Raj was sentenced to ten years' rigorous imprisonment under the Arms Act and for possession of the counterfeiting dies and minting machine.

On May 26th, 1932, the Jodhpur Police arrested Gurbaksh Singh, a Punjabi, and Fatehraj of Jodhpur, the first being in possession of a revolver and service ammunition. Gurbaksh Singh disclosed that he was a member of the revolutionary party and had been instructed by Dr. Mool Raj in Multan. He was an absconder in the Delhi Conspiracy case and was closely connected with a party in Karachi, which planned the robbery of a Customs cashier, the blowing up of the train of the Indian States Enquiry Committee, the murder of police officials in Jodhpur and the robbery of a wealthy contractor there. A conspiracy case was instituted against ten accused, of whom two, including Dr. Mool Raj, were acquitted. The others were sentenced to rigorous imprisonment ranging from 6 months to 2½ years. Gurbaksh Singh and Fatehraj were also convicted and sentenced to one year's rigorous imprisonment each in Jodhpur for the offences committed there.

Sind was again favoured with a peaceful period after this conspiracy had been squashed until, in the year 1933, a series of bomb outrages were perpetrated in Hyderabad.

On June 16th, 1933, a bomb was thrown between two British soldiers who were returning to barracks, injuring one of them slightly. On September 17th, a bomb was thrown at four British soldiers, injuring one man and the servant of an Indian who lived nearby. On the 12th October another bomb was thrown in the courtyard of a house in Sanhri Lane, Hyderabad, breaking a few panes and on the 27th November still another missile was thrown near two military policemen, but although one soldier swooned as a result of the explosion, no injuries were caused. In the second case a Mohammedan confessed to the crime, but afterwards retracted and was found to be mentally deranged. Further investigations showed that local Hindus were responsible for all four crimes, and four persons were sent for trial, of whom three were sentenced, Karsondas Liladhar and Virji Kalianji to six years' each and Khemji Khetsi to four years' rigorous imprisonment. There was no indication that these persons were connected with any influential terrorist party and the outrages were little more than school boy pranks. Another somewhat similar case occurred at Larkana on September 2nd, 1934, when a local boy, Daulatgir, was injured and burnt when a letter he was holding exploded. A search of his house produced chemicals and photographs of extreme seditionists.

No further incidents have occurred in Sind.

CHAPTER VIII.

MADRAS.

Madras Presidency has been comparatively free from terrorism, but from time to time has been visited by revolutionaries who have attempted to instil revolutionary principles into the local population. Vanchi Aiyar, who had been recruited by one of these itinerant seditionists, shot Mr. Ashe, District Magistrate of Tinnevelly, dead on June 17th, 1911. The investigation led to the disclosure of a conspiracy and nine men were eventually sent to prison. Thereafter, for many years, no terrorist crimes were committed in the Presidency, although a conspiracy was unearthed in Madura in 1931, when an attempt was made by two armed youths, on June 30th, to rob a clerk of a banking firm who was taking Rs. 30,000 to the Imperial Bank. In the course of the attempt the clerk was shot by one of the robbers. The investigation showed that a terrorist organisation had been formed in 1927 with its headquarters at Madura and with branches in Madras City and other towns of the Presidency. Arms were obtained from the French possessions on the Madras coast and shooting practice was carried out in the hills. Subscriptions were first obtained from sympathisers, but when these failed, Congress funds were diverted to the terrorists, and plans were made to augment these funds by robberies. Unsuccessful attempts were made in 1928 at Negapatam and in 1929 in Trichinopoly. Again, in 1930, an attempt was made to rob a postman in Madras City which resulted in the conviction of two members of the party. Another member was convicted for the attempted murder of his concubine in Madura, and the apparent motive for this crime was the acquisition of her money and jewellery for the party funds. Ambitious schemes for the commission of outrages, which included a proposal to attack the members of the Simon Commission and an attempt on the life of the Collector of Tanjore, failed to materialise. The investigation appears to have frightened the members of the conspiracy, many of whom courted imprisonment as civil resisters rather than face a trial as terrorists. The case was not sent for trial but the eighty-seven members scattered over nine districts were listed to facilitate surveillance over their activities.

The year 1932 saw a series of bomb outrages in Madras, but, fortunately, no great damage was done. In Madura, a bomb was thrown at the Central Police Station on April 21st, 1932 and another on May 13th, 1932. On July 21st a bomb was found in a drain of the Public Prosecutor's house in the same town. These outrages were traced to a disgruntled Congressman who was posing as a Police informer. In Tinnevelly, two bombs were thrown at a constable's house on May 28th, and another bomb was thrown in the police lines on June 2nd. Ramaswami Pillai was sentenced to three years' rigorous imprisonment for his part in this conspiracy, but his companions were acquitted. The Ramnad district was the scene of three explosions in July 1932. On the 27th a bomb was thrown into a foreign cloth dealer's shop at Virudhunagar, on the 29th at Manamadura, a bomb exploded in a deserted reading-room and on the 30th a post-box in the post-office wall was blown up at Rajapalayam.

Some months later, in April 1933, half a dozen bombs were found in a boat in Cocanada; one of these exploded and severely wounded an inquisitive coolie. Investigations disclosed the existence of a local secret society with terrorist aims. The organiser was Prathibada Bhayankara Venkatachari, who had formed the party in 1931. As a result of searches three revolvers, cartridges, daggers, chemicals, and gun-powder were found. Four dismantled bombs were also found in the backyard of the house of one of the accused. Various plans to commit dacoities and murder officials had been abortive, and the last, to murder a Deputy Superintendent of Police, was frustrated as the members had to hide their bombs in a boat, where the unfortunate coolies found them. From addresses found in Venkatachari's house it was learnt that the party had connections with known terrorists in the United Provinces, Bombay, the Punjab, and Bengal. Venkatachari, who was absconding, was arrested, on September 11th, 1933, at Kazipet railway station, and a revolver was found on his person. Two more revolvers and over 50 cartridges were found in his baggage. Nine persons were subsequently sentenced to various terms of imprisonment, but on appeal seven were acquitted, while the sentences of Venkatachari and K. Kamasastri under the Explosive Substances Act were reduced to seven and four years' rigorous imprisonment respectively. While undergoing trial, Venkatachari was found attempting to escape by boring a hole in the roof of his cell. For this he was sentenced to two years' rigorous imprisonment.

A much more serio us event took place at Ootacamund on April 26th, 1933 when four youths of the Hindustan Socialist Republican Army of Northern India, committed a daring bank robbery. They entered the Travancore National Bank, locked the doors, and, at the point of a revolver snatched up a cash-box and escaped in a taxi, the driver of which they had previously left bound in a thick forest. As they left the Bank, the culprits, who had taken about Rs. 3,000, fired a few shots. The car was found abandoned near Coimbatore on the following day, with ammunition and acids left behind in it. On the same evening the robbers were seen at Erode railway station by a Sub-Inspector. One of them took out a revolver and fired, but the Sub-Inspector was able to arrest him and also a second man, and to take possession of the revolver. The other two escaped, only to be caught at Tiruchingode. The four persons were Nityanand Watsayana, Kushiram Mehta, Banta Singh and Bachu Ram, all of the Punjab. This event was followed, on May 1st, 1933, by an explosion at Royapuram and it was found that a youth, later shown to be Roshan Lal, a terrorist absconder from the Punjab, had been killed by the bursting of a bomb, which he was carrying along the beach railway line near the Standard Oil Company's Depot. Enquiries in this connection led to the tracing of a suspicious group to a house in Royapuram, Madras, where opposition was shown, and an entry was forced. A bomb was thrown at the police party, injuring one constable, but after one of the men, Govind Ram had been shot dead, the other three, Hira Lal, Shambu Nath and Prem Parkash, were arrested. The house was found to be a regular laboratory for the manufacture of bombs, and dynamite, false wigs, and ammunition were recovered. Investigation showed that these accused with the four arrested in connection with the Bank robbery were of the same party, all of them being members of the Hindustan Socialist Republican Army of the Punjab. Roshan Lal and Shambu Nath were absconders and Nityanand was a brother of the Watsayana who was an accused in the Delhi Conspiracy Case. His father was employed in the Archæological Department at Ootacamund, but had remonstrated with Nityanand, who had left the paternal roof. This man made a full statement showing that the persons arrested had formed a party sent from the Punjab to work in Madras and that they were under the instructions of the notorious Sitanath De, the Bengal revolutionary who fostered terrorism in several provinces. For their part in the Ootacamund Bank Robbery Case, Nityanand, Kushi Ram, Banta Singh and Bachu Ram were sentenced to transportation for life, but on appeal the sentences were reduced to ten years' rigorous imprisonment. Shambhu Nath, who had abetted the offence was also sent to jail for ten years. Prem Parkash, and Shambhu Nath were sentenced to transportation for life and Hira Lal was sent to a Borstal institution for four years for their part in the opposition shown to the police when their bomb-factory was raided.

The cases just described were attributable to persons outside Madras, and there was nothing to show that terrorism had taken root in the Presidency until, on information received, certain extremist Congress volunteers, who were about to proceed to Ramnad district to commit a dacoity were arrested and found to be in possession of arms. Subsequent investigation disclosed the existence of a widespread revolutionary organisation, which owed its inception to the association in jails of Bengali political prisoners and convicted Congress volunteers. On release, a number of the volunteers had formed a central revolutionary organisation in Madras, variously styled as the Samyavadi Sangha or the Hindustan Socialist Republican Army, Madras Branch. The members of this central organisation belonged to East and West Godavari, Kistna, Guntur, Nellore, Tinnevelly, Madura, Ramnad, Tanjore and Coimbatore and also to Malabar. Arms were collected for the purpose of committing armed dacoities, robberies and assassinations. Several crimes were contemplated, and one of their plans was to send a packet containing silk handkerchiefs and a bottle of poisonous acids to every European officer in Madras at Christmas, so arranged that the person opening the bottle and those near him would be killed by the gases emitted. Twenty-one persons were sent for trial at Madras, and among the charges were a theft in Madras City, and a case of house-breaking in June 1933, a dacoity in a temple in Malabar in the same month, and preparation for two other dacoities. Three revolvers, three pistols and a quantity of ammunition were recovered from the accused. Two of the accused became approvers. Seventeen others were sentenced to terms ranging from one year to four years' imprisonment. The leader, Mukandlal Sarkar, *ex*-Secretary of the Trade Union Congress, received the highest sentence.

The conclusion of this case marked the end of terrorism in Madras, which had never been fertile ground.

CHAPTER IX.

CENTRAL PROVINCES.

The Central Provinces have always been comparatively free from terrorism although during the period before that with which this book deals there had been some activity when Rash Behari Bose had made his extensive plans for an uprising in 1915. Nilani Mohan Mukharji was deputed by Bose to induce the troops at Jubbulpore to join a rising planned by the Ghadr Party, but he only met with failure. After that, one of Rash Behari Bose's lieutenants, Vinayak Rao Kaple, who was absconding in the Benares Conspiracy Case, endeavoured to form a terrorist association in Jubbulpore, but his plot was disclosed and five men were interned. Kaple then associated with terrorists in Bengal and the United Provinces, but was murdered by other members of the party at Lucknow on the 9th February 1918. From that date until 1930 no terrorist activities came to light in the provinces but in that year, during the Civil Disobedience Campaign, some boys attempted to form a branch of the Hindustan Socialist Republican Army, although their effort was broken when nine of the members were convicted for house-breaking, a crime they had committed for the purpose of obtaining arms and cash. On April 7th of the same year a goldsmith of Narsinghpur district was killed by an explosion which took place in his house and a search of his dwelling produced a quantity of chemicals and Communist and terrorist literature. On July 23rd, 1931, two officers were stabbed in their berths in the Punjab Mail near Khandwa by two men, Yeshwant Singh of Damoh and Deonarayan Tiwari, a Brahmin of the United Provinces. Lt. Hext died of his wounds but Lt. Sheehan who had been on the top berth and had struggled with the assailants was not so seriously wounded and survived. The accused had acted in emulation of Bhagat Singh and Chandra Shekhar Azad, but no connection with any organisation was established. Yeshwant Singh and Tiwari were sentenced to death for the crime and an accomplice whose courage had failed at the last minute was sentenced to transportation for life. On August 1st, 1931, a bomb was thrown between the Divisional Commissioner and Scout Commissioner at a Boy Scout Rally at Burhanpur, but did not explode. This was followed on August 9th, 1931, by the finding of a bomb in the compound of the Government High School, Saugor. The infernal machine exploded when a sweeper threw it away but no one was injured. In the next year, 1932, during the investigations of the theft of revolvers from Betul and Nagpur it was discovered that a revolutionary group calling itself the "Bharat Sewa Sangh" had been formed about the end of 1930. Most of the members were students and a number of them were the sons of Government servants. Connections had been established in Wardha and Raipur. The party had planned dacoities near Nagpur, Chhindwara and Betul, but only one crime had been committed by the party, that of a theft of Rs. 1,200 in notes and cash from the railway staff at Hinganghat station on the night of June 9th, 1932. The revolvers had been obtained to help in the commission of crimes and some of the members admitted that the party was in possession of five weapons, three of which were actually recovered. No connections with other organisations were found. Fourteen persons were sent for trial, of whom one was an approver and after a protracted hearing, ten persons were sentenced to imprisonment for terms varying from two to five years for conspiracy, but on appeal two of the convicted men were acquitted.

In January 1933, it was found that a revolutionary group had been formed in Jubbulpore and was working in conjunction with Benares revolutionaries with the object of collecting arms, ammunition and material for bombs. They were known to have obtained at least one revolver by theft, but, owing to the fact that the identity of the informer became known nothing tangible resulted. In 1934, on August 27th, a bomb exploded in the main street of Sitabuldi, Nagpur, but, although the bazar was crowded, no one was hurt. Again on November 4th, 1934, a missile exploded near two police officers in Sitabuldi main bazar,

Nagpur and again no one was injured. Four persons, of whom one was an approver, were charged, and it was found that a sanyasi of Lahore had taught them to make bombs. The principal accused, Nago who had visited revolutionaries in Delhi, was sentenced to five years' rigorous imprisonment and the other two were acquitted.

Apart from these occasional outbreaks, the Central Provinces has been free from terrorism. True, in common with all provinces, revolutionary leaflets and posters have appeared from time to time, but, except for a few known individuals there has never been any reason to suspect the existence of a dangerous terrorist organisation. The fact that a number of students from the Central Provinces join the Benares University is a potential source of danger, but so far, this has fortunately not developed.

APPENDIX 1.

LIST OF CASES.

Date.		Place.	Nature.
Day.	Month.		
		1917.	
23rd	January ..	Kantapukur Lane, Calcutta.	Employees of a jute firm were relieved of Rs. 7,000 by four Bengalis.
24th	February	Paikerchar, Dacca, Bengal.	Two armed *Bhadraloks* robbed Rs. 1,200 cash.
5th	March ..	Lakhanda, Midnapore, Bengal.	Dacoity by 10 or 12 armed *Bhadraloks*.
7th	April ..	Goila Bazar, Bakarganj, Bengal.	Bomb thrown.
15th	April ..	Jamnagar, Rajshahi, Bengal.	Armed dacoity ; over Rs. 25,000 stolen.
7th	May ..	Armenian Street, Calcutta.	Goldsmith's shop raided by armed gang, and two brothers of owner mortally wounded. Ornaments worth nearly Rs. 5,500 taken by dacoits who left in taxicab and shot dead a companion who had been wounded.
20th	June ..	Rakhalbaruz, Rangpur, Bengal.	Armed dacoity with murder. About Rs. 30,000 stolen.
23rd	June ..	Godai, Rangpur, Bengal.	Armed dacoity.
17th	July ..	Augarpur, Mymensingh, Bengal.	Attempted dacoity.
26th	October	Abdullapur, Dacca, Bengal.	Armed dacoity, nearly Rs. 25,000 stolen.
2nd	November	Majhiara, Tippera, Bengal.	Armed dacoity, over Rs. 32,000 stolen and one person shot.
11th	November	Mainpuri, United Provinces.	Dacoity. Victim cut by sword and woman tortured with daggers, but only a few ornaments obtained.
30th	December	Kairail, Mymensingh, Bengal.	Armed dacoity, nearly Rs. 3,000 stolen.

Date. Day.	Month.	Place.	Nature.
		1918.	
21st	January	Auraiya, Etawah, United Provinces.	Sharraf robbed of box containing Rs. 600.
9th	February	Lucknow, United Provinces.	Vinayek Rao Kaple murdered in party quarrel.
16th	February	Mirpur, Mymensingh, Bengal.	Attempted robbery by armed youth.
15th	March ..	Haria, Dacca, Bengal	Dacoity. Cash and ornaments stolen.
18th	March ..	Sibpur, Mymensingh, Bengal.	Over Rs. 8,000 stolen by armed dacoits.
8th	May ..	Bogra, Bengal ..	A sub-inspector shot dead while searching a house.
9th	May ..	Kishoreganj railway station, Mymensingh, Bengal.	Constable shot, died subsequently.
27th	May ..	Atgharia, Pabna, Bengal.	In search for two absconders one fired at Assistant Superintendent of Police.
15th	June ..	Dacca Town, Bengal..	During house search for suspicious persons two suspects opened fire on police who returned fire killing one on spot and fatally wounding other. Sub-Inspector seriously wounded and head constable died of wounds the following day.
16th	June ..	Asutia, Mymensingh, Bengal.	Dacoity.
23rd	June ..	Parali, Hardoi, United Provinces.	House of Brahmin widow looted, maid servant shot dead and mistress tortured with dagger and by burning her fingers. Two villagers shot dead and loot valued at Rs. 10,000 taken away.
29th	June ..	Ramdi, Mymensingh, Bengal.	Attempted robbery by three men who found safe empty.
5th	November	Balakhal, of Hat, Tippera, Bengal.	Headless body of Akhil Chaudhri Datta found. Suspected by comrades to be police spy.

Date. Day.	Month.	Place.	Nature.
		1919.	
10th	January	Dhalla, Mymensingh, Bengal.	Five armed dacoits handed shopkeeper a letter demanding money but only secured Rs. 60.
19th	March ..	Jumapur, Mymensingh, Bengal.	Attempted armed dacoity but disturbed by alarm raised in village.
25th	June ..	Jumapur, Mymensingh, Bengal.	Attempted armed dacoity.
3rd	July ..	Maizkhapara Patuair, Mymensingh, Bengal.	Armed dacoity, about Rs. 900 stolen.
About 20th	September	Mymensingh, Bengal	Informer murdered by terrorists.
		1920.	
23rd	February	Nagargaon, Mymensingh, Bengal.	Armed dacoity.
14th	June ..	Raipara, Dacca, Bengal	Dacoity.
2nd	August ..	Gobindapur, Mymensingh, Bengal.	Attempted armed dacoity; dispersed by villagers.
2nd	August ..	Gobindapur, Mymensingh, Bengal.	Attempted dacoity.
7th	October	Azimnagar, Dacca, Bengal.	Armed dacoity. About Rs. 4,000 stolen by dacoits who arrived by boat.
9th	November	Gangulinagar, Dacca, Bengal.	Armed dacoity, over Rs. 4,600 stolen.
		1921.	
10th	January	Sangramkali, Mymen singh, Bengal.	Armed dacoity by large gang but only Rs. 365 stolen by dacoits who fired at villagers.
31st	December	Alka Road, Khulna, Bengal.	Gang attacked two persons and relieved them of Rs. 2,141.
		1922.	
22nd	June ..	Bareilly, United Provinces.	Constable murdered.
16th	July ..	Sararchar, Mymensingh, Bengal.	Bepin Chandra Shaha murdered as he was suspected of being police spy.

Date. Day.	Month.	Place.	Nature.
		1923.	
22nd	March ..	Paraikora, Chittagong, Bengal.	Armed dacoity in which two men were wounded and over Rs. 8,000 were carried away.
15th	May ..	Kona, Howrah, Bengal	Armed dacoity in which two men were murdered.
24th	May ..	Ultadinghi, Calcutta, Bengal.	P. O. robbery by 4 armed youths.
8th	June ..	Sankar Ghosh Lane, Calcutta, Bengal.	Attempted robbery by four armed youths.
19th	July ..	Goalpara Lane, Calcutta Bengal.	Robbery by four armed youths.
30th	July ..	Garpar Road, Calcutta, Bengal.	Robbery with murder by three youths.
3rd	August ..	Sankaritola, Calcutta, Bengal	Post office raided and post master killed.
14th	December	Battali, Chittagong, Bengal.	Highway robbery by four armed youths who stole Rs. 17,000 from railway clerks.
24th	December	Shullak, Bahar, Chittagong, Bengal.	Two youths arrested after running fight with police in which 5 villagers and one constable were wounded.
		1924.	
12th	January	Chowringhee Road, Calcutta, Bengal.	Mr. Day shot in mistake for Commissioner of Police.
27th	February	Ondal, Burdwan, Bengal.	Rs. 8,000 stolen from mail runner.
14th	March ..	Faridpur, Bengal ..	Youth injured by explosion while manufacturing bombs.
15th	March ..	Maniktola, Calcutta, Bengal.	Six live bombs and other materials and explosives found in raid
13th	April ..	Clive Street, Calcutta, Bengal.	Attempted murder of Mr. Bruce.
25th	May ..	Chittagong, Bengal ..	S. I. Prafulla Kumar Rae, murdered.

Date. Day.	Month.	Place.	Nature.
		1924—*contd.*	
22nd	August ..	Mirzapur Street, Calcutta, Bengal.	Bomb thrown at khaddar shop killing one person and injuring others in attack on suspected police spy.
5th	September	Noapara, Chittagong, Bengal.	Armed dacoity.
2nd/3rd	October	Between Dum Dum and Belghurriah, Bengal.	Santi Lal Chakrabartti acquitted accused in Mirzapur Street bomb case, murdered.
25th	December	Bamrauli, U. P. ..	Dacoity with murder.
		1925.	
9/10th	March ..	Bichpuri, U. P. ..	Dacoity.
24th	May ..	Dwarkapur, U. P. ..	Dacoity with murder.
3rd	August ..	Tollygunj, 24-Parganas, Bengal.	Highway robbery by two youths armed with dagger.
9th	August ..	Kakori, U. P. ..	Train dacoity with murder.
12th	September	Barisal, Bakarganj, Bengal.	Revolutionary stabbed.
10th	November	Dakhineswar, 24-Parganas, Bengal.	Bomb, revolver, pistol cartridges and chemicals recovered in raid.
10th	November	Sovabazar, Calcutta, Bengal.	Revolver, cartridges and literature seized in raid.
		1926.	
28th	May ..	Alipore, 24-Parganas, Bengal.	Rai Bhupendra Nath Chatarji Bahadur, Special Superintendent of Police, murdered in New Central Jail by Dakhineswar and Sovabazar prisoners.
		1927	
5th	May ..	Khilgram, Hooghli, Bengal.	Armed robbery by *bhadraloks.*
27th	August ..	Salkia, Howrah, Bengal	Find of 11 bomb-shells, revolver cartridges, etc.
13th	November	Benares, U. P. ..	Attempt to murder Rai J. N. Banarji Bahadur, Dy. S. P.

Date.		Place.	Nature.
Day.	Month.		
		1928.	
1st	March ..	Patuakhali, Barisal, Bengal.	Bomb thrown at constable who was injured slightly.
13th	March ..	Patuakhali, Barisal, Bengal.	Pleader stabbed while returning home.
4th	August ..	Bijhari, Faridpur, Bengal.	Suspected police spy stabbed.
8th	October	Manmad, Bombay ..	Bomb exploded in train killing 3 and injuring 8.
23rd	October	Lahore, Punjab ..	Bomb thrown near Roshnai Gate after Dushera Celebration killing 10 and injuring 50 persons.
9th	November	Bazidpur, Muzaffarpur, Bihar.	Dacoity.
17th	December	Lahore, Punjab ..	Mr. Saunders, A. S. P., and head constable Chanan Singh shot dead.
		1929.	
11th	January	Bahlolpur, Muzaffarpur, Bihar.	Dacoity.
10th	March ..	Barisal, Bengal ..	Sub-inspector stabbed to death.
5th	April ..	Goraul, Muzaffarpur, Bihar.	House-breaking.
8th	April ..	Delhi	Bhagat Singh and B. K. Dutt threw two bombs in the Legislative Assembly.
17th	April ..	Madaripur, Faridpur. Bengal.	Assault on constable.
13th	May ..	Saharanpur, U. P. ..	Recoveries of bombs, arms and ammunition.
8th	June ..	Maulania, Champaran, Bihar.	Dacoity with murder.
1st	August ..	Saharanpur. U. P. ..	Attempt on the life of Benarsi Lal, approver in the Kakori Conspiracy Case.
5th	August ..	Saharanpur, U. P. ..	Attempt on the life of Sheo Charan Lal, a suspected-informer.

Date. Day.	Month.	Place.	Nature.
		1929—*contd.*	
11th	September	Rajshahi, Bengal ..	Attempted mail dacoity in which one person was shot.
11th	September	Bhusawal, Bombay ..	Armed attack on police by two men when bombs were found in their trunks by the excise Staff.
29th	September	Poona, Bombay ..	Shivram Rajguru arrested
15th	October	Between Kup and Ahmedgarh, Punjab.	Attempt at train dacoity.
24th	November	Lahore, Punjab ..	Bomb explosion in a dharamsala.
3rd	December	Saratgunge, Mymensingh, Bengal.	Armed dacoity.
23rd	December	Delhi	Mine exploded under the Viceroy's special train near the Purana Quila.
27th	December	Pangmasua, Mymensingh, Bengal.	Armed dacoity.
		1930.	
22nd	January	Madaripur, Faridpur, Bengal.	Bomb exploded, injuring two persons.
1st	February	Mymensingh, Bengal	Satish Chandra Ray, an Assistant Teacher of the Ramananda Union H. E. School, was murdered at Kishoreganj.
21st	February	Jalgaon, Bombay ..	Attempt made with revolver by one Bhagwan Das, an under-trial prisoner in Bhusawal Bomb case, to murder the approver Jai Gopal. Jai Gopal and a sub-inspector of Police were wounded.
22nd	February	Amritsar, Punjab ..	Country-made bomb thrown at Principal, Khalsa College.
2nd	March ..	Jullundur, Punjab ..	Two cocoanut bomb-shells and a quantity of chemicals were found.
9th	March ..	Amritsar, Punjab ..	Three bombs exploded in front of the city kotwali.

Date. Day.	Month.	Place.	Nature.
		1930—*contd.*	
12th/13th	March	Chittagong, Bengal ..	Bomb exploded during experiments.
22nd	March ..	Barisal, Bengal ..	Bomb thrown on to roof of kotwali and exploded.
24th	March ..	Mymensingh, Bengal	Body of Bhupendra Raha Roy, *alias* Pola, found on railway line severely mutilated by being run over by train and bearing injuries caused by a sharp instrument.
7th	April ..	Narsinghpur, C. P. ..	A bomb explosion occurred in the house of a goldsmith, killing him.
12th	April ..	Calcutta, Bengal ..	Five or six *bhadraloks* decamped with Rs. 15,000 in G. C. notes from the *gaddi* of Messrs. Harish Chandra Sen and Ram Kanai Bhuiya at 23, Kali Kumar Banerji Lane, Tala.
14th	April ..	Simla, Punjab ..	Bomb thrown at constable in front of Police Reporting Room but failed to explode.
18th	April ..	Chittagong, Bengal ..	Terrorist party of Chittagong headed by Ananta Singh, attacked and looted the Auxiliary Force Armoury, the Telephone Exchange and the District Police Armoury.
23rd	April ..	Feni, Noakhali, Bengal	Ananta Lal Singh and three others were arrested when they fired on the police, three of whom were injured, and decamped.
29th	April ..	Khulna, Bengal ..	Articles worth Rs. 36 looted from house of Amrita Lal Ray, Samanta Sena.
7th	May ..	Chittagong, Bengal ..	Absconding insurgents while passing through Sikalbaha opened fire on villagers and escaped.
11th	May	Daltonganj, Bihar ..	Mail dacoity.

Date.		Place.	Nature.
Day.	Month.		
		1930—*contd.*	
16th	May ..	Shibpur, Howrah ..	Bomb thrown at house of the officer-in-charge of Shibpur Police Station.
19th	May ..	Multan, Punjab ..	Bomb thrown at Police.
26th	May ..	Sialkot, Punjab ..	Hindu youth killed while making bombs.
26th	May ..	Bhola, Bakarganj, Bengal.	Bomb explosion during experiments, killing one person.
27/28th	May ..	Ludhiana Distict, Punjab.	Two bombs thrown at railway line, for experimental purposes.
28th	May ..	Lahore, Punjab ..	Explosion occurred while certain members of Lahore revolutionary party were testing a dangerous bomb.
29th	May ..	Darbhanga, Bihar ..	An armed dacoity was committed at Jhajhra.
31st	May ..	Champaran, Bihar ..	An armed dacoity with attempted murder was committed at Dheluaha.
31st	May ..	Cawnpore, U. P. ..	Explosion of some chemicals while explosives for bombs were being prepared.
2nd	June ..	Mulchar, Dacca, Bengal	Postal overseer waylaid and robbed of Rs. 1,000 while going from Mulchar Police Station to Swarmgram Post Office.
2nd	June ..	Lahore, Punajb ..	Bomb exploded in a house on Bahawalpore Road which was used by revolutionaries as a depot.
6th	June ..	Lyallpur, Punjab ..	Bomb thrown in Chanab Club.
16th	June ..	Jhang, Punjab ..	Bomb thrown into Police Post.
19th	June ..	Rawalpindi, Lahore, Amritsar, Lyallpore, Gujranwala, Sheikhupura, Punjab.	Simultaneous explosion of six very powerful "booby trap" bombs.
1st	July ..	Bakarganj, Bengal ..	Bomb thrown at an Excise shop.

Date. Day.	Month.	Place.	Nature.
		1930—*contd.*	
2nd	July ..	Insein, Burma ..	Two revolver shots fired at two police officers from passing car ; no one was hit.
2nd	July ..	Peshawar Cantonment, N.-W. F. P.	At 8·45 P.M. bomb exploded under engine of Calcutta Mail train.
6th	July ..	Delhi	A dacoity committed at the Gadodia Store.
8th	July ..	Peshawar, N.-W. F. P.	A crude bomb exploded outside the house of a Honorary Magistrate.
8th	July ..	Howrah, Bengal ..	Bomb thrown at S. I.'s house.
15th	July ..	Peshawar Cantonment, N.-W. F. P.	An explosion occurred in one of the two old ornamental guns in the Mackeson Gardens.
19th	July ..	Rangpur, Bengal ..	Bomb thrown and exploded at police officers passing along Gaibandha Road in Gaibandha town.
20th	July ..	Lahore, Punjab ..	Bomb exploded in suit case belonging to Sikh member of Lahore revolutionary party, at a road side stall.
22nd	July ..	Moghulpura (Lahore), Punjab.	Bomb exploded inside a Sarai, while being tested by a member of secret organisation.
23rd	July ..	Rangpur, Bengal ..	Bomb exploded in a house, seriously injuring one man.
28th	July ..	Amritsar, Punjab ..	Two youths arrested at Railway station with two revolvers and some cartridges.
28th	July ..	Bhiwani, Hissar, Punjab.	Bomb thrown in City Police Station.
1st	August	Daltonganj, Bihar ..	Murder and robbery of mail-runner.
2nd	August ..	Mymensingh, Bengal	Constable shot at while arresting certain accused in the warehouse looting case.

Date. Day.	Month.	Place.	Nature.
		1930—*contd.*	
8th	August ..	Jhansi, U. P. ..	Laxmi Kant Pande attempted to assassinate Commissioner.
15th	August ..	Barisal, Bengal ..	Bomb thrown at S. I.'s quarters in Kotwali P. S.
25th	August ..	Calcutta, Bengal ..	Bombs thrown at Sir Charles Tegart, Commissioner of Police.
25th	August ..	Saidpur, G. R. P., Bengal.	Three persons assaulted postal peon carrying bags containing about Rs. 1,000 in cash at Shahatali Railway Station.
26th	August ..	Calcutta, Bengal ..	Bomb thrown in compound of Jorabagan Police Court.
27th	August ..	Calcutta, Bengal ..	Bomb thrown at Eden Gardens Police Out-Post.
28th	August ..	Barnagore, 24-Parganas, Bengal.	Armed dacoity.
29th	August ..	Calcutta, Bengal ..	Ratan Bhusan Hazra murdered at Deshbandhu Park.
29th	August ..	Dacca, Bengal ..	Mr. Lowman, I. G. of Police, Bengal, and Mr. Hodson, S. P., Dacca, were shot in the Mitford Hospital.
29th	August ..	Amritsar, Punjab ..	Bomb exploded near police barracks, by an axe accidentally falling on it.
30th	August ..	Mymensingh, Bengal..	Bomb thrown in house of Inspector Pabitra Bose of Mymensingh Detective Department.
30th	August ..	Mymensingh, Bengal..	Bomb thrown at Excise Sub-Inspector.
1st	September	Rangoon, Burma ..	A daylight highway robbery committed.
1st	September	Peshawar, N.-W. F. P.	Bomb of the Mills type, wrapped in cloth, found by a police inspector on return to his house at midnight.

Date.		Place.	Nature.
Day.	Month.		
		1930—*contd.*	
1st	September	Bannu, N.-W. F. P. ..	Bomb of the Mills type exploded in the house of City Inspector; no damage.
2nd	September	Gindapara, French Chandernagore.	Shooting affray and arrest of Chittagong absconders.
3rd	September	Rajshahi Railway Station, Bengal.	A Mail peon robbed of cash, etc., valued at Rs. 3,650
7th	September	Gouripur, Mymensingh, Bengal.	Bomb exploded during experiments, injuring one person.
8th	September	Ichapura, Dacca, Bengal.	Dacoity committed in Ichapura P. O., Serajdikhan, Rs. 1,347, which included private money and ornaments of the post-master were looted.
8th	September	Benares City, U. P. (Durgakund police outpost).	Bomb in a barley tin exploded when touched by elderly woman killing her.
16th	September	Karachi, Sind ..	A crude bomb thrown at the City Police Station. Exploded but no damage.
23rd	September	Khulna, Bengal ..	Bomb thrown in compound of P. S. where District Intelligence Branch Inspector and others were sitting.
24th	September	Gopalpur, Faridpur, Bengal.	Cash and ornaments worth Rs. 551 looted from houses of Chandni Charan Saha Poddar and Raj Kumar Saha Poddar at Gopalpur, P. S. Kalkini.
27th	September	Rawalpindi, Punjab ..	Bomb thrown, but did not explode.
29th	September	Karachi, Sind ..	A bomb exploded in Rewachand's Building.
4th	October	Lahore, Punjab ..	Attempt on life of K. B. Abdul Aziz, S. P.
8th	October	Ballia, U. P. ..	Cracker exploded in Middle School.

Date.		Place.	Nature.
Day.	Month.		
		1930—*contd.*	
9th	October	Bombay, Bombay ..	Shooting outrage near Lamington Road P. S. in which Sergeant Taylor and his wife were injured.
10th	October	Lohagora, Jessore, Bengal.	Bomb thrown at Itna Beat-house.
12th	October	Lahore, Punjab ..	Attempt on life of Sergeant Smyth of Lahore Police.
13th	October	Jamalpur, Mymensingh, Bengal.	Sub-Inspector of Mymensingh District, Intelligence Branch and his guard were shot at while trying to arrest two absconders in the Mymensingh Excise Warehouse looting case.
13th	October	Jamalpur, Bihar ..	Three unknown men fired five shots at police sub-inspector and constable.
15th	October	Panditpara, Mymensingh, Bengal.	Armed house robbery.
17th	October	Calcutta, Bengal ..	Dacoity with murder occurred at Armenian Street in the *gadi* of Manikchand Gopalchand, in which the culprits decamped with Rs. 2,346.
20th	October	Manauli, Ambala, Punjab.	Dacoity with murder.
23rd	October	Kalabaria, Barisal, Bengal.	Rs. 400 in cash looted from house of Jagatbandhu Bandopadhya, Nalchira.
28th	October	Delhi	Kailashpati, absconder in the Punjab-U. P. Conspiracy (1st Lahore Conspiracy) Case, arrested.
28th	October	Between Shubhinta and Nyaungchidauk Railway Stations.	4-Down Rangoon Mail was derailed.
30th	October	Jashodalpur, Mymensingh, Bengal.	Railway guard assaulted.
30th	October	Barisal, Bengal ..	Rs. 3,451 looted from house of Rajnath Banik, Madhabpasha, Babuganj,

Date. Day.	Month.	Place.	Nature.
		1930—*contd.*	
31st	October	Mymensingh, Bengal.	Property worth Rs. 35 looted from house of Chandra Nath Tewari, Sealdah.
1st	November	Rajshahi, Bengal ..	A peon of Rajshahi College waylaid and robbed of Rs. 368.
1st	November	Delhi	Dhanwantri, a listed absconder, attacked policemen who attempted to arrest him, with revolver.
2nd	November	Jessore, Bengal ..	Bomb thrown at Kotwali P. S.
4th	November	Mymensingh, Bengal	Dacoity committed in house of Kali Charan Bhattacharji, of Jashodal, in which cash and ornaments of unknown value were taken away.
4th	November	Lahore, Punjab ..	Two revolutionaries, Tehl Singh and Basheshar Nath fired revolver shots at police party deputed to arrest them.
7th	November	Lahore, Punjab ..	A bomb and explosive material found in house in Gawalmandi.
7th	November	Karachi, Sind ..	Bomb thrown at City Police Station.
8th	November	Mymensingh, Bengal	House of Umanath Majumdar, of Gangail, P. S. Kishoreganj, dacoited but nothing taken away
12th	November	Tangail, Bengal ..	Rs. 15,000 snatched away from Jamadar and two durwans of Messrs. R. Sim & Co., of Elashin, while taking a cash remittance by road from Tangail to Company's Office.
15th	November	Lahore, Punjab ..	Six revolvers and cartridges found by police.
16th	November	Gournadi, Barisal. Bengal.	Bomb thrown at Constables barracks.

Date.		Place.	Nature.
Day.	Month.		
		1930—*contd.*	
25th	November	Karachi, Sind ..	A practically completed bomb and bomb-making materials were recovered from house of one Tek Chand.
26th	November	Barisal, Bengal ..	Rs. 941 in cash carried away by dacoits from house of Sarat Kumar Guha, Raghunathpur.
27th	November	Jaraitola, Mymensingh, Bengal.	Armed dacoity by some 16 *bhadraloks* who looted cash and ornaments worth Rs. 2,141.
28th	November	Hyderabad, Sind ..	Crude bomb exploded in com pound of bungalow of D. S. P.
1st	December	Chandpur Railway Station, Bengal.	Inspector Tarini Mukharji of Railway Police, shot dead in mistake for I. G.
1st	December	Cawnpore, U. P. ..	Salig Ram Shukla attacked and wounded by revolver fire three men of a police search party.
8th	December	Calcutta, Bengal ..	Colonel Simpson, I. G. of Prisons, Bengal, fatally shot in Writers' Buildings.
8th	December	Dacca, Bengal ..	Bearer of Intermediate College, *dak* bag, waylaid and robbed of Rs. 2,093 which he was carrying to the Treasury.
11th	December	Comilla, Bengal ..	Bomb found on verandah of Dy. S. P.'s house.
14th	December	Patna, Bihar ..	Attempted armed robbery at Maharajgunj.
17th	December	Sialkot, Punjab ..	Bomb exploded in Government High School and two live bombs found in Murray College.
18th	December	Dacca, Bengal ..	Properties worth Rs. 2,145 were carried away from house of Kailash Chandra Banarji, of Paisagaon, Tangibari.

Date. Day.	Month.	Place.	Nature.
		1930—*concld.*	
22nd	December	Satkhira, Khulna, Bengal.	Powerful bomb thrown into house of a S. I.
23rd	December	Lahore, Punjab ..	H. E. the Governor of Punjab, fired at when leaving University Hall.
26th	December	Delhi, Delhi ..	A cigarette tin bomb found in 2nd class waiting room at Delhi Railway Station.
26th	December	Patna, Bihar ..	Bomb explosion at Maniganj.
27th	December	Ahmedabad, Bombay	Bomb exploded in house of a tailor seriously injuring him and a friend of his, both low class Congress workers.
27th	December	Benares, U. P. ..	Bomb exploded in compound of P. S. Chowk.
		1931.	
1st to 13th.	January	Benares, U. P. ..	Series of bomb explosions.
2nd	January	Cawnpore, U. P. ..	Asoka Kumar Bose attempted to assassinate Inspector Tika Ram, C. I. D., and a sub-inspector.
4th	January	Farrukhabad, U. P. ..	Bomb exploded against wall of Kotwali.
5th	January	Benares, U. P. ..	Attempt to rob Mail Van.
5th	January	Barisal, Bengal ..	Attempt made to rob P. O at Bazarkhola, Amanatganj.
6th	January	Between Harashpur and Gobindpur, Assam.	A mail robbery was attempted and a bomb was thrown at the pursuers.
6th	January	Kheri, U. P. ..	Three persons injured while making bomb.
11th	January	Cawnpore, U. P. ..	Bomb thrown into camp of Deputy Collector, but failed to explode.
11th	January	Mymensingh, Bengal	Rs. 22 looted when a dacoity occurred at Nilganj Railway Station, P. S. Bhairab.

Date. Day.	Month.	Place.	Nature.
		1931—*contd.*	
12th	January	Dacca, Bengal ..	A clerk of Bhowal Court of Wards, shot and wounded in an attempt at robbery.
12th	January	Hatigarh, Assam ..	A dacoity committed in which Rs. 3,420 in cash and half Government currency notes to the face value of Rs. 500 stolen.
12th	January	Maharbardi, Bombay City.	A crude cocoanut-shell bomb exploded while police were dispersing large crowd which had collected near the P. S. No damage.
13th	January	Ahmednagar, Bombay	Bomb thrown into compound of the sub-jail. Exploded but caused no damage.
14th	January	Mardan, N.-W. F. P...	Two Mills grenades recovered from the house of a Hindu.
18th	January	Bakargunj, Bengal ..	Man injured while trying to prepare a bomb which exploded.
20th	January	Bagerhat, Khulna, Bengal.	Attempted mail robbery by three youths who threatened guard of train with revolver.
20th/21st.	January	Peshawar, N.-W. F. P.	Country-made bomb placed on rails outside City Railway Station. It exploded on contact with wheels of an engine, but did no damage.
20th	January	Bagerhat, Bengal ..	Attempt to rob mail bag which contained insured cover valued at Rs. 834, from train.
20th	January	Cawnpore, U. P. ..	A bomb exploded in a Mohulla without injuring anyone.
26th	January	Dacca, Bengal ..	A postal peon robbed of Rs. 1,500 at Farashganj Road.
27th	January	Harinarayanpur, Nadia, Bengal.	Bomb thrown at an Excise Vendor's shop
31st	January	Lahore, Punjab ..	Empty bomb-shells and a small quantity of bomb-making materials found by police in house of a carpenter.

Date. Day	Month.	Place.	Nature.
		1931—*contd.*	
31st	January	Kamalganj, Assam ..	A mail robbery was committed.
6th	February	Benares, U. P. ..	A cocoanut-shell bomb found near kotwali.
6th	February	Benares, U. P. ..	A cocoanut-shell bomb exploded in the compound of a house occupied by a munsiff.
8th	February	Bakargunj, Bengal ..	Bomb exploded in a school library.
14th	February	Mymensingh, Bengal	Dacoity at Messrs. Ralli Bros. Agency, Jamalpur, Rs. 7,919 looted.
17th	February	Shahjahanpur, U. P.	A bomb exploded in a Dharamsala.
21st	February	Dacca, Bengal ..	A dacoity occurred at Suapara at which Rs. 2,022 was looted.
23rd	February	Barisal, Bengal ..	Bomb thrown into the District Intelligence Branch sub-inspector's house.
24th	February	Calcutta, Bengal ..	Explosion in a house in Ward Institution Street, a well-known haunt of terrorists.
27th	February	Allahabad, U. P. ..	Chandra Shekhar Azad shot dead.
2nd	March .	Dharampur, Assam ..	Highway robbery of mails was attempted.
5th	March ..	Tippera, Bengal ..	Highway mail robbery at Brahmanbaria P. O. when Rs. 10,942 was looted.
10th	March ..	Feni, Noakhali, Bengal	Robbery at Railway Station.
11th	March ..	Faridpur, Bengal ..	Dacoity at Kathalbari P. S. Palong, when Rs. 2,783 was looted.
12th	March ..	Barama, Chittagong, Bengal.	Dacoity by some 16 youths who decamped with cash and ornaments worth Rs. 3,082.

Date. Day.	Month.	Place.	Nature.
		1931—*contd.*	
14th	March ..	Peshawar, N.-W. F. P.	Country-made bomb thrown near the Kissa Khani P. S. but did not explode.
16th	March ..	Jamalpur, Mymensingh, Bengal.	Attempted murder of suspected police spy.
16th	March ..	Chittagong, Bengal ..	Assistant Sub-Inspector of Chittagong Intelligence Branch was shot at and wounded by Tarakeswar Dastidar at Barama, P. S. Patiya.
17th	March ..	Nadia, Bengal ..	Bomb thrown into house of District Intelligence Branch Inspector.
17th	March ..	Nadia, Bengal ..	Bomb thrown at Kotwali, P. S. Nadia.
17th	March ..	Nadia, Bengal ..	Bomb thrown into house of S. P.
24th	March ..	Benares, U. P. ..	Bomb thrown at P. S. Chowk.
25th	March ..	Benares, U. P. ..	Cocoanut-shell bomb found near P. S. Kotwali.
27th	March ..	Mymensingh, Bengal	Dacoity in house of Upendra Mazumdar, Khamargaon, P. S. Nandail, Rs. 2,249 stolen.
3rd	April ..	Chapra	Bomb thrown in house of Bettiah Raj Manager.
7th	April ..	Midnapur, Bengal ..	Mr. J. Peddie, I.C.S., District Magistrate assassinated.
7th	April ..	Palong, Faridpur, Bengal.	An armed mail dacoity occurred at Steamer Station, Rs. 1,540 looted.
10th	April ..	Mymensingh, Bengal	Three youths committed an armed robbery between Atharbari and Sohaji stations carrying off over Rs. 9,000.
11th	April ..	Patna, Bihar ..	Bomb explosion at Dharamsala Ghat.
12th	April ..	Lucknow, U. P. ..	Two boys injured when bomb which they found in a wall exploded.

Date. Day.	Month.	Place.	Nature.
		1931—*contd.*	
13th	April ..	Patna, Bihar ..	Two cocoanut bombs exploded in an empty school and one unexploded bomb found in school premises at Pahari.
14th	April ..	Ambala, Punjab ..	Two loaded revolvers, 24 live cartridges, an air-pistol and slugs and three rounds of automatic ammunition recovered from youth on train at Ambala.
17th	April ..	Delhi	Explosion in yard near Delhi Main Station.
17th	April ..	Rajshahi, Bengal ..	Dacoity at Ranibazar, Rs. 1,000 looted.
20th	April ..	Sealdah, Bengal ..	Armed robbery at Railway Station, Rs. 4,938 looted.
24th	April ..	Calcutta, Bengal ..	Bomb thrown at the Royal Calcutta Golf Club.
29th	April ..	Rander, Surat, Bombay	Boy injured when bomb materials exploded.
30th	April ..	Chunian, Punjab, Lahore.	Three Hindus arrested while preparing bombs. Explosive substances recovered.
1st	May ..	Bakargunj, Bengal ..	*Bhadralok* youths robbed a peon of Rs. 235 and shot a person who attempted to apprehend the culprits.
4th	May ..	Kup (P. S. Multan), Punjab.	Bombs thrown into Kup P. S. at night.
4th	May ..	Jalabari, Barisal, Bengal.	Four men attacked a mail peon and threw a bomb while retreating.
7th	May ..	Suchetgarh (on border of Jammu State), Punjab.	Police escort attacked by suspects.
7th	May ..	Noapara, Chittagong, Bengal.	Some 10 persons armed with daggers forced an entry into P. O. and after assaulting the P. M. and a peon decamped with Rs. 1,198.

Date. Day.	Month.	Place.	Nature.
		1931—*contd.*	
8th	May ..	Peshawar, N.-W. F. P.	Two country-made bombs found in Kissa Khani Bazar by servant of a bookseller
11th	May ..	Adampur, Punjab ..	Bomb exploded in hands of a Sikh carrying it and killed him.
11th	May ..	Mymensingh, Bengal	Two armed dacoities occurred at Sontiabazar, Rs. 540 and Rs. 650 being stolen.
15th	May ..	Patna, Bihar ..	Suspected police spy found murdered at Pribahore.
16th	May ..	Dacca, Bengal ..	Postal van robbed of Rs. 800.
20th	May ..	Mymensingh, Bengal	While returning from Court at Nutan Bazar the Court Inspector and his orderly were attacked by two youths armed with a crow bar and a hockey stick and the Inspector's revolver was stolen.
21st	May ..	Shahdara near Sheikhupura, Punjab.	Two men arrested with two revolvers one automatic pistol, five sticks of dynamite and some fuses.
21st	May ..	Cawnpore, U. P. ..	Cover, addressed to Superintendent of Police, exploded when opened.
22nd	May ..	Sidh Marja, Hoshiarpur, Punjab.	A bomb exploded seriously injuring an Akali Sikh.
2nd	June ..	Chittagong, Bengal ..	Find of tin canister bombs.
5th	June ..	Khulna, Bengal ..	Mail robbery at Samantasena, Rs. 70 looted.
6th	June ..	Cawnpore, U. P. ..	Two constables attacked by three friends of a 'wanted' revolutionary they were taking to lock-up.
10th	June ..	Cawnpore, U. P. ..	Bomb exploded, injuring a boy.
12th and 18th.	June ..	Bombay, Bombay ..	Bombs exploded in Gunpowder Street.

Date. Day.	Month.	Place.	Nature.
		1931—*contd.*	
15th	June ..	Tippera, Bengal ..	Bomb thrown at a liquor shop at Puran Bazar killing one fisherman on the spot and injuring another who died a few minutes later.
15th	June ..	Hajipur, Bihar ..	The Station Master and his Assistant were shot at while taking cash bags to train. S. M. died and Rs. 640 was looted.
16th	June ..	Mazagon, Bombay ..	Bomb explosion injuring a Hindu boy.
16th	June ..	Chittagong, Bengal ..	Armed dacoity by 30 or 40 persons at West Guzra—Rs. 4,326 stolen.
17th	June ..	Nayanpur, Bengal ..	Rs. 278 was looted from office of A. S. M., Nayanpur Railway Station, Assam-Bengal Railway.
18th	June ..	Mazagon, Bombay ..	Bomb explosion, injuring a Mohammedan boy.
20th	June ..	Cawnpore, U. P. ..	Armed robbery committed in a shop, Munim killed.
22nd/23rd.	June ..	Lucknow, U. P ..	Two young men on bicycles threw two bombs which exploded and fired four shots at an ekka (horse carriage).
28th	June ..	Patna, Bihar ..	Sub-Inspector of Police was killed and a head constable seriously wounded by the explosion of a bomb which was thrown at them by two revolutionaries, both of whom were injured also, one seriously.
30th	June ..	Bannu, N.-W. F. P. ..	Two bombs were found in possession of a labourer.
2nd	July ..	Gouripur, Iswarganj, Bengal.	3 peons of the Iswarganj Civil Court were robbed of Rs. 1,196 in a running train.
2nd	July ..	Near Gauripur Junction, Assam.	Armed dacoity committed Rs. 2,796 looted.

Date. Day.	Month.	Place.	Nature.
		1931—*contd.*	
7th	July ..	Nadia, Bengal ..	Attempt made to rob mails at Kumarkhali.
17th	July ..	Dacca, Bengal ..	Armed dacoity at Nitaiganj, Narayanganj, Rs. 8,479 looted.
18th	July ..	Cawnpore, U. P. ..	Attempt on life of Bir Bhaddar Tiwari, terrorist.
20th	July ..	Cawnpore, U. P. ..	Ramesh Mehta, a terrorist, was shot and wounded.
22nd	July ..	Poona, Bombay ..	Attempt on life of Acting Governor (Sir Ernest Hotson), while on a visit to the Ferguson College, Poona.
23rd	July ..	Nuthio Thar Village .. Taluqa, Sind.	Armed dacoity committed in which Rs. 4,697 was looted.
23rd	July ..	Barisal, Bengal ..	Attempted robbery at Narayangpur by youths who fired at the mail runners but missed.
23rd	July ..	Between Dongargaon and Mandwa on Bhusawal-Itarsi section, C. P.	Two European military officers travelling in a first class coupe of the 6-Up Punjab mail were stabbed, one of whom (Lieut. Hext) subsequently succumbed to his injuries.
24th	July ..	Barisal, Bengal ..	Attempted mail robbery at Narayanpur, Police Station Jhalakati.
27th	July ..	Alipore, 24-Parganas, Bengal.	Mr. Garlick, I.C.S., District and Sessions Judge, assassinated.
31st	July ..	Barisal, Bengal ..	Attempted mail robbery at Dharmaganj, P. S. Mendiganj.
31st	July ..	Tajhal, Rangpur, Bengal	Robbery by four *bhadraloks*.

Date. Day.	Month.	Place.	Nature.
		1931—*contd.*	
31st	July ..	Patna, Bihar ..	Two men injured while one was handling a bomb which fell and exploded. One of them subsequently died.
1st	August ..	Dacca, Bengal ..	Armed robbery at the Municipal office gate, Rs. 6,202 being looted.
1st	August ..	Binharpur, C. P. ..	Bomb thrown at Scout Rally.
4th	August ..	Mymensingh, Bengal	House dacoity at Kachilahati by armed youths who stole Rs. 3,458.
4th	August ..	Mymensingh, Bengal	Armed dacoity at Nandail Road Bazar Station, Rs. 395 being looted.
4th	August	Mymensingh, Bengal	Armed house robbery at Kachilahati.
6th	August ..	Cawnpore, U. P. ..	Employee of a cloth merchant attacked and robbed.
9th	August ..	Saugor, U. P. ..	A dangerous bomb found in Government High School.
10th	August ..	Farukhabad, U. P. ..	Bomb exploded in a school desk.
10th	August ..	Dacca, Bengal ..	Armed robbery at Saraswati Samaj, Rs. 627 looted.
10th	August ..	Allahabad, U. P. ..	Bomb thrown at a sub-post-office, injuring a boy.
11th	August ..	Cawnpore, U. P. ..	Raja Ram Zalim, a suspected terrorist, shot.
12th	August ..	Chapra, Bihar ..	Two youths arrested at Railway Station with one six-chambered revolver, an old pattern double barrel pistol (loaded), some gunpowder and chloroform.
15th	August ..	Delhi	Revolver found in house of two Sikhs in Hauz Qazi.
15th	August ..	Kot Najibullah. N.-W. F. P., ..	A youth, who was apparently preparing a bomb, was injured when it exploded.

Date.		Place.	Nature.
Day.	Month.		
		1931—*contd.*	
18th	August ..	Benares, U. P ..	Bomb exploded in the Dassaswamedh Police outpost.
21st	August ..	Mymensingh, Bengal	Attempt made on life of Mr. A. Cassells, C.I.E., I.C.S., Divisional Commissioner, Dacca, at Tangail.
21st	August ..	Burhanpur, C. P. ..	Cocoanut bomb thrown into a scout rally at Marathi school at which the Divisional Commissioner was present. The bomb did not explode.
22nd	August ..	Phulwaria, Saran ..	Last of four attempts at dacoity in Phulwaria where two were injured by bomb explosion, resulted in Chapra conspiracy case.
23rd	August ..	Faridpur, Bengal ..	7 live bombs and some explosives found in Govindapur, P. O.
23rd	August ..	Saran, Bihar ..	Series of bomb explosions at Phulwaria.
30th	August ..	Chittagong, Bengal ..	K. B. Asanullah, Inspector of Police, was assassinated.
30th	August ..	Rajshahi, Bengal ..	Armed dacoity by *bhadraloks*.
3rd	September	Dacca, Bengal ..	Armed robbery of postal money amounting to Rs. 348 at the junction of Hare and Wyre Street.
8th	September	Burdwan, Bengal ..	Bomb thrown into compound of Kalna P. S.
9th	September	Hooghly, Bengal ..	A highway robbery occurred at Mankunda.
9th	September	Burdwan, Bengal ..	Bomb thrown into compound of Kalna P. S.
10th	September	Burdwan, Bengal ..	Bomb thrown into the Officer Commanding's quarters, Memari P. S.
11th	September	Khulna, Bengal ..	Armed dacoity at Raghunathpur, P. S. Bagerhat, Rs. 2,000 stolen.
13th	September	Mymensingh, Bengal ..	Armed dacoity in house of Bhagaban Saha of Niamatpur, P. S. Karimganj.

Date. Day.	Month.	Place.	Nature.
		1931—*contd.*	
17th	September	Rajshahi, Bengal ..	Rs. 2,333 stolen.
			Bomb thrown into Boalia P. S. compound but did not explode.
18th	September	Rajshahi, Bengal ..	Attemped mail dacoity near Ghoramara Post Office.
19th	September	Mymensingh, Bengal	3 *bhadraloks* held up mail runner at point of revolver and looted bags.
2nd	October	Calcutta, Bengal ..	Dacoity in the gaddi of Krista Ch. Sanatan Pal, Canal West Road, Maniktola. Rs. 300 which was looted was recovered.
3rd	October	Birbhum, Bengal ..	Mail peon at Dubrajpur assaulted and robbed of 4 mail bags.
5th	October	Dacca, Bengal ..	Armed dacoity in shop of Sushil Mohan Sahai, Madhabdi Bazar, P. S. Narsingdi.
8th	October	Benares, U. P. ..	Three bombs recovered in a house-search exploded in the Police Station malkhana next day.
10th	October	Khulna, Bengal ..	Dacoity in house of Satish Ch. Malakar, P. S. Taltalla, Rs. 412 looted.
10th	October	Mymensingh, Bengal	Attempted dacoity in house of Hriday Pal, Kalabandha, P. S. Melandah.
12th	October	Mymensingh, Bengal	Dacoity in house of Purna Ch. Saha, Kamalpur, P. S. Rajitpur, Rs. 900 looted.
13th	October	Dacca, Bengal ..	Two persons robbed a bullion merchant of Rs. 2,479, at Tanti Bazar.
13th	October	Dacca, Bengal ..	Armed robbery of Rs. 28,000 in cash which was being sent from the Imperial Bank to the Post Office.
16th	October	Dacca, Bengal ..	Rs. 83 robbed from Jinardi Railway Station Office.

Date.		Place.	Nature.
Day.	Month.		
		1931—*contd.*	
17th	October	Burdwan, Bengal ..	Dacoity in house of Nurjan Malik of Khagragoria.
20th	October	Mymensingh, Bengal	A postal runner was robbed of Rs. 1,272 near Nagargaon, P. S., Katiadi.
21st	October	Faridpur, Bengal ..	Dacoity in house of Radha Krishan Deb Nath of Chandani, P. S. Naria, Rs. 994 looted.
28th	October	Mymensingh, Bengal	Armed dacoity in jute agency of Rukhini Kanta Sarkar, Gochihata, P. S. Katiadi, Rs. 1,245 looted.
28th	October	Dacca, Bengal ..	Attempt to assassinate Mr. Durno, I.C.S., District Magistrate.
29th	October	Calcutta Bengal ..	Attempt to murder Mr. Villiers, President, European Association, in his office at Clive Buildings.
10th	November	Rajshahi, Bengal ..	Armed mail robbery at Dharbila, P. S. Charghat, Rs. 195 being looted but recovered afterwards.
11th	November	Faridpur, Bengal ..	Armed dacoity in house of Radha Madhab Pal, of North Madhyapara, Palong, Rs. 1,950 stolen.
11th	November	Mymensingh, Bengal	Attempt made to shoo Inspector Monoranjan Chaudhri at Rajballavpur, Sherpur.
16th	November	Faridpur, Bengal ..	Armed mail robbery at Kanaikati, Madaripur, Rs. 2,500 being looted.
21st	November	Bakarganj, Bengal ..	Two explosive crackers thrown into Baishari P. O.
24th	November	Jalaun, U. P. ..	Second murderous attack on Bir Bhaddar Tiwari.
4th	December	Mymensingh, Bengal	Armed dacoity in house of Abdul Majid of Seorakanda, P. S. Tangail, Rs. 2,608 looted.

Date. Day.	Month.	Place.	Nature.
		1931—*concld.*	
7th	December	Dinajpur, Bengal ..	Dacoity in house of Mohendra Nath Sarkar, of Darimonpur, P. S. Hemtabad, Rs. 100 looted.
14th	December	Tippera, Bengal ..	Mr. C. G. B. Stevens, I.C.S., District Magistrate fatally shot.
15th	December	Faridpur, Bengal ..	Mail bags containing Rs. 1,900 looted near Naria Steamer Station.
18th	December	Dacca, Bengal ..	Armed dacoity in house of Mohanta Nath of Telirbag, P. S. Tangibari, Rs. 677 looted.
26th	December	Champaran, Bihar ..	Dacoity at Dhaka.
28th	December	Mymensingh, Bengal	On his way back from renewing his licence a man was relieved of his gun by some 6 persons near Tarakandi.
30th	December	Calcutta, Bengal ..	An important witness in the Maniktola dacoity case, was fatally shot at No. 52, Gouribari Lane.
		1932.	
3rd	January	Dacca, Bengal ..	Armed robbery committed by four persons in a shop at Kamalaghat, Mirkadim, Munshiganj.
4th	January	Dacca, Bengal ..	Attempt to rob clerk and durwan at Munshiganj Middle English School. Durwan wounded by revolver bullet.
8th	January	Tippera, Bengal ..	6 *bhadraloks* boarded mail van of train after leaving Natherpatua and ransacked mail bags after threatening guard with revolvers and daggers.
9th	January	Mymensingh, Bengal	Armed dacoity by *bhadraloks* who robbed a merchant of Rs. 700.

Date.		Place.	Nature.
Day.	Month.		
		1932—*contd.*	
11th	January	Mymensingh, Bengal	Dacoity committed in house at Swarikanda, P. S. Netrakona.
11th	January	Faridpur, Bengal ..	Bomb thrown at police boat at Goala.
12th	January	Farukhabad, U. P. ..	Bomb found hanging from lamp-post.
18th	January	Between Bengal Natherpetua and Uttardah Railway Stations.	Mails robbed by six persons on Assam-Bengal Railway.
18th	January	Faridpur, Bengal ..	Dacoity committed in house at Sotashi, P. S. Bhusna.
19th	January	Dacca, Bengal ..	Sergeant Bourne of the City Police assaulted by 4 unknown persons who stole his revolver.
22nd	January	Howrah, Bengal ..	Dacoity committed in house at Kalyanchak, P. S. Amta.
22nd	January	Patihal Railway Station, Bengal.	Bomb thrown at compartment occupied by District Magistrate, Howrah, at Patihal Railway Station, on Howrah-Amta Railway.
23rd	January	Allahabad, U. P. ..	Yashpal arrested.
25th	January	Sadisopur, Bihar ..	Train derailed.
26th	January	Lucknow, U. P. ..	Bomb thrown at a policeman on duty at Aminabad crossing but failed to explode.
27th	January	Futwa, Bihar ..	Train derailed.
1st	February	Lucknow, U. P. ..	Bomb thrown at Aminabad crossing.
2nd	February (?).	Delhi	Fragments of bomb found on G. I. P. Railway line which runs from Delhi to Agra.
5th	February	Bhagalpur, Bihar ..	Murder of a Mahant and robbery at Amarpur.
6th	February	Calcutta, Bengal ..	Attempt on life of Governor.

Date. Day.	Month.	Place.	Nature.
		1932—*contd.*	
6th	February	Hooghly, Bengal ..	Five persons arrested at Raghubati, P. S. Haripal with a revolver, a pistol and cartridges while about to commit a dacoity.
6th	February	Azamgarh, U. P. ..	Bomb exploded in main bazar, injuring nine persons.
6th 7th	February February	Amritsar, Punjab ..	Two parcels of bombs from Rawalpindi seized.
7th	February	Khulna, Bengal ..	Dacoity in house at Maghia, Kailashkati, P. S. Kachua.
10th	February	Mymensingh, Bengal	Armed Dacoity in house at Massimpur, Bhabanipur, Kuliarchar.
10th	February	Mymensingh, Bengal	Dacoity by 6 *bhadraloks* at Madhakhola.
12th	February	Murshidabad, Bengal	Armed robbery by 4 men at Banwaribad.
15th	February	Mymensingh, Bengal	Dacoity in house at Chowali Charpara, P. S. Mirzapur.
15th	February	Faridpur, Bengal ..	Dacoity at Saldah by youths who stole Rs. 1,085.
17th	February	Dacca, Bengal ..	6 persons waylaid mail runners at Gangadharpatti and took away insured covers valued at Rs. 1,095.
18th	February	Dacca, Bengal ..	Mail dacoity at Gangadharpatti near Munshiganj.
23rd	February	Mymensingh, Bengal	Dacoity at Agency of Messrs. Ralli Brothers at Atharbari, P. S. Iswarganj.
23rd 8th	February to April.	Allahabad, U. P. ..	Series of bomb explosions.
27th	February	Mymensingh, Bengal	Dacoity in house at Sararchar P. S. Bajitpur.

Date.		Place.	Nature.
Day.	Month.		
		1932—*contd.*	
27th	February	Between Assam Shaistaganj and Habibganj.	Four masked men, armed with revolvers and daggers entered the mail van of a passenger train and overpowered the man in attendance at the point of a revolver and dagger and looted all the mail bags.
28th	February	Mymensingh, Bengal	Robbery at Sararchar P. O.
2nd	March ..	Rajshahi, Bengal ..	Three youths attempted to rob a mail runner near the Boalia P. O., P. S. Ghoramara.
5th	March ..	Jessore, Bengal ..	Dacoity in house at Uttar Bagdanga, Narail.
11th	March ..	Murshidabad, Bengal	Three bombs thrown into quarters of Sub-Divisional Officer, Kandi.
12th	March ..	Lahore, Punjab ..	Gold lace firm raided by four terrorists.
14th	March ..	24-Parganas, Bengal	Five persons arrested with implements for committing dacoity at Agarpara.
14th	March ..	Dacca, Bengal ..	Dacoity in a house at Teghari.
15th	March ..	Faridpur, Bengal ..	A mail dacoity with murder at Charmuguria P. O., P. S. Madaripur.
15th	March ..	Faridpur, Bengal ..	Dacoity in house at Saldah, P. S. Naria.
15th	March ..	Dacca, Bengal ..	Mail robbery committed by three *bhadraloks* armed with revolvers at Lalbag, P. S. Lalbag.
22nd	March ..	Bakarganj, Bengal ..	Mail runner attacked and robbed of mails at Nalchiti Steamer Ghat Road.
24th	March ..	Mymensingh, Bengal	Robbery in house at Sararchar P. S. Bajitpur, by two persons.
28th	March ..	Dacca, Bengal ..	Mail robbery at Ichapura P. S. Sirajdikhan.

Date. Day.	Month.	Place.	Nature.
		1932—*contd.*	
28th	March ..	Rangpur, Bengal ..	Tents in camp of Settlement Officer, Lalmonirhat, set fire to, for purpose of stealing revolvers of officers.
1st to 5th April		Banda, U. P. ..	Combustibles dropped into post-boxes.
1st	April ..	Benares, U. P. ..	Five persons arrested while removing bricks from one of the piers of the Dufferin Bridge over the Ganges.
2nd	April ..	Nadia, Bengal ..	Bomb thrown at Plasseypara.
3rd	April ..	Betul, C. P. ..	A ·455 bore revolver stolen from house of retired sub-inspector of police.
4th	April ..	Berhampur, Bengal ..	Attempt made to rob a man by two youths armed with daggers on road to railway station (near cemetery).
5th	April ..	Bakargunj, Bengal ..	Mail robbery on Keora Road, P. S. Jhalakati.
5th	April ..	Tripura State, Bengal	A house dacoity committed at Agartola.
6th	April ..	Dacca, Bengal ..	Dacoity by 8 *bhadraloks* who robbed two youths of Rs. 108.
8th	April ..	Lucknow, U. P. ..	Bomb exploded in a main street.
11th	April ..	Howrah, Bengal ..	Bomb thrown at Amta P. S. but only injured a goat.
11th	April ..	Calcutta, Bengal ..	Mail robbery with murder in Hari Mohan Roy Lane, Belliaghata.
12th	April ..	Rangpur, Bengal ..	Merchant attacked and robbed by three youths armed with revolvers in a running train, near Nilphamari Railway Station.
13th	April ..	Faridpur, Bengal ..	Mail robbery at Jobsa Steamer Station, P. S. Naria.
15th	April ..	Calcutta, Bengal ..	Dacoity in a shop at No. 8A South Sealdah Road.

Date.		Place.	Nature.
Day.	Month.		
		1932—*contd.*	
16th	April ..	Dacca, Bengal ..	Youth admitted to hospital suffering with injuries caused with explosives.
21st	April ..	Calcutta, Bengal ..	Bomb exploded in vestibule of the Head Office of Messrs. Martin & Co., Mission Row.
21st	April ..	Madura, Madras ..	Bomb thrown at Police Station.
30th	April ..	Midnapore, Bengal ..	Mr. R. Douglas, I.C.S., District Magistrate, shot dead.
April & May	..	Allahabad, Lucknow, Agra, U. P.	Telegraph wires cut in many places.
2nd	May ..	Salem, Madras ..	Bomb thrown at Sub-Magistrate's house.
4th	May ..	Benares, U. P. ..	Explosion cracked wall of house—other explosives recovered.
9th	May ..	Hardoi, U. P. ..	Bomb exploded in Superintendent of Police's compound.
10th	May ..	Sitapur, U. P. ..	Bomb exploded outside house of Superintendent of Police.
11-12th May	..	Ludhiana, Punjab ..	Telegraph wires cut.
11th	May ..	Bakarganj, Bengal ..	Dacoity in house at Changaldanda, Banaripara.
13th	May ..	Madura, Madras ..	Bomb thrown at police station.
13th	May ..	Dacca, Bengal ..	Train dacoity between Tezgaon and Dacca in which three merchants were robbed of Rs. 32,000, the culprits shot at and wounded the guard who came to see why the train had stopped.
14th	May ..	Tippera, Bengal ..	Mail robbery on District Board Road, Rajnagar.
17th	May ..	Faridpur, Bengal ..	Mail robbery in which one dacoit was killed, at Angaria, P. S. Palong.

Date. Day.	Month.	Place.	Nature.
		1932—*contd.*	
18th	May	.. Chittagong, Bengal ..	Parcel exploded in Lamabazar P.O., injuring a packer of the P. O.
21st	May	.. Faridpur, Bengal ..	Mail robbery at Kaneswar.
26th	May	.. Dacca, Bengal ..	The guard constable of a retired judge struck from behind and robbed of his loaded revolver.
27th	May	.. Cawnpore, U. P. ..	Arms and explosives recovered in house search. One shell bore initials H. S. R. A.
27th	May	.. Howrah, Bengal ..	Bomb explosion injured three experimenters.
28th	May	.. Tinnevelly, Madras ..	Two bombs thrown at Constable's house, but did not explode.
29th	May	.. Mymensingh, Bengal	Dacoity in house at Kamalpur, Rs. 8,125 looted.
31st	May	.. Hooghly, Bengal ..	*Bhadraloks* robbed a man of Rs. 130 which he had just drawn from the Savings Bank at Gourhate.
2nd	June	.. Tinnevelly, Madras ..	Bomb thrown at Constable's house in police lines.
3rd	June	.. Hyderabad, Sind ..	Hans Raj *alias* Wireless arrested. He was a very important member of the Hindustan Socialist Republican Association and an absconder in the 2nd Lahore Conspiracy Case.
4th	June	.. Allahabad, U. P. ..	Revolver thrown on railway line.
5th	June	.. Mymensingh, Bengal	A house dacoity with murder at Ramnagarpara, Kuniati.
5th	June	.. Allahabad, U. P. ..	Bomb found in Hewett Road.
6th	June	.. Bhagalpur, Bihar ..	Post Office dacoity at Sabour.
9th	June	.. Hinganghat (Wardha), C. P.	Rs. 1,403 stolen from the railway station safe.
11th	June	.. Jessore, Bengal ..	Attempted dacoity at Sarulia by armed youths.
11th	June	.. Tinnevelly, Madras ..	Two bombs found in house search.

Date. Day.	Month.	Place.	Nature.
		1932—*contd.*	
12th	June ..	Faridpur, Bengal ..	Bomb thrown at train at Rajbari Railway Station, Eastern Bengal Railway in which the District Magistrate and Superintendent of Police, Faridpur, were travelling.
13th	June ..	Tippera, Bengal ..	Dacoity with murder in a house at Mograbazar.
13th	June ..	Chittagong, Bengal ..	Captain Cameron shot dead while leading a military raid on an absconders' den at Dhalghat, Patya.
14th	June ..	Sabour Post Office ..	Last of 3 attempts on the Post Office by a gang using cracker bombs.
14th	June ..	Mymensingh, Bengal	Dacoity in a house at Binnahati.
20th	June ..	Agra, U. P. ..	Bomb exploded at a secret political meeting.
23rd	June ..	Bihpur	Two men were arrested with 2 bombs. This and the Sabour occurrences resulted in Bhagalpur conspiracy.
25th	June ..	Rajshahi, Bengal ..	Armed dacoity at Hatiandaha.
27th	June ..	Dacca, Bengal ..	Babu Kamakhya Sen, Sub-Deputy Magistrate, shot dead in house.
2nd	July ..	Nagpur, C. P. ..	A ·455 bore revolver stolen from the bungalow of the City Superintendent of Police.
2nd	July ..	Jessore, Bengal ..	A highway robbery was committed on the Bypara Road.
6/7th	July ..	Jhansi, U. P. ..	Cocoanut bomb exploded.
12th	July ..	Mymensingh, Bengal	Armed dacoity in which a man was shot dead and another wounded.
13th	July ..	Agra, U. P. ..	Armed dacoity by about half a dozen men who entered the house of a rich businessman.

Date.		Place.	Nature.
Day.	Month.		

1932—*contd.*

Day	Month	Place	Nature
16th	July ..	Mymensingh, Bengal	Armed dacoity in house at Gangailpara-Taliapara. The culprits wounded four persons with buckshot and escaped in boats.
18th	July ..	Barisal, Bengal ..	Dacoity with murder in a house at Singa.
19/20th	July ..	Agra, U. P. ..	Explosion in the house of one of the accused in Agra dacoity case.
20th	July ..	Delhi	Constable on traffic duty near Qudsia Bagh attacked.
21st	July ..	Madura, Madras ..	Bomb thrown at Public Prosecutor's house.
22nd	July ..	Cawnpore, U. P. ..	Ten bombs recovered.
22nd	July ..	Birbhum, Bengal ..	Armed dacoity.
27th	July ..	Ramnad, Madras ..	Bomb thrown at foreign cloth-shop in Virudhanagar.
27th	July ..	Dacca, Bengal ..	Murder of Sub-Deputy Magistrate.
29th	July ..	Comilla, Bengal ..	Mr. Ellison, Superintendent of Police, Tippera, shot dead.
29th	July ..	Ramnad, Madras ..	Bomb found in reading-room at Manamadura.
30th	July ..	Ramnad, Madras ..	Post box in Rajapalayam blown up.
5th	August ..	Calcutta, Bengal ..	First attempt to shoot Sir Alfred Watson, Editor of "The Statesman", at Chowringhee. The assailant committed suicide.
5th	August ..	Agra, U. P. ..	Four revolvers, two pistols, acid, etc., recovered in house of Bacha Babu, leader of the Agra gang.
13th	August ..	Madura, Madras ..	Bomb recovered from passenger in train.
15th	August ..	Dacca, Bengal ..	Train dacoity committed by four or five *bhadralok* youths armed with revolvers between Dacca and Tezgaon Railway stations.

Date. Day.	Month.	Place.	Nature.
		1932—*contd.*	
15th	August ..	Bogra, Bengal ..	Two youths armed with revolvers robbed servants of Bogra Coronation School of school-fees.
15th	August ..	Faridpur, Bengal ..	Dacoities in two houses at Charmuguria, Madaripur.
22nd	August ..	Dacca, Bengal ..	Attempt to shoot Mr. C. Grassby, Additional Superintendent of Police, Dacca, at the Nawabpur railway crossing.
29th	August ..	Jessore, Bengal ..	Attempted armed dacoity at Brahmandanga.
30th	August ..	Chittagong, Bengal ..	Dacoity in house at West Noapara, by eight persons who posed as police officers.
1st	September	Faridpur, Bengal ..	Five persons arrested in a boat with arms, while on way to commit a dacoity at Bhangeswardi, P. S. Bhusna.
7th	September	Dacca, Bengal ..	Highway robbery by three youths armed with a pistol and daggers was committed near the Dacca Railway Station.
10th	September	Burdwan, Bengal ..	Dacoity by armed *bhadralok* at Begutia, and shot a pursuer dead.
14th	September	Jessore, Bengal ..	Armed dacoity at Brahmandanga Bazar.
14th	September	Dacca, Bengal ..	Armed dacoity at Shomepara.
15th	September	Faridpur, Bengal ..	An armed youth attempted to snatch away mail bags from mail peon near the Khankhanapur railway station.
15th	September	Burdwan, Bengal ..	House robbery with murder at Begutia, P. S. Memari.

Date. Day.	Month.	Place.	Nature.
		1932—*contd.*	
24th	September	Chittagong, Bengal ..	European Institute at Pahartali, raided by terrorists led by woman terrorist, who eventually committed suicide. One European lady killed and several Europeans and Anglo-Indians wounded.
25th	September	Faridpur, Bengal ..	Dacoity was committed in Lonesingh post office.
26th	September	Faridpur, Bengal ..	Dacoity committed in a house at Panjia, Keshabpur.
27th	September	Dughar, Assam ..	Cash and ornaments valued at Rs. 15,400 stolen in a dacoity which is suspected to have been committed by terrorists.
28th	September	Calcutta, Bengal ..	Second attempt on life of Sir Alfred Watson, Editor of "The Statesman", near Strand Road.
12th	October	Bankura, Bengal ..	Mail robbery at Kamarpukur by four *bhadraloks* who chloroformed the mail-runner.
19th	October	Panvel, Bombay ..	Attempt was made on the life of Sub-Divisional Magistrate, Northern Division, Kolaba, at Panewal.
29th	October	Tippera, Bengal ..	Armed dacoity at Mandabag.
1st	November	Tippera, Bengal ..	Dacoity in house at Medda, Brahmanbaria.
5th	November	Dacca, Bengal ..	Attempt to rob mails at Islampur, P. S. Dhamrai. The peon was shot in the neck.
9th	November	Bettiah, Bihar ..	Phanindra Nath Ghosh, an approver in the Lahore Conspiracy Case of 1930 and in the Maulania Dacoity was fatally stabbed by two youths. One Ganesh Gupta was also fatally wounded by the assailants when he tried to prevent their escape.

Date. Day.	Month.	Place.		Nature.
		1932—*concld.*		
11th	November	Midnapore, Bengal	..	Armed dacoity.
17th	November	Dacca, Bengal	..	Highway robbery on Sutrapur Road.
18th	November	Rajshahi, Bengal	..	Attempt was made to murder Mr. Luke, Superintendent, Rajshahi Jail.
19th	November	Dacca, Bengal	..	Dacoity in house at Panchasar, P. S. Munshiganj.
20th	November	Tippera, Bengal	..	Attempt to murder a suspected spy at Kalikatcha, Sarail.
22nd	November	Hardoi, U. P.	..	Express train stopped by two youths who pulled the communication cord, fired at, and wounded the guard.
29th	November	Noakhali, Bengal	..	Armed youths committed a dacoity at Bijoypur, and used bombs.
11th	December	Burdwan, Bengal	..	Bomb exploded, injuring one person.
18th	December	Birbhum, Bengal	..	Armed dacoity.
		1933.		
3rd	January	Howrah, Bengal	..	Mail dacoity at Baramaria, P. S. Amta.
4th	January	Dinajpur, Bengal	..	Dacoity at Chirirbandar.
4th	January	Tippera, Bengal	..	Dacoity in house at Nalua.
4th	January	Agra, U. P.	..	Three youths tried to relieve a postman of Rs. 4,475.
5th	January	Cawnpore, U. P.	..	Police subjected to revolver fire when arresting a revolutionary absconder.
7th	January	Barisal, Bengal	..	Bomb explosion at Basukati.
9th	January	Dacca, Bengal	..	Two *bhadralok* youths attacked Private Flavell with iron rods on Savage Road, P. S. Lalbag, in order to steal his revolver.

Date		Place.	Nature.
Day.	Month.		
		1933—*contd.*	
12th	January	Sylhet, Assam	Four *bhadraloks* went out in a taxi at Chandpur, turned the car, chloroformed driver and handyman, assaulted two mail runners from Sylhet to Sunamganj, took their bags and got away with Rs. 5,000-6,000 in insured covers and about Rs. 400 in cash.
27th	January	Birbhum, Bengal ..	Dacoity at Rampurhat.
30th	January	Near Gaya ..	Postal robbery.
31st	January	Mymensingh, Bengal ..	Dacoity at Bajitpur.
2nd	February	Sitapur, U. P. ..	Postman carrying Rs. 633 cash and stamps worth Rs. 77 was held up at the point of a revolver by two young men who seized the cash bag.
5th	February	Cawnpore, U. P. ..	Bomb found at police outpost, Sirki Mohal.
7th	February	Sylhet, Assam ..	Dacoity and murder of a boy.
17th	February	Chittagong, Bengal ..	Arrest of Surja Sen at Gariala.
20th	February	Lyallpur, Punjab ..	Dacoity.
21st	February	Birbhum, Bengal ..	Dacoity at Sainthia.
25th	February	Benares, U. P. ..	A merchant carrying silver and currency notes was attacked and shot by two men.
1st	March ..	Tippera, Bengal ..	Dacoity.
6th	March ..	Birbhum, Bengal	Dacoity at Subalpur.
9th	March ..	French Chandernagore	Commissioner of Police assassinated.

Date.		Place.	Nature.
Day.	Month.		
		1933—*contd.*	
13th	March ..	Sylhet, Assam ..	Six *bhadralok* youths attacked a mail runner at Itakhola and when surrounded by villagers one of them (Ashit Bhattacharji) opened fire killing one villager and wounding two. Four of the dacoits were arrested later on.
14th	March ..	Bankura, Bengal ..	Dacoity at Hatya.
16th	March ..	Madras	A revolver found in Governor's box in Legislative Council Hall.
25th	March ..	Bombay	Bomb thrown in Empire Cinema, injuring one person.
1st	April ..	Noakhali, Bengal ..	Dacoity at Tarakucha.
6th	April ..	Bombay	Bomb thrown in Empire Cinema, but did not explode.
7th	April ..	Bombay	Road robbery when a school master was relieved of the pay of his staff. Investigation disclosed the existence of the terrorist group "Anand Mandal", which was organised by one of the acquitted accused in the Lamington Road Shooting Case of 1930.
14th	April ..	Dacca, Bengal ..	Attempt made by two armed youths on cycles to rob a jeweller in Lalchand Makim's Lane, P. S. Sutrapur.
15th	April ..	Cocanada, Madras ..	Six bombs found in a boat, one of which was unwittingly exploded by a cooly, who was wounded.
18th	April ..	Tippera, Bengal ..	Dacoity at Gouripur Post Office.

Date. Day.	Month.	Place.	Nature.
		1933—*contd.*	
21st	April ..	Ahmedabad, Bombay	Following two unsuccessful attempts to set fire to two foreign cloth shops, two men, suspected to be the culprits, were arrested.
26th	April ..	Ootacamund, Madras	Four individuals dressed in khaki shirts and shorts, and armed with revolvers, entered Travancore National Bank, and decamped with Rs. 3,000 in cash. They were subsequently arrested and convicted.
26th	April ..	Erode, Madras ..	Sub-Inspector wounded in arresting two of accused in Bank robbery case.
1st	May ..	Royapuram, Madras	Roshan Lal, absconder from Punjab, killed by explosion of a bomb he was carrying on the beach.
2nd	May ..	Barhee	Down Punjab Mail derailed.
18th	May ..	Chittagong, Bengal	When suspected shelter was surrounded by police and military at Gahira, Anwara, certain armoury raid and terrorist absconders opened fire on the Government forces. Two absconders, *viz.*, Tarakeshwar Dastidar and Miss Kalpana Dutt, were arrested. No casualties.
21st	May ..	Lucknow, U. P. ..	Dangerous bomb placed in the drain of Police outpost, Aminabad.
22nd	May ..	Calcutta, Bengal ..	When No. 136/3B, Cornwallis Street, a suspected shelter of absconders, was surrounded by police, absconders opened fire wounding Special Branch Inspector N. Bhattacharji. Three dangerous absconders, including two who had escaped from custody, were arrested.

Date. Day.	Month.	Place.	Nature.
		1933—*contd.*	
22nd	May ..	Khulna, Bengal ..	Attempt made to rob mail between Fakirhat and Rangdia.
24th	May ..	Bankura, Bengal ..	Mail robbery at Kanchanpur Road.
28th	May ..	Jessore, Bengal ..	Dacoity.
29th	May ..	Allahabad, U. P. ..	Seven post boxes tampered with on Ghadr Day.
13th	June ..	Dacca, Bengal ..	Mail dacoity at Falshatia, P. S. Manikganj.
16th	June ..	Rajshahi, Bengal ..	A local merchant while taking an insured cover containing Rs. 1,000 to the Ghoramra P. O. was attacked and robbed by three youths at Ranibazar, Boalia.
16th	June ..	Hyderabad, Sind ..	Bomb thrown by two youths on bicycles near two British soldiers who were walking in a street. One of the soldiers was slightly injured in the neck.
28th	June ..	Bankura, Bengal ..	Armed mail robbery at Deruabari, P. S. Kotulpur.
6th	July ..	Sonepur	Baikunth Shukul, absconder in the Approver Murder Case was caught with a loaded bomb.
18th	July ..	Barisal, Bengal ..	Dacoity at Kirthipasha.
2nd	August ..	Barisal, Bengal ..	Dacoity at Agalpasha.
22nd	August ..	Mymensingh, Bengal	Murder of Dhirendra De at Jamalpur.
2nd	September	Shamshernagar, Assam	Mail dacoity.
2nd	September	Midnapur, Bengal ..	Mr. B. E. J. Burge, I.C.S., District Judge shot. Two of his assailants were killed.
17th	September	Hyderabad, Sind ..	Bomb thrown at four British soldiers.
24th/25th	September.	Lahore, Punjab ..	Bomb thrown into compound of Lohari Gate Police Post.
12th	October	Hyderabad, Sind ..	Bomb thrown.
13th	October	Birbhum, Bengal ..	Mail dacoity at Suri.

Date. Day.	Month.	Place.	Nature.
		1933—*concld.*	
20th	October	Rangpur, Bengal ..	Dacoity at Naldanga.
24th	October	Rangpur, Bengal ..	Train robbery at Kurigram.
28th	October	Dinajpur, Bengal ..	A party of 15 youths, carrying arms, raided Hili Railway Station and got away with cash and mail bags, after wounding a postal peon, a railway mechanic and four coolies. The Postal peon died. Seven of the dacoits were arrested by the police later on same day.
30th	October	Lahore, Punjab ..	Two persons arrested with bomb in tonga on the Mall.
7th	November	Azamgarh, U. P. ..	Bomb exploded in mosque.
27th	November	Hyderabad, Sind ..	Bomb thrown at two military policemen.
4th	December	Madhabani, Bihar ..	Sub-Inspector assaulted and wounded with kukri by an absconder.
5th	December	Sonaru, Sylhet, Assam	Mail dacoity by five armed *bhadraloks*.
17th	December	Saran, Bihar ..	Constable assaulted at Sonepore.
23rd	December	Sitapur, U. P. ..	A youth was injured when trying to make a bomb.
25th	December	Mymensingh, Bengal	Dacoity at Karimganj.
		1934.	
7th	January	Chittagong, Bengal ..	Murderous attack on Europeans at a cricket match.
8th	January	Chittagong, Bengal ..	Murder at Gariala.
13th	February	Sylhet, Assam ..	Dacoity at Sardabaz.
17th	February	Dinajpur, Bengal ..	Dacoity at Kakna.
20th	February	Mymensingh, Bengal	Attempted dacoity at Kulia char. One dacoit killed.
24th	February	Chittagong, Bengal ..	Dacoity at Bathna.

Date.		Place.	Nature.
Day.	Month.		
		1934—*contd.*	
2nd	March ..	Sylhet, Assam ..	Armed robbery by four *bhadraloks* at Kalighat.
20th	March ..	Umednagar, Assam ..	Mail robbery by two armed youths.
21st	March ..	Dinajpur, Bengal ..	Dacoity at Tilini.
21st	March ..	Dacca, Bengal ..	Dacoity.
10th	April ..	Dacca, Bengal ..	When challenged three Hindu youths fired at party of Mohammedans killing one and wounding another at Deobhog.
22nd	April ..	Birbhum, Bengal ..	Attempted robbery at Kalitola in a prostitute's house.
23rd/26th	April ..	Sholapur, Bombay ..	Series of five bomb explosions during textile strike.
27th	April ..	Bombay	Armed attack on Mr. Sweetland.
30th	April ..	Poona, Bombay ..	Student injured when a package on his cycle handbar exploded.
6th	May ..	Howrah, Bengal ..	Bomb thrown into the Sibpur Police Station.
8th	May ..	Darjeeling, Bengal ..	Murderous attack on Governor of Bengal at Lebong Races.
15th	May ..	Barisal, Bengal ..	Dacoity at Abhoynil.
2nd	June ..	Tippera, Bengal ..	Dacoity with murder at Hajiganj Railway Station
11th	June ..	Lakhimpur, Assam ..	Dacoity at Tinsukia.
22nd	June ..	Sholapur, Bombay ..	Bomb thrown at European spinning-master's bed.
25th	June ..	Poona, Bombay ..	Bomb apparently intended for Mr. Gandhi, exploded injuring twelve persons.
4th	July ..	Dacca, Bengal ..	Murder at Savar.
9th	July ..	Arale, Bombay ..	Boy injured when package, with which he was playing, exploded.
13th	July ..	Dinajpur, Bengal ..	Dacoity at Batta

Date. Day.	Month.	Place.	Nature.
		1934—*concld.*	
27th	August ..	Sitabuldi, C. P. ..	Bomb exploded in main street.
2nd	September	Larkana, Sind ..	Boy injured when a letter he was posting exploded.
18th	September	Sylhet, Assam ..	Mail robbery at Jalsuka by two youths who wounded the Assistant Sub-Inspector who led a pursuit party.
21st	September	Dacca, Bengal ..	Murder at New Chasara.
13th	October	Mymensingh, Bengal	Dacoity at Gangail.
4th	November	Sitabuldi, C. P. ..	Bomb exploded in main street.
		1935.	
28th	January	Dinajpur, Bengal ..	Dacoity at Kalitola.
15th	February	Dacca, Bengal ..	Assault on an Assistant Sub-Inspector.
2nd	April ..	Jessore, Bengal ..	Mail robbery at Kamini Khali.
4th	June ..	Faridpur, Bengal ..	Murder at Thanapara.
15th	June ..	Faridpur, Bengal ..	Sub-Inspector murdered at Goalundo by a Chittagonian *detenu*.
3rd	July ..	Dacca, Bengal ..	Murder near Government House.
6th	December	Rangpur, Bengal ..	Assault on Sub-Inspector at Rowmani Police Station.
		1936.	
12th	January	Dacca, Bengal ..	Dacoity at Makuhati.
4th	April ..	Noakhali, Bengal ..	Arrest of an absconder of Chittagong at Shahadebpur after shooting affray.
21st	April ..	Rangpur, Bengal ..	Train robbery between Kurigram and Tograihat.
3rd	July ..	Dacca, Bengal ..	Murder of Hira Chakraborti, a suspected Police Spy.
19th	September	Mymensingh, Bengal	Robbery from an old woman at Tangail.

APPENDIX 2.

ACCUSED IN THE MAIN INTER-PROVINCIAL CASES.

MAINPURI CONSPIRACY CASE.

Accused.

Name.	District.	Province.	Sentence.
Gopi Nath ..	.. Jasrana ..	U. P. ..	7 years.
Karhori Lal ..	.. Bewar ..	U. P. ..	3 years.
Sidh Gopal ..	.. Chandrika ..	U. P.(?) ..	5 years.
Prabhakar ..	.. Alipur ..	U. P. ..	5 years.
Chandradhar ..	.. Mainpuri ..	U. P. ..	5 years.
Ḍammi Lal ..	.. Alipur ..	U. P. ..	7 years.
Rajȧ Ram ..	.. Deokali ..	U. P. ..	3 years.
Kali Charan	.. Shahjahanpur	U. P. ..	Acquitted.
Sheo Charan Lal	.. Etah ..	U. P. ..	5 years.
Fateh Singh	.. Cawnpore ..	U. P. ..	5 years.
Makundi	.. Etawah ..	U. P. ..	3 years.

Approvers.

Name.	District.	Province.
Somdeo Sharma	.. Fyzabad ..	U. P.
Dalpat Singh	.. Mainpuri ..	U. P.

KAKORI CASE.

Offences.

1. Conspiracy.
2. Bamrauli dacoity.
3. Bichpuri dacoity.
4. Dwarkapur dacoity.
5. Kakori train dacoity.

Accused.

Name.	District.	Province.	Sentence.
Ram Prasad Bismil ..	Shahjahanpur	U. P. ..	Hanged.
Ashfaqullah Khan ..	Shahjahanpur	U. P. ..	Hanged.
Rajendra Nath Lahiri ..	Benares and Pabna.	U. P. and Bengal.	Hanged.
Roshan Singh ..	Shahjahanpur	U. P. ..	Hanged.
Jogesh Chandra Chatterji	Dacca ..	Bengal ..	Transportation for life.
Sachinda Nath Bakhshi..	Benares and Jhansi.	U. P. ..	Transportation for life.
Sachindra Nath Sanyal ..	Benares and Allahabad.	U. P. ..	Transportation for life.
Makundi Lal	Etawah ..	U. P. ..	Transportation for life.
Govind Charan Kar *alias* D. N. Chaudhuri.	Dacca ..	Bengal ..	Transportation for life.
Manmotho Nath Gupta ..	Benares ..	U. P. ..	14 years' R. I.
Raj Kumar Sinha ..	Cawnpore ..	U. P. ..	10 years' R. I.
Ram Kishan Khattri ..	Chanda ..	C. P. ..	10 years' R. I.
Suresh Chandra Batta-chariya.	Cawnpore and Benares.	U. P. ..	10 years' R. I.
Vishnu Saran Dublis ..	Meerut ..	U. P. ..	10 years' R. I.
Banwari Lal	Rae Bareli ..	U. P. ..	5 years' R. I.
Bhupendra Nath Sanyal	Benares and Allahabad.	U. P. ..	5 years' R. I.
Prem Kishan Khanna ..	Shahjahanpur	U. P. ..	5 years' R. I.
Ram Dulare Trivedi ..	Cawnpore ..	U. P. ..	5 years' R. I.
Parnawesh Kumar Chatterji	Jubbulpore	C. P. ..	4 years' R. I.
Ram Nath Pande ..	Benares ..	U. P. ..	3 years' R. I.

Approvers.

Benarsi Lal ..	Shahjahanpur	U. P.
Indu Bishan Mitra ..	Shahjahanpur	U. P.

Absconding.

Chandar Shekhar Azad ..	Benares ..	U. P.

LAHORE CONSPIRACY CASE. No. 1 OF 1930.

Accused.

Name.	District.	Province.	Sentence.
Bhagat Singh	Lahore ..	Punjab ..	Hanged.
Sukh Dev, *alias* Dyal, *alias* Swami, *alias* Villager, son of Ram Lal.	Lyallpur ..	Punjab ..	Hanged.
Shivaram Rajguru *alias* "M", *alias* Ram guru *alias* Raghunath.	Benares ..	U. P. ..	Hanged.
Kishori Lal Rattan, *alias* Deo Datt Rattan, *alias* Mast Ram Shastri.	Hoshiarpur	Punjab ..	Transportation for life.
Jai Dev *alias* Harish Chander.	Hardoi ..	Bengal ..	Transportation for life.
Sheo Varma *alias* Parbhat *alias* Harnarain *alias* Ram Narain Kapur.	Hardoi ..	Bengal ..	Transportation for life.
Gaya Parshad *alias* Dr. B. S. Nigham *alias* Ram Lal *alias* Ram Nath *alias* Desh Bhagat.	Cawnpore ..	U. P. ..	Transportation for life.
Mahabir Singh *alias* Partab of Shahpur Tehla.	Etah ..	U. P. ..	Transportation for life.
Bijoy Kumar Sinha *alias* Bachu.	Cawnpore	U. P. ..	Transportation for life.
Kanwal Nath Trivedi *alias* Kamal Nath Tewari.	Champaran	Bihar ..	Transportation for life.
Kundan Lal *alias* Partap has proved to be Bhagwan Das Mahor *al* Gunthala arrested at Bhusawal.	Benares ..	U. P. ..	7 years' R. I.
Prem Dutt *alias* Master *alias* Amrit Lal.	Gujrat ..	Punjab ..	5 years' R. I.

Absconders.

Name.	District.	Province.	Sentence.
Chandar Shekar Azad *alias* Panditji *alias* Quicksilver.	Benares ..	U. P. ..	(Shot dead in February 1931).
Kailash Patti *alias* Kali Charan.	Azamgarh ..	U. P. ..	Arrested in Delhi.
Bhagwati Charan *alias* B. C. Vohra.	Lahore ..	Punjab	(died as result of bomb explosion in May 1930).
Yashpal	Dharmsala ..	Punjab (arrested in U. P.).	
Satgur Dayal Awasthi ..	Cawnpore ..	U. P. ..	Arrested.

Approvers.

Name.	District.	Province.	Sentence.
Jai Gopal *alias* Harbans Lal *alias* Gopal *alias* Kishan Chand.	Gujranwala	Punjab.	
Phonindra Nath Ghosh *alias* Dada.	Champaran ..	Bihar.	
Manmohan Bannerji *alias* Manohar Bannerji.	Champaran ..	Bihar.	
Lalit Kumar Mukarji ..	Allahabad ..	U. P.	
Hans Raj *Vohra* *alias* Tarlok Chand.	Lahore ..	Punjab	
Ram Saran Dass ..	Kapurthala State.	Punjab ..	(Ram Saran Dass and Brahm Dutt were later convicted to 1½ years R. I. each for perjury.)
Brahm Dutt *alias* Monmohan ..	Cawnpore ..	U. P.	

LAHORE CONSPIRACY CASE, No. 2 OF 1930.

Accused.

Name.	District.	Province.	Sentence.
Inderpal	Kangra ..	Punjab ..	Transportation for life.
Rup Chand	R. Pindi ..	Punjab ..	Transportation for life.
†Jahangiri Lal	Sheikhupura	Punjab ..	Transportation for life.
Gulab Singh	R. Pindi ..	Punjab ..	Transportation for life.
Kundan Lal	Benares ..	U. P. ..	Transportation for life.

Name.	District.	Province.	Sentence.
Nathu Ram	R. Pindi	Punjab	7 years' R. I.
Sardar Singh	Muttra	Punjab	4 years' R. I.
Gurbakhsh Singh	Gujranwala	Punjab	4 years' R. I.
Bhim Sen	Sheikhupura	Punjab	4 years' R. I.
Sukh Dev Raj	Gurdaspur	Punjab	3 years' R. I.*
Sita Ram	Jhelum	Punjab	2 years' R. I.
†Kundan Lal	Sheikhupura	Punjab	2 years' R. I.
Hari Ram	R. Pindi	Punjab	2 years' R. I.
Gokal Chand	Sheikhupura	Punjab	2 years' R. I.
Krishen Lal	Jhelum	Punjab	2 years' R. I.
Harnam Singh	R. Pindi	Punjab	2 years R. I.
Bishen Dass	R. Pindi	Punjab	(Died during course of trial

Absconders.

Name	District	Province	Remarks
Yash Pal	Kangra	Punjab	Arrested U. P.
Hansraj (Wireless)	Lyallpur	Punjab	Arrested Sind.
Lekh Ram	Hissar	Punjab.	
Prem Nath	Lahore	Punjab.	
Mussumat Prakasho	Lahore	Punjab	Arrested Delhi.
‡Mussumat Durga Devi	Lahore	Punjab	Arrested Punjab.
Chandra Shekhar Azad	Benares	U. P.	(Killed in Allahabad while offering resistance to police).
‡Mussumat Soshila	Gujrat	Punjab.	
‡Prof. Sanpuran Singh Tandon.	Lahore	Punjab	Arrested Punjab.
‡Chailbihari	Delhi.		

* To run concurrently with 3 years R. I. awarded in a separate case under the Arms Act.

† Brothers.

‡ Surrendered, but no proceedings were conducted against them.

DELHI CONSPIRACY CASE.

Accused.

Name.	District.	Province.	On withdrawal of case. Sentence.
1. Vidha Bhusan ..	Chapra ..	Bihar ..	Interned under Reg. III of 1818.
2. Khiali Ram ..	Agra ..	U. P. ..	
3. Dhanwantri ..	Gurdaspur ..	Punjab ..	Tried u/s 307, I. P. C. & 19, Arms Act, & sentenced to 7 years' R. I.
4. N. K. Nigham ..		Delhi ..	Tried u/s 20, Arms Act, & sentenced to 2 years' R. I.
5. Vishwanath Rao Vaishampayan.	Jhansi ..	U. P.	Tried u/s 46 & 5, Explosives Act & sentenced to 2 years' R. I. but acquitted by High Court.
6. Potdar			
7. Sachchidananda Watsayana.	Jullundur ..	Punjab ..	Tried u/s 46, Explosives Act, but acquitted by High Court.
8. B. P. Jain ..	Meerut ..	U. P. ..	Tried u/s 46, Explosives Act. Sentenced 3 years.
9. Babu Ram Gupta ..	Etah ..	U. P. ..	Tried u/s 6, Explosives Act. Acquitted by High Court.
10. Kapur Chand ..	..	Delhi ..	Tried u/s 46 5, Explosives Act, and 19, Arms Act. 3 years' R. I.

DEOGHAR CONSPIRACY CASE.

Sailendra Nath Chakravartti.	Allahabad ..	U. P. ..	7 years' R. I.
Upendra Kumar Dhar .	Sylhet and Comilla.	Assam-Bengal.	7 years' R. I.
Surendra Nath Bhattacharya.	Dacca ..	Bengal ..	5 years' R. I.

Name.	District.	Province.	Sentence.
Birendra Nath Bhattachariya.	Dacca ..	Bengal ..	5 years' R. I.
Sukhendu Bikas Dutt ..	Chittagong	Bengal ..	5 years' R. I.
Prasad Chandra Chattarji	Hooghly and Howrah.	Bengal ..	5 years' R. I.
Sushil Kumar Sen ..	Barisal and Hailakandi.	Bengal-Assam.	5 years' R. I.
Bijon Kumar Bannerji ..	Howrah ..	Bengal ..	5 years' R. I.
Atul Krishna Dutt ..	Khulna ..	Bengal ..	3 years' R. I.
Lakshmi Kanta Ghose ..	Howrah ..	Bengal ..	3 years' R. I.
Biswa Mohan Sanyal ..	Nadia ..	Bengal ..	3 years' R. I.

GAYA CONSPIRACY CASE.

Name.	District.	Province.	Sentence.
Shyama Charan Barthwar	Gaya and Benares.	Bihar and U. P.	Seven years' R. I. and fine of Rs. 200 in default 6 months' R. I.
Dr. Kesho Prasad ..	Gaya ..	Bihar ..	
Biswanath Prasad ..	Darbhanga, Gaya and Benares.	Bihar and U. P.	
Sahadeo Singh ..	Gaya ..	Bihar ..	Five years' R. I. and fine of Rs. 200 in default 6 months' R. I
Satrughana Saran Singh ..	Gaya ..	Bihar ..	
Jagdeo Lohar	Gaya ..	Bihar ..	
Mithilesh Kumar Singh ..	Gaya ..	Bihar ..	Four years' R. I. and fine of Rs 200 in default 6 months' R. I.
Pramatha Nath Mukharjee	Hooghly and Daltonganj.	Bengal and Bihar.	
Lala Prasad	Gaya ..	Bihar ..	
Jagatdeo Malaviya ..	Allahabad .	U. P. ..	Three years' R. I.
Kedar Nath Malaviya ..	Allahabad ..	U. P. ..	
Mahant Bhagwan Dass ..	Gaya ..	Bihar ..	Two years' R. I. and fine of Rs. 150 in default 6 months' R. I.
Ganesh Prasad Varma ..	Gaya and Daltonganj.	Bihar ..	
Radha Mohan	Gaya ..	Bihar ..	Two years' R. I.
Bijay Kumar Das Gupta	Chittagong and Benares.	Bengal and U. P.	
Deodhari Prasad Jadav ..	Gaya ..	Bihar ..	One year's R. I.

INTER-PROVINCIAL CONSPIRACY CASE.

Name.	District.	Province.	Sentence.
Prabhat Chandra Chakrabartti.	Tippera and Calcutta.	Bengal ..	Transportation for life.
Jitendra Nath Gupta ..	Faridpur and Calcutta.	Bengal ..	Transportation for life.
Sitanath De	Faridpur ..	Bengal ..	Transportation for life.
Narendra Prosad Ghosh	Mymensingh	Bengal ..	14 years' transportation.
Dhirendra Nath Bhattacharji.	Tippera ..	Bengal ..	14 years' transportation.
Purnananda Das Gupta	Dacca ..	Bengal ..	14 years' transportation.
Kishori Mohan Das Gupta	Noakhali and Calcutta.	Bengal ..	7 years' R. I.
Manindra Lal Chaudhury	Chittagong	Bengal ..	7 years' R. I
Paresh Guha	Dacca ..	Bengal ..	7 years' R. I.
Satyandra Narayan Majumdar.	Jessore and Calcutta.	Bengal ..	7 years' R. I.
Pravat Kumar Mitra ..	Hooghly and Calcutta.	Bengal ..	7 years' R. I.
Jotin Chakrabartti ..	Tippera and Calcutta.	Bengal ..	7 years' R. I.
Dwigendra Nath Talapattra	Rajshahi & Calcutta.	Bengal ..	7 years' R. I.
Haripada De	Dacca and Calcutta.	Bengal ..	7 years' R. I.
Niranjan Ghoshal ..	Faridpur ..	Bengal ..	7 years' R. I.
Amulya Chandra Sen Gupta.	Dacca ..	Bengal ..	7 years' R. I.
Amiya Kumar Pal ..	Dacca and Calcutta.	Bengal ..	7 years' R. I.
Hem Chandra Bhattacharji.	Chittagong and Calcutta.	Bengal ..	6 years' R. I.
Jyotish Chandra Majumdar.	Tippera and Calcutta.	Bengal ..	6 years' R. I.
Bimal Bhattacharji ..	Mymensingh and Calcutta.	Bengal ..	6 years' R. I.
Surendra Dhar Chaudhuri	Tippera and Calcutta.	Bengal ..	6 years' R. I.

Name.	District.	Province.	Sentence.
Abani Mohan Bhattacharji	Tippera and Calcutta ..	Bengal ..	5 years' R. I.
Sudhir Chandra Bhattacharji.	Tippera ..	Bengal ..	3 years' R. I.
Shyam Behari Lal Sukla	Shahjahanpore and Calcutta.	Bengal .. and U. P.	3 years' R. I.
Santosh Chatarji ..	Faridpur and Calcutta.	Bengal ..	3 years' R. I
Sushil Kumar Roy Chakravarty.	Faridpur ..	Bengal ..	3 years' R. I.
Indu Bhushan Majumdar	Barisal and Calcutta.	Bengal ..	3 years' R. I.
Probodh Kumar Ghosh ..	Calcutta ..	Bengal ..	3 years' R. I.
Abani Ranjan Sarkar ..	Khulna ..	Bengal ..	1 year's R. I.

KARACHI CONSPIRACY CASE.

Name.	District.	Province.	Sentence.
1. Gurbaksh Singh ..	Ichra, Lahore	Punjab ..	2½ years' R. I.
2. Birji	Karachi ..	Sind ..	1 year's R. I.
3. Munshiram ..	Narawal, Sialkot.	Punjab ..	1 year's R. I.
4. Fatehraj	Jodhpur ..	..	2½ years' R. I.
5. Boor Singh ..	Jermiasingh, Gurdaspur.	Punjab ..	6 months' R. I.
6. Mukandalal ..	Punjab and	Karachi ..	1 year's R. I.
7. Sadhu Singh ..	Sialkot ..	Punjab ..	1 year's R. I.
8. Diwan Chand ..	Budha Tola, Sialkot.	Punjab ..	1 year's R. I.
9. Birendra Nath Pande	Cawnpore ..	U. P. ..	Acquitted.
10. Doctor Moolraj ..	Multan ..	Punjab ..	Acquitted.
11. Hari Singh (Approver)	Muttra ..	U. P. ..	Pardoned.

APPENDIX 3.

SELECTED TERRORIST PUBLICATIONS.

The Revolutionary Pamphlet.

A four-page pamphlet dated the 1st January 1925, issued over the signature of Vijay Kumar, President, Central Council, The R. P. of India, was probably the production of Sachindra Nath Sanyal as extracts from notes in the same phrasing were found in a note-book when he was arrested in 1925. The pamphlet was very widely distributed, by hand and by post, in Bengal, the U. P. and the Punjab and a few copies were sent to editors in other provinces.

THE REVOLUTIONARY.

AN ORGAN OF THE REVOLUTIONARY PARTY OF INDIA.

INDIA—1ST JANUARY 1925.

Vol. I. No. I.

(*Every honest Indian should read the whole of it and circulate it among his friends.*)

Manifesto of the Revolutionary party of India.

" Chaos is necessary to the birth of a new star " and the birth of life is accompanied by agony and pain. India is also taking a new birth, and is passing through that inevitable phase, when chaos and agony shall play their destined role, when all calculations shall prove futile, when the wise and the mighty shall be bewildered by the simple and the weak, when great empires shall crumble down and new nations shall arise and surprise humanity with the splendour and glory which shall be all its own.

This new power, which is shaking the world from its very depths, this new spirit, which is working miracles behind the scene, is also manifesting itself in the young blood of India and is taking the shape of a movement which is despised and ignored by the wise and the learned, and is being described as the wild dreams of a few mad men. This remarkable movement is the revolutionary movement of young India.

This revolutionary movement has unnerved the weak, has inspired the robust and the healthy and has confounded the worldly wise and the learned. This movement can never be crushed just as much as the coming of the spring can never be thwarted. It will never die out until it has fulfilled the mission for which it has taken its birth. Tyrants will oppress it, the faithless will taunt it, and the confounded will denounce it ; but thoughts and ideas can never be crushed by the sword, and the noble impulse that takes birth in the very depths of our being can neither be ignored nor taurted.

This revolutionary movement is the manifestation of the new life that has taken birth in the nation. To denounce this life is to denounce one's own understanding.

Twenty years of ruthless repression has not been able to crush it. Scathing denunciations by the renowned public leaders have not been able to arrest its steady growth. The movement stands mightier to-day than what it was before. The prospects of this revolutionary party were never so bright as they are today. The future is assured.

Let no Indian deny the existence of this revolutionary party in order to denounce the repressive measures of the foreign rulers. The foreigners have no right to rule over India and therefore they must be denounced and driven out, not that they have committed any particular act of violence or crime. These are the natural consequences of a foreign rule. This foreign rule must be abolished. They have no justification to rule over India except the justification of the sword, and therefore the revolutionary party has taken to the sword. But the sword of the revolutionary party bears ideas at its edge.

The immediate object of the revolutionary party in the domain of politics is to establish a Federal Republic of the United States of India by an organised and armed revolution. The final constitution of this Republic shall be framed and declared at a time when the representatives of India shall have the power to carry out their decisions. But the basic principles of this Republic shall be universal suffrage, and the abolition of all systems which make the exploitation of man by man possible; *e.g.*, the railways and other means of transportation and communication, the mine and other kinds of very great industries such as the manufacture of steel and ships, all these shall be nationalised. In this Republic the electors shall have the right to recall their representatives if so desired, otherwise the democracy shall become a mockery. In this Republic, the legislature shall have the power to control the exeeutives and replace them whenever necessity will arise.

The revolutionary party is not national but international in the sense that its ultimate object is to bring harmony in the world by respecting and guaranteeing the diverse interests of the different nations; it aims not at competition but at co-operation between the different nations and states, and in this respect it follows the footsteps of the great Indian Rishis of the glorious past and of Bolshevik Russia in the modern age. Good for humanity is no vain and empty word with the Indian revolutionaries. But the weak, the coward and the powerless can do no good either to themselves or to humanity.

With regard to the communal questions, the revolutionary party contemplates to grant whatever rights the different communities may demand, provided they do not clash with the interests of other communities and they lead ultimately to hearty and organic union of the different communities in the near future.

In the domain of economic and social welfare the party will foster the spirit of co-operation in as large a scale as possible. Instead of private and unorganised business enterprises, the party prefers co-operative unions.

In the spiritual domain the party aims at establishing the truth and preaching it that the world is not "Maya"—an illusion to be ignored and despised at but that it is the manifestation of the one indivisible soul, the supreme source of all power, all knowledge, and all beauty.

This revolutionary party has its own policy and its own programme. It cannot for obvious reasons divulge all its secrets. But when it will become quite sure that the government happens to know more than our own people, then the public will also be informed of its plans and methods without any hesitation at all.

This revolutionary party pursues the policy of co-operation when posssible and dissociation where necessary with the Congress and its different parties. But this party views all constitutional agitations in the country with contempt and ridicule. It is a mockery to say that India's salvation can be achieved through constitutional means, where no constitution exists. It is self-deception to say that India's political liberty can be attained through peaceful and legitimate means when the enemy is determined to break the peace at his own convenience and the fine phrase "legitimate" looses all its charm and significance when one pledges himself to maintain peace at all costs.

Our public leaders hesitate to speak in plain terms that India wants complete autonomy free from foreign control. They perhaps are ignorant of the fact that nations are born through the inspirations of great ideals. The spiritual ideal which hesitates to accept this spirit of complete autonomy can hardly be called spiritual though it may seemingly appear the most sublime. The time has come to speak the truth in the most unmistakeable terms and to place before the nation an ideal worth the name.

The ideal before us is to serve humanity in an organised way. This ideal can never be realised by India so long as she remains in bondage and slavery, so long as India remains British India. In order that India may realise her ideal she must have a separate and independent existence. This independence can never be achieved through peaceful and constitutional means. Even a child can understand that the laws that govern British India are not made by the Indians nor can they have any control over them. British India can never be transformed into a Federal Republic of the United States of India through the British laws and constitutions. Young Indians! Shake off your illusions, face realities with a stout heart, and do not avoid struggles, difficulties and sacrifices. The inevitable is to come. Do not be misguided any more. Peace and tranquillity you cannot have and India's liberty can never be achieved through peaceful and legal means. The following memorable words of a great English author Mr. Robertson may serve to make the wise men of India wiser still.

"The movement and programme of reform was mainly the achievement of Irish and Protestant leaders, to whom British statesmen had revealed the fatal secret that England could be bullied but not argued into justice and generosity" (England under the Hanoverians, p. 197). Indian public leaders are still ignorant of this "fatal secret" or else they are foolishly wise to ignore it.

The wise men of India say that it is absurd to cherish the hope that India can be re-conquered by the force of arms, though they forget that it is equally or more absurd to believe that a handful of Englishmen have kept under subjugation by the force of arms, one-fifth of the whole human race. Posterity may well doubt the authenticity of this fact that a handful of Englishmen ever ruled over the Indian continent, it is so inconceivable.

A few words more about terrorism and anarchism. These two words are playing the most mischievous part in India today. They are being invariably misapplied whenever any reference to the revolutionaries is to be made, because it is so very convenient to denounce the revolutionaries under that name. The Indian revolutionaries are neither terrorists nor anarchists. They never aim at spreading anarchy in the land, and therefore they can never properly be called anarchists. Terrorism is never their object and they cannot be called terrorists. They do not believe that terrorism alone can bring independence and they do not want terrorism for terrorism's sake, although they may at times resort to this method as a very effective means of retaliation. The present government exists solely because the foreigners have successfully been able to terrorise the Indian people. The Indian people do not love their English masters, they do not want them to be here; but they do help the Britishers simply because they are terribly afraid of them; and this very fear resists the Indians from extending their helping hands to the revolutionaries, not that they do not love them.

This official terrorism is surely to be met by counter terrorism. A spirit of utter helplessness pervades every strata of our society and terrorism is an effective means of restoring the proper spirits in the society without which progress will be difficult. Moreover the English masters and their hired lackeys can never be allowed to do whatever they like, unhampered, unmolested. Every possible difficulty and resistance must be thrown in their way. Terrorism has an international bearing also, because the attentions of the enemies of England are at once drawn towards India through the acts of terrorism and revolutionary demonstrations and the revolutionaries are thereby able to form an alliance with them, and thus expedite the speedy attainment of India's deliverance. But this revolutionary party has deliberately abstained itself from entering into this terrorist campaign at the present moment even at the greatest of provocations in the form of outrages committed on their sisters and mothers by the agents of a foreign government, simply because the party is waiting to deliver the final blow. But when expediency will demand it the Party will unhesitatingly enter into a desperate campaign of terrorism, when the life of every officer and individual who will be helping the foreign rulers in any way will be made intolerable, be he Indian or European, high or low. But even then the party will never forget that terrorism is not their object, and they will try incessantly to organise a band of selfless and devoted workers who will devote their best energies towards the political and social emancipation of their country. They will always remember that "the making of nations requires the self-sacrifice of thousands of obscure men and women who care more for the idea of their country, than for their own comfort or interest, their own lives or the lives of those whom they love".

(Sd.) VIJAY KUMAR,

President, Central Council,

The R. P. of India.

THE HINDUSTAN REPUBLICAN ASSOCIATION.

Name.—

The name of the association shall be the Hindustan Republican Association.

Object.—

The object of the association shall be to establish a Federated Republic of the United States of India by an organised and armed revolution.

The final form of the constitution of the Republic shall be framed and declared by the representatives of the people at the time when they will be in a position to enforce their decisions.

The basic principle of the republic shall be universal suffrage and the abolition of all systems which make any kind of exploitation of man by man possible.

Constitution—Governing Body :—

The governing body of the association shall be the Central Council composed of the representatives of every province of India. All decisions of the Central Council shall be arrived at by unanimous consent. The Central Council shall be vested with absolute powers.

The principal function of the Central Council shall be to supervise, adjust and co-ordinate the activities in the different provinces of which it shall have full knowledge.

The Central Council shall be in direct charge of the work to be carried on in countries outside India.

Provincial Organisation.—

There shall be a committee ordinarily of five (5) men representing the five (5) different departments of the association in every province which shall regulate all the activities of the association in the province.

All decisions of the committee shall be arrived at by unanimous consent.

Departments.—

Every provincial organisation shall have the following departments :—

1. Propaganda.
2. Collection of men.
3. Collection of Funds and Terrorism.
4. Collection and storage of arms and ammunitions.
5. Foreign connection.

1. *Propaganda* shall be carried on :—

(*a*) by an open and a secret press,

(*b*) through private conversations,

(*c*) through public platforms,

(*d*) through a system of organised Kathas, and

(*e*) through magic lantern slides.

2. *Collection of men* shall be done by organisers in charge of different districts.

3. *Funds* shall be collected generally by means of voluntary subscriptions and occasionally by contributions exacted by force. In extreme cases of repressions by agent or agents of a foreign government it shall be the duty of the association to retaliate in whatever form it shall consider suitable.

4. Every effort shall be made to arm every member of the association; but all such arms shall be stored at different centres and be used according to the directions of the provincial committee only.

No arms shall be removed from any place in the district or used without the knowledge and the permission of the district organiser or the officer in-charge of this department.

5. *Foreign connection.*—This department shall carry on its work under the direct orders from the C. C.

District organiser—His duties.—

The district organiser shall be in sole charge of the members of his district.

He shall try to start branches of this association in every part of his district. In order to have efficient recruitment he should keep himself in touch with the different public bodies and institutions in his district.

The district organisers shall be subordinate in every way to the provincial committee who shall supervise and direct all their activities.

The district organisers must see that the members are divided into separate groups and the different groups do not know each other.

So far as possible the district organiser of any province must not know the activities of each other and if possible they must also not know each other by person or by name.

No district organiser shall leave his station without previously informing his superior.

Qualifications of a District Organiser.—

1. He must have the tact and the ability to guide and handle men of different temperaments.

2. He must have the capacity to grasp political, social and economical problems of the present day with special reference to his Motherland.

3. He must be able to grasp the spirit of the history of India, with special reference to the particular civilization which India has evolved.

4. He must have faith in the mission and the destiny of a free India, which is to bring harmony in the different spheres of human activities both spiritual and material.

5. He must be courageous and self-sacrificing without which all his brilliant qualities will have no real value.

Provincial Council and Central Council.—

P. C. and C. C. members must see that every member of this association gets full scope and ample opportunity to develop and use his individual abilities, without which the association will tend to disintegrate.

PROGRAMME.

All the activities of the association shall be divided into two parts :— public and private.

Public.—

1. To start associations in the forms of clubs, libraries, seva sammitis and the like.

2. To start labour and peasant organisations. Suitable men must be engaged on behalf of the association to organise and control the labourers in the different factories, the railways and in the coalfields, and instil into their minds that they are not for the revolution but that the revolution is for them.

Similarly the Kisans must also be organised.

3. To start weekly paper in every province to propagate the idea of an independent Indian Republic.

4. To publish booklets and pamphlets with a view to enlighten the public as to the course of events and the current of thoughts as prevalent in the countries outside India.

5. To utilise and influence the Congress and other public activities as far as possible.

Private.—

(*a*) To establish a secret press and through it to publish such literature which cannot easily be published openly.

(*b*) To circulate such literature.

(*c*) To establish branches of this association in every part of the country, district by district.

(*d*) To collect funds in as many ways as possible.

(*e*) To send suitable men to foreign countries where they may get military or scientific training so that they may become military or scientific experts to take charge of armies and ammunition factories at the time of open rebellion.

(*f*) To import arms and ammunitions and also to manufacture them, as far as possible, in the country.

(*g*) To remain in close touch and to co-operate with the Indian revolutionaries outside India.

(*h*) To get the members of the association enlisted into the present army.

(*i*) To enlist the sympathy of the public to our cause by occasional retaliatory measures and propaganda and thus create a band of sympathisers.

Membership.

All members shall be recruited by organisers in charge of different districts in every province. Every member must be ready to devote his whole time for the association and to risk his life if necessary.

He must obey the commands of the district organiser implicitly.

He should develop his own initiative and remember that the success of the association depends much on the resourcefulness, the initiative and the sense of duty of its individual members.

He must behave in a manner that may not prejudice the cause for which his association stands or may not do any harm directly or indirectly to this organisation.

No member of this association shall belong to any other organisation without the consent of the district organiser.

No member shall leave his station without informing the district organiser about it.

Every member must try to avoid being suspected of revolutionary connections by the police or public.

Every member must remember that his individual behaviour and mistakes might lead to the ruin of the whole organisation.

No member shall conceal anything from the district organiser as far as his public life is concerned.

Members who will betray shall be punished either with expulsion or death.

The authority of punishment shall rest entirely with the "P. C."

THE HINDUSTAN SOCIALIST REPUBLICAN ASSOCIATION.

Manifesto.

The Philosophy of the Bomb.

Introductory.

Recent events, particularly the congress resolution on the attempt to blow up the Viceregal Special on the 23rd December 1929, and Gandhi's subsequent writings in 'Young India', clearly show that the Indian National Congress, in conjunction with Gandhi, has launched a crusade against the revolutionaries. A great amount of public criticism, both from the press and the platform, has been made against them. It is a pity that they have all along been, either deliberately or due to sheer ignorance, misrepresented and misunderstood. The revolutionaries do not shun criticism and public scrutiny of their ideals, or actions. They rather welcome these as chances of making those understand, who have a genuine desire to do so, the basic principles of the revolutionary movement and the high and noble ideals that are a perennial source of inspiration and strength to it. It is hoped that this article will help the general public to know the revolutionaries as they are and will prevent it from taking them for what interested and ignorant persons would have it believe them to be.

Violence or non-violence.

Let us, first of all, take up the question of violence and non-violence. We think that the use of these terms, in itself, is a grave injustice to either party for they express the ideals of neither of them correctly. Violence is physical force applied for committing injustice, and that is certainly not what the revolutionaries stand for. On the other hand, what generally goes by the name of non-violence is in reality the theory of soul-force, as applied to the attainment of personal and national rights through courting suffering and hoping thus to finally convert your opponent to your point of view. When a revolutionary believes certain things to be his right, he asks for them, pleads for them, argues for them, wills to attain them with all the soul-force at his command, stands the greatest amount of suffering for them, is always prepared to make the highest sacrifice for their attainment, and also backs his efforts with all the physical force he is capable of. You may coin what other word you like to describe his methods but you cannot call it violence, because that would constitute an outrage on the dictionary meaning of that word. Satyagraha is insistance upon Truth. Why press, for the acceptance of Truth, by soul-force alone? Why not add physical force also to it? While the revolutionaries stand for winning independence by all the forces, physical as well as moral, at their command, the advocates of soul-force would like to ban the use of physical force. The question really, therefore, is not whether you will have violence or non-violence, but whether you will have soul-force plus physical force or soul-force alone.

Our Ideal.

The revolutionaries believe that the deliverance of their country will come through Revolution. The Revolution, they are constantly working and hoping for, will not only express itself in the form of an armed conflict between the foreign government and its supporters and the people, it will also usher in a New Social Order. The revolution will ring the death knell of Capitalism and class distinctions and privileges. It will bring joy and prosperity to the starving millions who are seething today under the terrible yoke of both foreign and Indian exploitation. It will bring the nation into its own. It will give birth to a new State—a new social order. Above all, it will establish the Dictatorship of the Proletariat and will for ever banish social parasites from the seat of political power.

Terrorism.

The revolutionaries already see the advent of the revolution in the restlessness of youth, in its desire to break free from the mental bondage and religious superstitions that hold them. As the youth will get more and more saturated with the psychology of revolution, it will come to have a clearer realisation of national bondage and a growing, intense, unquenchable thirst for freedom. It will grow, this feeling of bondage, this insatiable desire for freedom, till, in their righteous anger, the infuriated youth will begin to kill the oppressors. Thus has Terrorism been born in the country. It is a phase, a necessary, an inevitable phase of the revolution. Terrorism is not the complete Revolution and the Revolution is not complete without Terrorism. This thesis can be supported by an analysis of any and every revolution in history. Terrorism instils fear in the hearts of the oppressors, it brings hopes of revenge and redemption to the oppressed masses, it gives courage and self-confidence to the wavering, it shatters the spell of the superiority of the ruling class and raises the status of the subject race in the eyes of the world, because it is the most convincing proof of a nation's hunger for Freedom. Here in India, as in other countries in the past, Terrorism will develop into the Revolution and the Revolution into Independence, social, political and economic.

Revolutionary Methods.

This then is what the revolutionaries believe in, this is what they hope to accomplish for their country. They are doing it both openly and secretly and in their own way. The experience of a century. long and world-wide struggle, between the masses and the governing class, is their guide to their goal and the methods they are following have never been known to have failed.

The Congress and the Revolutionaries.

Meanwhile, what has the congress been doing ? It has changed its creed from Swaraj to Complete Independence. As a logical sequence to this, one would expect it to declare a war on the British Government. Instead, we find, it has declared war against the Revolutionaries. The first offensive of the Congress came in the form of a resolution deploring the attempt made on the 23rd December 1929, to blow up the Viceroy's special. It was drafted by Gandhi and he fought tooth and nail for it, with the result, that it was passed by a trifling majority of 81 in a house of 1,713. Was even this bare majority a result of honest political convictions ? Let us quote the opinion of Sarla Devi Chaudhrani, who has been a devotee of the Congress all her life, in reply. She says, "I discovered in the course of my conversations with a good many of the Mahatma's followers that it was only their senses of personal loyalty to him that was keeping them back from an expression of their independent views and preventing them from voting against any resolution whatsoever that was fathered by Mahatmaji". As to Gandhi's arguments in favour of his proposition, we will deal with them later, when we discuss his article, "The Cult of the Bomb" which is more or less, an amplification of his speech in the congress. There is one fact about this deplorable resolution which we must not lose sight of, and that is this. Inspite of the fact, that the congress is pledged to non-violence and has been actively engaged in carrying on propaganda in its favour for the last ten years, and, inspite of the fact also, that the supporters of the resolution indulged in abuse, called the revolutionaries 'cowards' and described their actions as 'dastardly'—and one of them even threateningly remarked, that if they wanted to be lead by Gandhi, they should pass this resolution without any opposition—inspite of all this, the resolution could only be adopted by a dangerously narrow majority. That demonstrates, beyond the shadow of a doubt, how solidly the country is backing the revolutionaries. In a way Gandhi deserved our thanks for having brought the question up for discussion and thus having shown to the world at large that even the congress—that stronghold of non-violence—is at least as much, if not more, with the revolutionaries than with him.

Gandhi on War Path.

Having achieved a victory which cost him more than a defeat, Gandhi has returned to the attack in his article "The Cult of the Bomb". We will give it our closest attention before proceeding further. That article consists of three things, his faith, his opinion and his arguments. We will not discuss what is a matter of faith with him because reason has little in common with faith. Let us then take such of his opinions as are backed by arguments and his arguments proper, against what he calls violence and discuss them one by one.

Do the Masses believe in non-violence ?

He thinks that on the basis of his experience during his latest tour in the country, he is right in believing that the large masses of Indian Humanity are yet untouched by the spirit of violence and that non-violence has come to stay as a political weapon. Let him not delude himself on the experiences of his latest tour in the country. Though it is true that the average leader confines his tours to places where only the mail train can conveniently land him, while Gandhi has extended his tour limit to where a motor car can take him, the practice, of staying only with the richest people in the places visited, of spending most of his time on being complimented by his devotees in private and public and of granting Darshan, now and then, to the illiterate masses, whom he claims to understand so well, disqualifies him from claiming to know the mind of the masses. No man can claim to know a people's mind by seeing them from the public platform and giving them Darshan and Updesh. He can at the most claim to have told the masses what he thinks about things. Has Gandhi, during recent years mixed in the social life of the masses ? Has he sat with the peasant round the evening fire and tried to know what he thinks ? Has he passed a single evening in the company of a factory labourer and shared with him his vows ? We have, and therefore we claim to know what the masses think. We assure Gandhi, that the average Indian, like the average human being, understands little of the fine theological niceties about 'Ahinsa' and 'loving one's enemy'. The way of the world is like this. You have a friend: you love him, sometimes so much that you even die for him. You have an enemy, you shun him, you fight against him and if possible, kill him. The gospel of the revolutionaries is simple and straight. It is what it has been since the days of Adam and Eve and no man has any difficulty about understanding it. We affirm that the masses of India are solidly with us because we know it from personal experience. The day is not far off when they will flock in their thousands to work the will of the Revolution.

The Gospel of Love.

Gandhi declares that his faith in the efficacy of non-violence has increased. That is to say, he believes more and more, that through his gospel of love and self-imposed suffering, he hopes someday to convert the foreign rulers to his way of thinking. Now, he has devoted his whole life to the preaching of his wonderful gospel and has practised it with unwavering constance, as few others have done. Will he let the world know how many enemies of India he has been able to turn into friends ? How many O'Dwyers, Dyers, Readings and Irwins has he been able to convert into friends of India ? If none, how can India be expected to share his growing faith', that he will be able to persuade or compel England to agree to Indian Independence through the practice of non-violence.

What would have happened.

If the bomb, that burst under the Viceroy's special, had exploded properly, one of the two things suggested by Gandhi would have surely happened. The Viceroy would have either been badly injured or killed. Under such circumstances there certainly would have been no meeting between the leaders of political parties and the Viceroy. The uncalled for and undignified attempt on the part of these individuals, to lower the national prestige by knocking at the gates of the Government House with the beggar's bowl in their hands and Dominion Status on their lips, inspite of the clear terms of the Calcutta Ultimatum, would have been checkmated and the nation would have been the better off for that. If, fortunately, the explosion had been powerful enough to kill the Viceroy, one more enemy of India would have met a well deserved doom. The author of the Meerut prosecutions and the Lahore and Bhusawal persecutions can appear a Friend of India only to the enemies of her Freedom. Inspite of Gandhi and the Nehrus and their claims to political sagacity and statesmanship, Irwin has succeeded in shattering the unity between different political parties in the country, that had resulted from the boycott of the Simon Commission. Even the congress today is a house divided against itself. Who else, except the Viceroy and his olive tongue, have we to thank for our grave misfortunes ? And yet there exist people in our country who proclaim him a Friend of India !

The Future of the Congress.

There might be those who have no regard for the congress and hope nothing from it. If Gandhi thinks that the revolutionaries belong to that category, he wrongs them grievously. They fully realise the part played by the congress in awakening, among the ignorant masses, a keen desire for freedom. They expect great things of it in the future. Though they hold firmly to their opinion. that so long as persons like Sen Gupta. whose wonderful intelligence compels him to discern the hand of the C. I. D. in the late attempt to blow up the Viceroy's Special, and persons like Ansari, who think abuse the better part of argument and know so little of politics as to make the ridiculous and fallacious assertion that no nation had achieved freedom by the Bomb, have a determining voice in the affairs of the congress, the country can hope little from it, they are hopefully looking forward to the day, when the mania of non-violence would have passed away from the congress, and it would march arm in arm with the revolutionaries to their common goal of Complete Independence. This year it has accepted the ideal which the revolutionaries have preached and lived upto for more than a quarter of a century. Let us hope the next year will see it endorse their methods also.

Violence and Military Expenditure.

Gandhi is of opinion that as often as violence has been practised in the country, it has resulted in an increase of military expenditure. If his reference is to revolutionary activities during the last twenty-five years we dispute the accuracy of his statement and challenge him to prove his statement with facts and figures. If, on the other hand, he had the wars that have taken place in India since the British came here in mind, our reply is that even his modest experiment in Ahinsa and Satyagrah which had little to compare in it with the wars for independence, produced its effect on the finances of the Bureaucracy. Mass action, whether violent or non-violent, whether successful or unsuccessful, is bound to produce the same kind of repercussions on the finances of a state.

The Reforms.

Why should Gandhi mix up the revolutionaries with the various constitutional reforms granted by the government ? They never cared or worked for the Morley-Minto Reforms, Montague Reforms and the like. These the British Government threw before the constitutionalist agitators to lure them away from the right path. This was the bribe paid to them for their support to the government in its policy of crushing and uprooting the revolutionaries. These toys—as Gandhi calls them—were sent to India for the benefit of those, who, from time to time, raised the cry of 'Home Rule', 'Self-Government', 'Responsible Government', 'Full Responsible Government', 'Dominion Status' and such other constitutional names for slavery. The revolutionaries never claim the Reforms as their achievements. They raised the standard of independence long ago. They have lived for it. They have ungrudgingly laid their lives down for the sake of this ideal. They claim that their sacrifices have produced a tremendous change in the mentality of the people. That their efforts have advanced the country a long way on the road to Independence, is granted by even those who do not see eye to eye with them in politics.

The Way of Progress.

As to Gandhi's contention that violence impedes the march of progress and thus directly postpones the day of freedom, we can refer him to so many contemporary instances where violence has led to the social progress and political freedom of the people who practised it. Take the case of Russia and Turkey for example. In both countries the party for progress took over the state organisation through an armed revolution. Yet social progress and political freedom has not been impeded. Legislation, backed by force, has made the masses go 'double march' on the road of progress. The solitary example of Afghanistan cannot establish a political formula It is rather the exception that proves the rule.

Failure of Non-Co-operation.

Gandhi is of opinion that the great awakening in the people, during the days of non-co-operation, was a result of the preaching of non-violence. It is wrong to assign to non-violence the widespread awakening of the masses which, in fact, is manifested where ever a programme of direct action is adopted. In Russia, for instance, there came about widespread awakening among the peasants and workers, when the communists launched forth their great programme of Militant Mass Action, though nobody preached non-violence to them. We will even go further and state that it was mainly the mania for non-violence and Gandhi's compromise mentality that brought about the disruption of the forces that had come together at the call of Mass Action. It is claimed that non-violence can be used as a weapon for righting political wrongs. To say the least, it is a novel idea, yet untried. It failed to achieve what were considered to be the just rights of Indians in South Africa. It failed to bring 'Swaraj within a year' to the Indian masses inspite of the untiring labours of an army of national workers and one and a quarter crores of rupees. More recently, it failed to win for the Bardoli peasants what the leaders of the Satyagraha movement had promised them—the famous irreducible minimum of Gandhi and Patel. We know of no other trials non-violence has had on a country-wide scale. Up to this time, non-violence has been blessed with one result—Failure. Little wonder then, that the country refuses to give it another trial. In fact Satyagraha as preached by Gandhi is a form of agitation—a protest, leading up invariably, as has already been seen, to a compromise. It can hardly be of any use to a nation striving for national independence which can never come as the result of a compromise. The sooner we recognise, that there can be no compromise between independenc and slavery, the better.

Is it a new era ?

'We are entering upon a new era' thinks Gandhi. The mere act of defining swaraj as Complete Independence, this technical change in the congress constitution, can hardly constitute a new era. It will be a great day indeed when the congress will decide upon a country-wide programme of Mass Action, based on well recognised revolutionary principles. Till then the unfurling of the flag of Independence is a mockery and we concur with the following remarks of Sarla Devi Chaudharani, which she recently made, in a press interview.

"The unfurling of the Flag of Independence", she says "at just one minute after midnight of the 31st December 1929 was too stagy for words—just as the G. O. C. and the assistant G. O. C. and others in gaudy uniforms were card board Grand Officers Commanding".

"The fact that the unfurling of the flag of Independence lay hanging in the balance till midnight of that date, and that the scales might have been turned at even the eleventh hour fifty-ninth minute had a message from the Viceroy or the Secretary of State come to the Congress granting Dominion Status, proves that Independence is not a heart hunger of the leaders but that the declaration of it is only like a petulant child's retort. It would have been a worthy action of the Indian National Congress if Independence was achieved first and declared afterwards". It is true that the congress orators will henceforth harangue the masses on Complete Independence instead of Dominion Status. They will call upon the people to prepare for a struggle in which one party is to deliver blows and the other is simply to receive them, till beaten and demoralised beyond hope of recovery ! Can such a thing be named a struggle and can it ever lead the country to Complete Independence ? It is all very well to hold fast to the highest ideal worthy of a nation, but it is none the less necessary to adopt the best, the most efficacious and tried means, to achieve it ere you become the laughing stock of the whole world.

No Bullying please.

Gandhi has called upon all those who are not past reason to withdraw their support from the revolutionaries and condemn their actions so that ' our deluded patriots may, for want of nourishment to their violent spirit, realise the futility of violence and the great harm that violent activities have every time done'. How easy and convenient it is to call people deluded, to declare them to be past reason, to call upon the public to withdraw its support and condemn them so that they may get isolated and be forced to suspend their activities, specially when a man holds the confidence of an influential section of the public! It is a pity that Gandhi does not and will not understand revolutionary psychology inspite of his life-long experience of public life. Life is a precious thing. It is dear to every one. If a man becomes a revolutionary, if he goes about with his life in the hollow of his hand ready to sacrifice it at any moment, he does not do so merely for the fun of it. He does not risk his life merely because sometimes, when the crowd is in a sympathetic mood, it cries ' Bravo ' in appreciation. He does it because his reason forces him to take that course, because his conscience forces him to take that course, because his conscience dictates it. A revolutionary believes in reason more than anything. It is to reason, and reason alone, that he bows. No amount of abuse and condemnation, even if it eminates from the highest of the high, can turn him from his set purpose. To think, that a revolutionary will give up his ideals if public support and appreciation is withdrawn from him, is the highest folly. Many a revolutionary has, ere now, stepped on to the scaffold and laid his life down for the cause, regardless of the curses that the constitutionalist agitators rained plentifully upon him. If you will have the revolutionaries suspend their activities, reason with them squarely. That is the one and the only way. For the rest let their be no doubt in anybody's mind. A revolutionary is the last person on earth to submit to bullying.

An Appeal.

We take this opportunity to appeal to our countrymen—to the youth, to the workers and peasants, to the revolutionary intelligentsia —to come forward and join us in carrying aloft the banner of freedom. Let us establish a new order of society in which political and economic exploitation will be an impossibility. In the name of those gallant men and women, who willingly accepted death so that we, their descendants, may lead a happier life, who toiled ceaselessly and perished for the poor, the famished, and exploited millions of India, we call upon every patriot to take up the fight in all seriousness. Let nobody toy with the nation's freedom, which is her very life, by making psychological experiments in non-violence and such other novelties. Our slavery is our shame. When shall we have courage and wisdom enough to be able to shake ourselves free of it? What is our great heritage of civilisation and culture worth if we have not enough self-respect left in us to prevent us from bowing surveillance to the commands of foreigners and paying homage to their flag and king ?

Victory or death.

There is no crime that Britian has not committed in India. Deliberate misrule has reduced us to paupers, has 'bled us white'. As a race and a people we stand dishonoured and outraged. Do people still expect us to forget and to forgive ? We shall have our revenge—a people's righteous revenge on the Tyrant. Let cowards fall back and cringe for compromise and peace. We ask not for mercy and we give no quarter. Ours is a war to the end—to Victory or Death.

Long live revolution!

Kartar Singh,

President,

Hindustan Socialist Republican Association.

---

*THE HINDUSTAN SOCIALIST REPUBLICAN ASSOCIATION.

MANIFESTO.

"THE FOOD ON WHICH THE TENDER PLANT OF LIBERTY THRIVES IS THE BLOOD OF THE MARTYR."

For decades this life blood to the plant of India's liberty is being supplied by revolutionaries. There are few to question the magnanimity of the noble ideals they cherish and the grand sacrifices they have offered, but their normal activities being mostly secret the country is in dark as to their present policy and intentions. This has necessitated the Hindustan Socialist Republican Association to issue this manifesto.

This association stands for Revolution in India in order to liberate her from foreign domination by means of organised armed rebellion. Open rebellion by a subject people must always in the nature of things be preceded by secret propaganda and secret preparations. Once a country enters that phase the task of an alien Government becomes impossible. It might linger on for a number of years but its fate is sealed. Human nature, with all its prejudices and conservatism, has a sort of instinctive dread for Revolution. Upheavals have always been a terror to holders of power and privilege. Revolution is a phenomenon which nature loves and without which there can be no progress either in nature or in human affairs. Revolution is certainly not unthinking, brutal campaign of murder and incendiarism ;

---

*Circulated at the Lahore Congress in December 1929.

it is not a few bombs thrown here and a few shots fired there : neither it is a movement meant to destroy all remnants of civilization and blow to pieces time-honoured principles of Justice and Equity. Revolution is not a philosophy of despair or a creed of desperadoes. Revolution may be *anti*-God but is certainly not *anti*-Man. It is a vital, living force which is indicative of eternal conflict between the Old and the New, between Life and Living Death, between Light and Darkness. There is no concord, no symphony, no rhythm without revolution. 'The music of the spheres' of which poets have sung, would remain an unreality if a ceaseless Revolution were to be eliminated from the space. Revolution is Law, Revolution is Order and Revolution is the Truth.

The youths of our Nation have realized this Truth. They have learnt painfully the lesson that without Revolution there is no possibility of enthroning Order, Law and Love in place of chaos and Legal Vandalism and Hatred which are reigning supreme today. Let no one, in this blessed land of ours, run with the idea that the youths are irresponsible. They know where they stand. None knows better, than their own selves, that their path is not strewn with roses. From time to time thay have paid a fairly decent price for their Ideals. It does not, therefore, lie in the mouth of anybody to say that youthful impetuosity has feasted upon platitudes. It is no good to hurl denunciatory epithets at our Idealogy. It is enough to know that our Ideas are sufficiently active and powerful to drive us on aye, even to gallows.

It has become a fashion these days to indulge in wild and meaningless talk of non-violence. Mahatma Gandhi is great and we mean no disrespect to him if we express our emphatic disapproval of the methods advocated by him for our country's emancipation. We would be ungrateful to him if we do not salute him for the immense awakening that has been brought about by his non-co-operation movement in the country. But to us the Mahatma is an impossible visionary. Non-violence may be a noble Ideal, but it is a thing of the morrow. We can, situated as we are, never hope to win our freedom by mere non-violence. The world is armed to the very teeth. And the world is too much with us. All talk of peace may be sincere, but we, of the slave Nation, cannot, and must not, be led away by such false Idealogy. What Logic, we ask, is there in asking the country to traverse a non-violent path when the world atmosphere is surcharged with violence and exploitation of the weak ? We declared with all the emphasis we can command that the youths of the Nation cannot be lured by such mid-summer-night's dream.

We believe in violence, not as an end in itself but as a means to a Noble End. And the votaries of non-violence, as also the advocates of Caution and circumspection will readily grant this much at least that we know how to suffer for, and to act upto, our convictions. Shall we here recount all those sacrifices which our comrades have offered at the altar of our common Mother? Many a heart-rending and soul-stirring scene has been enacted inside the four walls of His Majesty's Prison: We have been taken to task for our Terroristic Policy. Our answer is that terrorism is never the object of revolutionaries, nor do they believe that terrorism alone can bring independence. No doubt the revolutionaries think, and rightly, that it is only by resorting to terrorism alone that they can find a most effective means of retaliation. The British Government exists, because the Britishers have been successful in terrorising the whole of India. How are we to meet this official terrorism? Only counter-terrorism on the part of revolutionaries can checkmate effectively this bureaucratic bullying. A feeling of utter helplessness pervades society. How can we overcome this fatal despondency? It is only by infusing a real spirit of sacrifice that that lost self-confidence can be restored. Terrorism has its Inter-national aspect also. England's enemies, which are many, are drawn towards us by effective demonstration of our strength. That in itself is a great advantage.

India is writhing under the yoke of imperialism. Her teeming millions are today a helpless prey to poverty and ignorance. Foreign domination and economic exploitation have unmanned the vast majority of the people who constitute the workers and peasants of India. The position of the Indian Proletariat is, today, extremely critical. It has a double danger to face. It has to bear the onslaught of Foreign Capitalism on one hand and the treacherous attack of Indian Capital on the other. The latter is showing a progressive tendency to join forces with the former. The leaning of certain politicians in favour of Dominion Status shows clearly which way the wind blows. Indian Capital is preparing to betray the masses into the hands of Foreign Capitalism and receive as a price of this betrayal, a little share in the Government of the country. The hope of the proletariat is, therefore, now centred in Socialism which alone can lead to the establishment of Complete Independence and the removal of all social distinctions and privileges.

The future of India rests with the youths. They are the salt of the earth. Their promptness to suffer, their daring courage and their radiant sacrifice prove that India's future in their hands is perfectly safe. In a moment of realization the late Deshbandhu Dass said, "The youths are at once the hope and glory of the Motherland. Theirs is the inspiration behind the movement. Theirs is the sacrifice. Theirs is the victory. They are torch-bearers on the road to Freedom. They are the pilgrims on the road to Liberty."

Youths-ye-soldiers of the Indian Republic, fall in! Do not stand easy, do not let your knees tremble. Shake off the paralysing effects of long lethargy. Yours is a noble Mission. Go out into every nook and corner of the country and prepare the ground for future Revolution which is sure to come. Respond to the clarion call of duty. Do not vegetate. Grow! Every minute of your life you must think of devising means so that this your ancient land may arise with flaming eyes and fierce yawn! Sow the seeds of disgust and hatred against British Imperialism in the fertile minds of your fellow youths. And the seeds shall sprout and there shall grow a jungle of sturdy trees, because you shall water the seeds with your warm blood. Then a grim and terrible earthquake having a universally destructive potentiality shall inevitably come along with portentous rumblings, and this edifice of Imperialism will crash and crumble to dust, and great shall be the fall thereof. And then and not till then, a new Indian Nation shall arise and surprise humanity with the splendour and glory all its own. The wise and the mighty shall be bewildered by the simple and the weak.

Individual liberty shall be safe. The sovereignty of the proletariat shall be recognised. We court the advent of such Revolution. Long live Revolution !!!

Kartar Singh,
President.

Printed at the Republican Press, Erehwon, India.

Copy of the notice found pasted on the gate of St. John's College, Agra.

Long live Revolution.

"WITHOUT LIBERTY LIFE IS NOT WORTH LIVING."

Youths ye are the source of liberty, the hope of the country, nay the saviour of the motherland. Loyalty to this tyranny and exploitation makes you traitor to your country by summarily disposing off and launching many of your brothers to eternity.

Make India another Ireland and the reins of Government are in your hands. Without the least agitation you should meet the scaffold even as a yogi enters the samadhi. The appetite for revolution is apt to grow with what it feeds on.

Remember the words of an Englishman who says "we have the power of life in our hands and I assure you we spare not.........."

Atrocities were committed in the burning of villages and massacre of innocent inhabitants at which Mohammad Tughlak himself would have stood ashamed. They have sewed Mohammedans in pig skin and smeared them with pork fat before execution during the mutiny and then burning their bodies and they have forced Hindus to defile themselves. It is plain enough from Russels diary.

They did not deliberately hang Indians but burnt them in their villages. The Englishmen did not hesitate to boast that they had spared no one and that peppering away at niggers was pleasant past time enjoyed amazingly.

An Englishman is almost suffocated with indignation when he reads that Chambers or Miss Jernnings was hacked to death by a dusky ruffian but in native history or legends and tradition it may be recorded against our people that mothers, wives and children with less familiar names fell miserable victims to the first swoop of English vengeance.

Our C.I.D. friends must remember the report of Montgomery Martin:

> "All the city people were bayonated on the spot when our army entered Delhi, the number was considerable when I tell you that in some houses 40 or 50 persons were hiding, they were not mutineers but residents of city who trusted to our **Well Known Mild Rule of Pardon,** I am glad to say that they were disappointed."

Further they warned that they stake their lives if they come in our way. British officials should take long furloughs and go home. We hold humanity sacred but Government our enemy.

We thank the Principal, Agra College and the Warden, Medical School for the loyalty they have shown to the Government. The students should condemn the action of that boy who took the Manifesto to the Principal. A social boycott is sufficient for such a traitor.

Get yourself enlisted soon. More you will find next week at this very place.

Long Live Revolution.

BRANCH OFFICE : Kailash Singh,

Naudab, Budaon. *President.*

Typed at the branch office of Hindustan Republican Association Erehwon, India.

NOTE 1. The antiques are in red in the original.

2. The Poster appeared in Agra in January 1930.

Copy of a leaflet found in the Mechuabazar Street, search (December 1929).

The Youths of Bengal.

"From the seeming stillness of the sea of Indian humanity a veritable storm is about to break out."

The critical moment for the fire-worshipping youthful sons (anarchists) of Bengal to bring the truth into reality has come. It has become necessary to stem the tide of the hideous oppressions that are being practised on the men and women of this country by the power-puffed and oppressive foreign rulers in the name of law and order. Since the beginning of the 20th century and up till now many youths of the country sacrificed completely their youthful qualities in order to stop the tide, some by welcoming hangman's rope, some by receiving bullet wounds, some by courting imprisonment in solitary cells and some by welcoming transportation in distant islands. That midnight dawned with the self-sacrifice of the revolutionary hero, Khudiram, Rudra (violence) worshipper, Kanialal and the bloody revolutionary Satyen. Then slowly as the light of day began to be scorching the fertile soil of Bengal was reddened with the hot blood of the many revolutionary heroes maddened with the joy of shedding blood. The Bengali youths with great pains have not been able to forget up till now the offering of Jatin Mukherji and Nalini Bagchi of that age. Then, when the political sky of India bacame surcharged with the vilification of the anarchists consequent on the agitation of non-violent non-co-operation, and when Mohandas Gandhi, the inaugurator of non-co-operation, and who is confident in English co-operation himself, smelt nothing but blunder in this extraordinary self-sacrifice, the embracing of death by dreadful soldier Gopinath by breaking the stillness, explained to the confounded Rudra worshippers (anarchists) of Bengal which was the road to freedom. In search of that path many youths ran recklessly, and in their attempt to destroy the blood-sucking of the covetous ruler, they, according to the custom of a dependent country, sacrificed themselves as a bloody offering in that fearful oblation with fire. But unfortunately, in spite of it the stillness of the country did not break. The inanimateness of the nation remained unmovingly fixed like a heavy chain and the helpless nation sank down in dolefulness. The matter of regret is that if anyone ever wants to draw a ray of light in this great night of New Moon, then there will rise from all quarters an uproar of incantation of "non-violence" or there will come out a false hoax of something very great. If any one ever giving out owing to mortal anguish and says "No, I shall never bear silently this sort of wrong-doing by the foreigner. Anyhow I shall try to make a campaign with my little power against it"—it will at once be proclaimed by the self-sufficient leaders that this is the work of a spy. In this way the so-called grandiloquent leaders want to pulverise the movement of a nation's life; because it strikes at the root of their proficiency—hurts their leadership.

The extreme proof of barbarism of the fiendish English people is the murder of Jatindranath in the Lahore Prison House. Bengali Youths! Will it not drag you now towards a bloody campaign? Will the fascination of untruth keep you as imbecile even now? Young Bengalis? Will not your revolutionary spirit stir up to play with fire at the self-sacrifice of Jatin? Will it not blossom like a red lotus? Will not the proof of convetousness of the English Government, the merciless oppressions on all quarters and the harrowing persecutions teach you to think seriously where your path lies? Do not select a wrong path being stupefied by the old leaders of Bengal. Stand on your legs. You will find that your strength is irresistible and unlimited. You will be in a position to crumble everything. What is your fear? What is your anxiety? This is how a nation awakes. Flare up with the fire of vengeance for the annihilation of foreign enemies. You will find that the victory is yours. History bears testimony to this. Read and learn the history of Pearse—the gem of young Ireland and you will find how noble is his sacrifice; how he stimulated new animation in the nation, being mad over independence. When everybody was reluctant to die he alone proclaimed loudly—"I cannot live. Even if I am alone I shall have to come to the field of activity with the banner of an armed revolution in order to bring vigour in the life of this inanimate nation. With my death a hundred heroes will spring up who will triumph over death, who with their fresh blood prepare the steps to Independence of Young Ireland in the next era". Pearse died and by so dying he roused in the heart of the nation an indomitable desire for armed revolution. Who will deny this truth? That lion of a hero did not tremble owing to the inferiority of his number—that revolutionary was not moved at the request of the old man. This is his peculiarity. Oh, the party of men deprived of everything—open your eyes and see where your position is. So, the call to break the bondage has come today and you will have to respond to that call. You will have to make the place of the enchained Bharat Mata in the world glorious, and it would be a matter of pride if you will have to stand alone at the outset against the despotism of the blood-thirsty English.

No fear there is no fear

He who will give his life completely

will sustain no loss.

SECRET.

EXTRACT FROM PAGES 244-245, VOLUME I, OF THE PROCEEDINGS OF THE COURT OF SPECIAL TRIBUNAL, CHITTAGONG.

The Indian Republican Army, Chittagong Branch, hereby declares today the lives of all Englishmen and white-skinned Anglo-Indians who are prejudicial to the interest of Indian freedom, forfeited to it. It also entreats all the members of **The Indian Republican Army** and the people of Chittagong to begin a vigorous campaign of murdering these people wherever found to avenge the murders of their forefathers and thus to relieve the country of the pernicious exploitations which they are doing in this land of OURS.

The Indian Republican Army further declares that any person who will be able to produce any Englishman, woman or child of any age to its headquarters, dead or alive, will be amply rewarded.

BY ORDER,

PRESIDENT IN COUNCIL,

Indian Republican Army,

Chittagong Branch

INDEX.

A

PAGE.

B.

PAGE.

C.

D.

PAGE.

E.

F.

PAGE.

PAGE.

I.

PAGE.

J

PAGE.

PAGE.

K.

PAGE.

PAGE.

M.

PAGE.

N.

PAGE.

O.

P.

PAGE.

Q.

R.

PAGE.

PAGE.

S.

PAGE.

PAGE.

PAGE.

PAGE.

PAGE.

PAGE.

T.

W.

Y.

Z